THE OFFSHORE YACHT

THE OFFSHORE YACHT

YACHT

Tim Thornton

ADLARD COLES LIMITED
GRANADA PUBLISHING
London Toronto Sydney New York

Adlard Coles Ltd
Granada Publishing Ltd
8 Grafton Street, London W1X 3LA

First published in Great Britain by
Adlard Coles Ltd 1984

British Library Cataloguing in Publication Data
Thornton, Tim
    The offshore yacht.
    1. Yacht-building
    I. Title
    623.8'223   VM331

ISBN 0-229-11681-7

Typeset by Activity Ltd, Salisbury, Wiltshire
Printed and bound in Great Britain by
R.J. Acford, Chichester, Sussex

Contents

v

Contents

Contents

Contents

Preface

Sailing boats have changed in many ways over the last two decades. Many of these have developed from the introduction of mass-produced fibreglass boats, which has resulted in a large growth in the number of participants in the sport. This growth has resulted in a more technologically orientated approach to the sport, with new materials being used to build lighter or cheaper craft, and the increasing use of microprocessors in instrumentation and navigation systems to name but two fields. Also, the pressures of racing have resulted in great strides in deck layouts, whilst the need for high sales in production cruisers has resulted in improved interior layouts.

However, relatively little design information is passed down to the yachtsman, and what is made available tends to be shrouded in half truths or mathematical formulae. This book discusses each aspect of yacht design in straightforward language, so that the reader may obtain a good working knowledge of the subject without getting lost in the depths of knowledge required by a professional designer.

I should like to thank all the individuals and firms who have helped in the preparation of this work. Particular thanks to Neil Dawtry for his comments on electrical systems, Paul Gallagher for comments on hull design and construction, and Rob Humphreys for comments on the IOR, and for allowing me to use many of his drawings; also to William Payne for help with the photos, and to Barbara Gentle for typing the manuscript.

Tim Thornton

Foreword

Anyone who has followed the construction of a yacht from start to completion will have witnessed a metamorphosis that rivals much that even nature can offer. In through the yard doors go drums of resin, rolls of fibreglass, bits of wood and boxes and boxes of miscellaneous items. Then some time later the doors open and out comes this beautiful object – a complex being with a personality unique to itself. Its temperament, performance and style are a function of the way the component parts have been configured and of the three-dimensional form to which it has been shaped. In fact one can draw a further analogy with nature in that the process of natural selection extends to yacht design, where generally only the most successful ideas and concepts are perpetuated and enhanced in future development.

From conception through execution nothing happens to a yacht without some decision being taken – be it by designer, builder or owner – and for every decision there are many alternative permutations available. To have followed a cohesive path through this maze of possible options is a measure of the success of the final product, and in *The Offshore Yacht* Tim Thornton has set out to explain the logic behind the design, construction and commissioning of a yacht, delving into the intricacies that set one boat apart from another. He has given himself a broad platform, looking at monohulls and multihulls, cruising yachts and racing yachts. He unravels many mysteries for the newcomer to sailing, and coincidentally offers the more experienced a host of information to chew over. The scope of the book is vast and in it the reader will find extensive discussion and information on design philosophy, construction methods, rig considerations, the deck and interior layout, as well as the mechanical and electrical aspects of a yacht. And for the more committed racing man there is a meaty section where the various handicap systems are explained, in particular the International Offshore Rule which is made comprehensible even to those who had long given up hope of understanding it.

Tim's researches have been extensive and the material he conveys is right up to date, with conspicuous references to modern keywords like Kevlar, Mylar, Decca and Satnav. His understanding of his subject is self-evident and with a breadth of experience that extends from competitive small boat sailing to participation in a trans-Atlantic race he is well qualified to comment on his chosen topics. As a reference work, or simply as a book to read, *The Offshore Yacht* will be a very useful addition to any yachtsman's library.

Rob Humphreys

Chapter 1

The Lines Plan

What Size Yacht?

When considering the purchase or design of a yacht, the first factor to be decided upon is her size. This will directly govern her cost, her speed, and the amount of living space on board.

The cost of a yacht rises rapidly as her size increases. This is not only due to the increasing size of her hull and rig, but also because of the heavier scantlings and larger fittings required, and the more extensive internal joinery. Typically the cost of the bare hull and deck amounts to only one third of the total cost of the boat.

The speed potential of a yacht varies with the square root of her waterline length, as will be shown later in this chapter. The average speed of a boat (in knots) will lie between $0.8\sqrt{\text{LWL}}$ and $1.0\sqrt{\text{LWL}}$ for monohulls and cruising multihulls, whilst racing multihulls may maintain speeds some 50% higher. A doubling of the waterline length will increase the average speed by some 40%, and so larger yachts are capable of making considerably faster passages than small ones. The penalty for this extra speed is a larger sail plan, requiring more crew to handle the boat.

It is wrong to judge the internal accommodation solely by the number of berths, as some designs cram in a large number of berths as a selling point; this only results in a cramped interior with insufficient stowage space. However, on any boat there should be a berth for each crew member to use when in harbour, and a sea berth for each off-watch crew member to use when at sea.

A further consideration is the effect that the weight of the crew and stores will have on the yacht's performance. Each crew member, together with his stores and personal gear, will weigh in at 300 – 400 lb for a seven-day cruise, and 500 – 700 lb for a five-week voyage. To put this into perspective, a 30-foot yacht going off on a month's cruise with four crew on board could easily have her displacement increased by 25%. Obviously this will affect light displacement designs by a

1

greater amount than heavier boats, as the extra weight will represent a greater percentage of the boat's displacement. For this reason, multihull owners in particular must resist the temptation to fill their boat's cavernous interior with stores and equipment.

Monohull or Multihull?

Although the majority of boat owners will no doubt continue to sail monohulls, multihulls have developed to a point where they are worthy of serious consideration.

The two main advantages to the cruising yachtsman are the large amount of internal accommodation and deck space, together with the absence of heel. This results in greatly increased comfort and a marked reduction in crew fatigue. Against this there is the possibility of a capsize. However, the majority of capsizes that occur are due to racing boats carrying too much sail, and could be prevented by prudent seamanship.

Fig. 1.1   The floats on this trimaran can be swung in (as shown) to reduce her beam for berthing and towing.

For events such as OSTAR and the Round Britain Race a multihull is essential for a good finishing position. Early designs lacked windward ability, but efficient centreboard design has now overcome this problem. Some boats used scantlings that proved to be too light, resulting in structural failures, but sufficient design experience has now been acquired for this to be less common. It could be eliminated almost entirely if the yachtsmen and designers were prepared to accept a slight weight penalty. Unfortunately, as these machines rely on ultra-light weight for their speed it is not possible to have a cruiser/racer without a marked reduction in performance.

The great advantage of monohulls is that they are unable to be permanently capsized. Also, due to their large numbers, there is a much greater variety of designs on the market, and greater opportunity for racing. In addition, the greater ability of monohulls to carry weight means that it is possible to have the yacht comfortably fitted out with only a slight reduction in performance.

Reading the Lines Plan

Figure 1.2 shows the lines plan of a yacht. The complex curves of the hull are defined by taking slices through the hull in several planes. The waterline is divided into eleven stations, numbered from 0 at the bow to 10 at the stern, and the transverse section at each station is shown in the body plan; additional sections are usually added at the ends of the yacht, where the shape changes rapidly. Whilst it is normal practice to use eleven stations, some designers use thirteen or even twenty-one on large craft. The waterlines are shown in the plan view, and the buttocks in the profile drawing. Note that each of these slices appears as a straight line in the other two views.

The accuracy of a line is at its greatest when it is perpendicular to the shape of the boat. Thus, to improve definition at the turn of the bilge, diagonals are used. These appear as straight lines on the body plan, and are drawn out on the lower half of the plan view.

The lines plan may also show the curve of areas, drawn over the diagonals. This shows how the immersed volume of the hull is distributed along its length, and ensures that there are no sudden changes in hull section. At one stage it was believed that this curve was a key factor in assessing the wavemaking resistance of the hull, but this is no longer held to be the case.

It is worth noting that the design waterline is only an approximation to its actual position. It is usually drawn for the half load condition, that is, carrying half of the estimated weight of crew, stores and equipment. Thus in practice the yacht will float above or below her design waterline depending upon what is on board.

The Elements of Hull Design

The three aims of hull design are low resistance, high stability, and good directional control. Unfortunately, all designs have to reach a balance between these factors, as their requirements are to some extent contradictory.

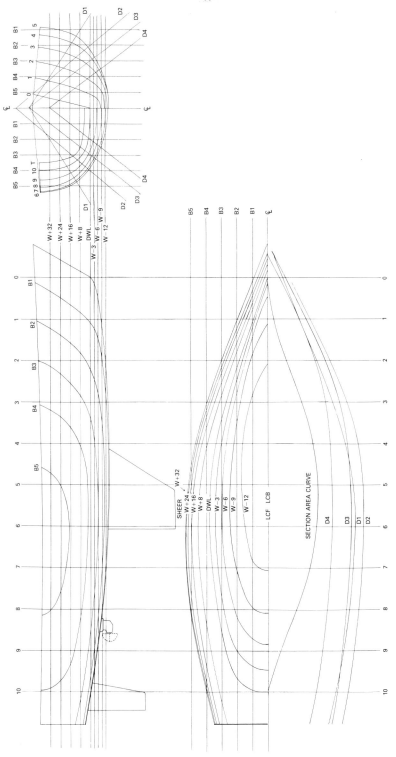

Fig. 1.2(a). The lines plan of a 30-foot fast cruiser. *LCB* is the longitudinal centre of buoyancy, *LCF* the longitudinal centre of flotation.

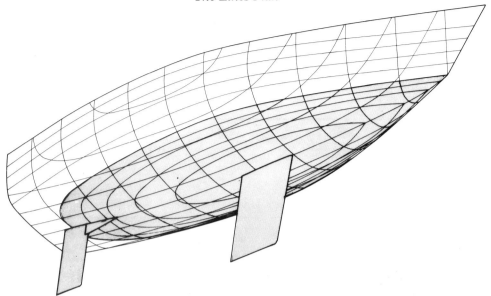

Fig 1.2(b). A perspective view of the lines plan, showing the interrelationship of the lines. The diagonals have not been drawn on in the interests of clarity.

The resistance of the hull springs from several sources. The viscosity of the water gives rise to frictional resistance and eddy-making resistance; pressure disturbances on the air/sea interface result in wavemaking resistance. The need to counteract the side force of the sails results in induced drag and, in the case of monohulls, drag due to heeling. Finally, the need to sail through waves results in drag due to pitching, heaving and yawing.

The yacht must have sufficient stability to enable her to carry sufficient sail for good performance. Creating stability is no problem with multihulls, but with monohulls the requirements for good stability are contradictory to the requirements for low resistance.

Finally, directional stability incorporates manoeuvrability and the balance of the yacht. Good handling properties are obviously required if the crew are to be able to get the best out of the yacht.

Hull Resistance

Frictional resistance

As water flows past the hull, the region close to the hull is slowed by friction between the hull and the water; the closer the water is to the hull, the more it is retarded. Ultimately, the film of water in direct contact with the hull is stopped completely. The thickness of this boundary layer, as it is known, increases from almost zero at the stem to about 1.5% of the waterline length at the transom.

Frictional resistance is proportional to the hull's wetted area, and rises approximately in proportion to the square of the speed. However, because of

5

scaling factors determined by the Reynolds Number, large yachts have slightly less resistance per unit of wetted area than smaller ones travelling at the same speed, a 60-foot yacht having a frictional resistance per unit area some 5% less than a 30-foot yacht.

The resistance can be reduced by designing the boat with as small a wetted area as possible, and by having as smooth a hull surface as possible. Surface imperfections are particularly harmful at high speeds and on large boats.

The only way to produce a smooth finish is through hard work with filler and wet and dry paper; for the best performance it is worth going down to the finest grade paper available. For minimum drag, a 22-foot waterline boat should not have any roughnesses greater than 0.001 inch; for a 60-foot waterline the critical value decreases to 0.0006 inch.

Development of the fin keel and separate rudder has drastically reduced the wetted surface area of the hull, and in some cases has been taken to its logical conclusion of lifting keels or centreboards. The other avenue for development is the shape of the hull. For a given displacement, the wetted area is least in hulls with a short waterline length, full ends, and semicircular sections. Unfortunately, this also results in high wavemaking resistance and low stability, so the designer has to reach a compromise here.

As can be seen in Fig. 1.3, frictional resistance is dominant at speeds below about $0.8\sqrt{\mathrm{LWL}}$, and remains significant up to speeds of $1.0\sqrt{\mathrm{LWL}}$. Thus low frictional resistance is particularly important when sailing to windward, and off the wind in light and moderate airs. However, at higher speeds it quickly becomes insignificant compared to the wavemaking resistance.

Eddy resistance

If the run of the boat is brought in too sharply, the water is unable to follow the shape of the hull. Instead, it separates from the hull and degenerates into a mass of eddies that are dragged along behind the hull, resulting in increased resistance. It is particularly detrimental at speeds below $0.4\sqrt{\mathrm{LWL}}$ and when surfing conditions prevail.

It is difficult to predict exactly when separation is likely to occur, and tank tests are not much help due to scaling problems. However, as a rough guide, separation can be expected if the angle of the water flow is greater than about 13° to the waterline and centreline. Large boats can tolerate a more pinched-in stern than smaller ones, though, due to the same scale effects that affect tank tests. Separation is easily initiated by any local imperfections, and so it is particularly important to have a smooth paint finish in the stern, with no protruding skin fittings.

Eddy resistance is only likely to be significant on heavy displacement boats, as the need to squeeze a large volume into a short length must result in sharply

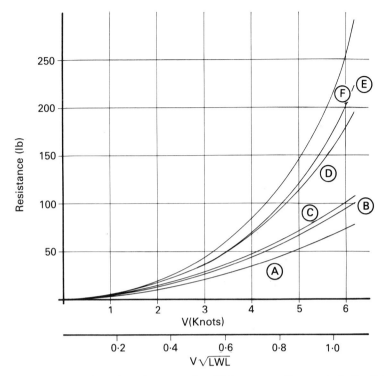

Fig. 1.3(a). Windward resistance of a 33-foot waterline monohull. Ⓐ Hull friction drag. Ⓑ Keel profile drag. Ⓒ Rudder profile drag. Ⓓ Wavemaking resistance. Ⓔ Resistance due to heeling. Ⓕ Induced drag.

tapered ends. The situation can be considerably improved by the use of a bustled stern. This gives a greater vertical distribution of the hull volume in the run, with water well below the waterline following the waterlines, and water near the surface following the buttocks. Figure 1.4 shows the run of a heavy displacement yacht both with and without a bustle, and it can be seen that the bustled stern gives the water a gentler path to follow.

Wavemaking resistance

The most obvious source of resistance, to the yachtsman, is wavemaking, which is also the least well understood from the designer's point of view. There are two aspects of the water flow that are responsible for the creation of waves.

Firstly, as Fig. 1.5 shows, the flow round the hull is initially slowed at the stem, then accelerated as it passes the midship section, and finally slowed again when it is brought together at the stern. There is a build-up of pressure where the water is slowed, causing the water to be pushed up into a wave crest; conversely, where the water is accelerated the water pressure drops, and a wave trough develops. This

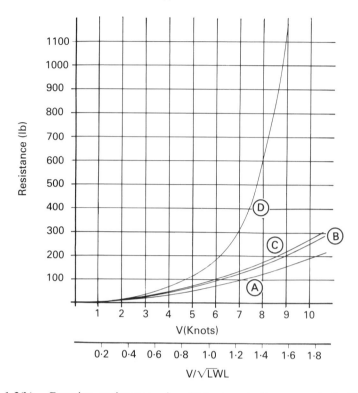

Fig. 1.3(b). Running resistance of a 33-foot waterline monohull. Ⓐ Hull friction drag. Ⓑ Keel profile drag. Ⓒ Rudder profile drag. Ⓓ Wavemaking resistance.

crest-trough-crest formation is present at all speeds, and travels along with the vessel. It dominates wavemaking resistance at the upper end of the speed range.

The second type of wave pattern is set up wherever there is a sudden disturbance to the water flow. All hulls have a wave system at the bow, together with a smaller one at the stern. However, if there are any sudden changes in shape along the hull, such as chines, additional weaker wave systems may appear. The wave system, shown in Fig. 1.6, has two components: a diverging wave train that immediately parts company with the hull, and a transverse wave train that remains in contact with the hull. The wavemaking resistance is largely governed by these bow and stern waves at low speeds.

The magnitude of the wavemaking resistance is dependent upon the magnitude of the total wave system, which is obtained by combining all the component systems. Thus when the waves counteract one another the resistance is relatively low, and when they reinforce one another the resistance is relatively high.

As the wavelength of the wave system varies with the square root of the boat's speed, when comparing boats of different sizes one should use the speed:length

8

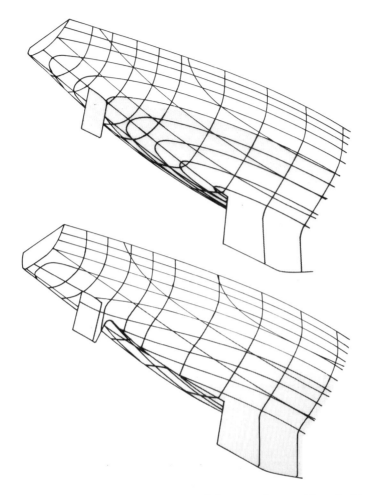

Fig. 1.4. The run of a heavy displacement 5.5-metre, drawn with and without a bustle.

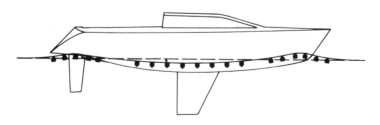

Fig. 1.5. The pressure wave around a hull. Areas of high pressure at the stem and stern create wave crests, whilst a pressure drop amidships results in a trough. The arrows show the line of action of the forces; the dashed line is the static waterline.

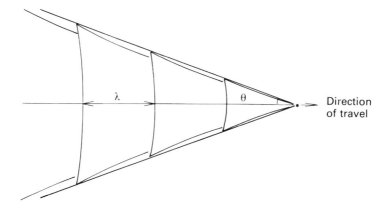

Fig. 1.6. Bow wave pattern. Although strongest at the bow, this wave pattern is also formed at the stern, and weaker wave patterns may form at chines, or the keel when well heeled. This wave pattern is sometimes called the Kelvin wave system. The angle θ remains constant at 19.5°, but λ varies: $\lambda = 2\pi \times V_s^2/g$ or $\lambda = 0.557V_s^2$, where V_s is measured in knots.

ratio, $V{:}\sqrt{\text{LWL}}$, if the wave systems, and thus the wavemaking resistances, are to be comparable.

At a speed of about $1.34\sqrt{\text{LWL}}$ (commonly called the hull speed) all three wave systems combine to give large crests at the bow and stern, and a large trough amidships. This results in a marked rise in resistance, especially in heavy displacement designs, and a considerable increase in thrust is required if the boat is to break through this resistance hump.

Once the waterline length has been fixed, displacement is the crucial factor in determining resistance. A light displacement hull has relatively little bulk, and so creates little fuss as it progresses through the water. The displacement:length ratio is used to assess the underwater bulk of a hull, and is given by $\triangle/(0.01\text{LWL})^3$, in units of tons and feet; Fig. 1.7 shows how the resistance varies with the displacement:length ratio. The lighter hulls have considerably less resistance at all speeds, and in particular have a much less marked increase in resistance at high speed. This is why racing multihulls, with their very low displacement:length ratios, are capable of such high speeds.

Monohulls have displacement:length ratios ranging from 90 for very light-weight designs, through to 300 or more for heavy boats. Upwind speeds are limited to $1.1\sqrt{\text{LWL}}$; off the wind, lightweight boats can achieve speeds of $2.0\sqrt{\text{LWL}}$, but those with a displacement:length ratio in excess of 200 will seldom exceed hull speed.

Multihulls should have their displacement:length ratio calculated on the assumption that just one hull carries the weight of the vessel, as this approximates to the situation when sailing hard. Displacement:length ratios range from about 140 for heavy cruising designs, down to as little as 40 for racing craft. Thus even

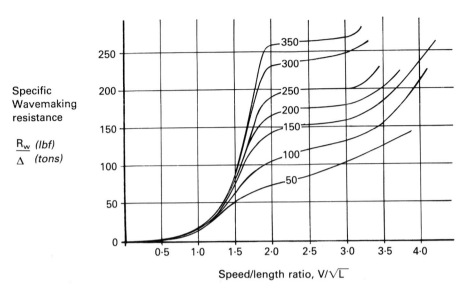

Fig. 1.7. Wavemaking resistance of a series of high-speed displacement hulls at various speed:length ratios.

cruising designs can expect to sail faster than most monohulls, and racing designs can achieve speeds of up to $1.5\sqrt{LWL}$ upwind, rising to $3.5\sqrt{LWL}$ downwind.

The prismatic coefficient (C_p) shows how the designer has distributed the immersed volume of the hull longitudinally, and is given by:

$$C_p = \nabla/(LWL \times \text{maximum sectional area})$$

A low value indicates a design with fine ends and a large midship section, whilst a high value indicates a more slender overall hull shape with fuller ends. Monohulls have values ranging between 0.52 and 0.59, but some multihull designers have used values as high as 0.7.

At speeds below $1.0\sqrt{LWL}$ most of the wavemaking resistance comes from the pressure disturbances at the ends of the hull, and so a low prismatic shape with its fine ends is preferred. As the speed increases, though, the rest of the hull becomes increasingly involved in wavemaking; thus a higher prismatic form is favoured, giving a more slender overall shape. However, at speeds below about $0.5\sqrt{LWL}$ the predominance of frictional resistance favours a high prismatic coefficient. This is because the reduction in wetted surface area is of more importance than a slight increase in wavemaking resistance at these low speeds.

The other ratio affecting wavemaking resistance is that of the waterline beam to the depth of the canoe body, $BWL:T_c$. Sometimes the ratio $LWL:BWL$ is used, but $BWL:T_c$ is to be preferred as it is independent of the displacement:length ratio and prismatic coefficent.

As the wave system is due to the presence of the air/sea interface, it might be

11

expected that a low beam:draught ratio will have little resistance, due to having a narrow waterline beam and a large proportion of the hull volume well below the water's surface. Although this argument is valid at low speeds, another effect comes into play at high speeds.

As can be seen in Fig. 1.5, there is a region of low pressure beneath the hull. At speed it sucks the hull down, effectively increasing the displacement. A series of tank tests on yacht hulls has shown that at low speeds a hull with a beam:draught ratio of 3.0 was best, but this was supplanted by a model with a ratio of 4.0 at a speed of $1.1\sqrt{LWL}$, and at speeds above $1.5\sqrt{LWL}$ a value of 5.3 offered least resistance. The wider, flatter hull sections have less suction due to their shallower draft, and also make it easier for water to flow down from the surface, resulting in a lower pressure differential.

Fig. 1.8. Tank testing a half-ton model. This 6-foot model is large enough to avoid most scaling problems, though it may be slightly too large for the size of the tank. Note how the long, full overhang aft helps to extend the waterline length; the pattern of the bow wave is also clearly visible. (*Courtesy Rob Humphreys.*)

We now come to the shape of the ends of the hull. The bows need to part the water as gently as possible, so as to minimise the size of the bow wave. This suggests straight waterlines to give a small angle of entry, coupled with a shallow forefoot. The angle of entry can be further reduced by moving the point of maximum beam further aft, so long as it is not detrimental to the shape of the stern. If the prismatic coefficient requires plenty of volume in the bows, this is best achieved by increasing the depth of the forefoot, rather than by filling out the waterlines.

The shape of the run varies a great deal from boat to boat, and the optimum form is highly dependent upon the speed potential of the boat. In slow boats, such as heavy displacement monohulls, or those designed to excel to windward or in light airs, a fine, double-ended stern is best. This minimises the wetted surface area, creates only a small stern wave, and reduces the likelihood of flow separation. As most of the water follows the waterlines, the point of maximum beam should be fairly well forward, so that the waterlines close as gently as possible.

As the maximum speed of the design increases, the stern should become wider and shallower for two reasons. Firstly, referring to Fig. 1.5, it can be seen that the stern wave has a forwards pressure component; if energy can be extracted from this, the resistance will clearly be reduced. This is achieved by having a shallow, gentle run to the buttocks, flattening the stern wave.

A second reason for a powerful stern is that at speeds greater than about $1.4\sqrt{\text{LWL}}$ the boat squats down by the stern. This effectively means that the boat is sailing uphill, and so the resistance is increased. The trim may alter by about 2.5° at a speed of $2.0\sqrt{\text{LWL}}$, resulting in a drag penalty of 4.4% of the boat's displacement – greater trim angles naturally result in greater increases in resistance. A wide, flat stern will provide plenty of buoyancy aft, and so reduce any squatting to a minimum.

The same effect works in reverse when the boat is surfing down waves. The wide transom now lifts the stern to the following sea, and the weight of the boat acts to increase her speed, helping her to ride the wave.

Heeled resistance

Monohulls build up their stability by heeling; this affects the boat's hydrodynamics in two ways. Figure 1.9 shows the waterlines of the hull drawn in Fig. 1.2 when heeled to 25°; the marked asymmetry of the hull can clearly be seen, and in particular the increased curvature to leeward. As may be expected, this causes increased drag. In addition, the waterlines are similar to a cambered aerofoil and so a lift force is developed, sucking the boat down to leeward, increasing the angle of leeway.

The drag penalty can easily amount to 15% or 20% when heeled to 30°, and the angle of leeway may be increased by as much as 2° to counteract the negative lift produced by the hull. The effect is greatest in boats with high beam:draught ratios, and to a lesser extent high displacement:length ratios, as these factors produce relatively large amounts of asymmetry.

WINDWARD

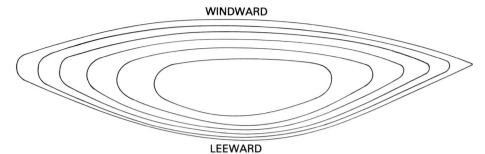

LEEWARD

Fig. 1.9. The lines of the boat shown in Fig. 1.2, shown heeled to 25°. Note that the leeward waterlines have much greater curvature, causing a drop in pressure which results in the wave trough to leeward, and also causes more leeway. Also, the centre of the waterlines no longer follows the boat's centreline, but runs from the bows to the leeward quarter.

The amount of asymmetry can be reduced by careful shaping of the hull above the waterline. A short overhang and little flare to the bow sections minimise the fullness on the lee side of the bow, and amidships the absence of flare reduces the asymmetry. If there is a long, low overhang aft, it will quickly become immersed when heeled, increasing the waterline length and helping prevent separation of the flow.

The creation of lift

When sailing on the wind, the rig produces a side force which has to be counteracted by the hull. This is achieved by sailing at an angle of leeway, λ, so that the keel and rudder produce a lift force. The canoe body is not an efficient producer of lift due to its shallow sections, and the negative lift it produces when heeled.

As the force developed by a foil acts in a direction approximately perpendicular to its surface, a drag component, the induced drag, is inevitably associated with lift. The magnitude of the induced drag is proportional to the angle of leeway; even on a well designed yacht, the induced drag can amount to as much as a quarter of the total resistance when sailing close-hauled.

In addition to the induced drag, there is profile drag. This term includes all the drag components except induced drag, that is, skin friction, separation drag, and drag due to the thickness and section of the foil; all these components arise due to the viscosity of water. Additionally, the proximity of the keel to the surface on monohulls when heeled may result in some additional wavemaking drag resistance.

The combined area of the keel and rudder is of prime importance. If it is too great, the angle of leeway will be small, but the frictional resistance will be excessive; if too small, performance off the wind will be improved by the reduction in frictional resistance, but upwind pointing will be poor and the

14

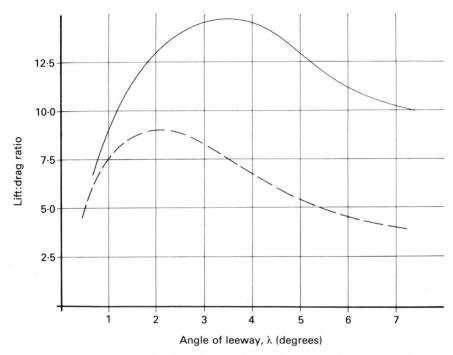

Fig. 1.10. Lift:drag ratios for a keel and a rudder. The rudder curve – shown dashed – has a lower lift:drag ratio, and reaches its optimum value at a lower angle of leeway, due to the turbulent wake of the keel.

induced drag excessive. The optimum angle of leeway lies at around 3° or 4°, requiring a combined area of keel and rudder amounting to 3–5% of the windward sail area. Beamy hulls obviously need larger keels to counteract the negative lift produced by the hull; on the other hand boats capable of high upwind speeds can have smaller keels. This is because both the keel's lift and the rig's sideforce vary with the square of the speed, and fast boats can attain a greater ratio of boatspeed to apparent wind speed. The drawback is that when the keel area is too small, if boat speed drops off, for example when coming out of a tack, performance will be poor until the helm bears off to regain boatspeed.

A large proportion of induced drag is due to a vortex trailing from the tip of the keel; this is formed by water twisting round the tip from the high pressure to the low pressure face, that is, from the leeward to the windward side. The strength of this vortex can be reduced by moving as much of the keel as possible away from the tip, and also by reducing the size of the tip in proportion to the keel area. This explains the marked superiority of deep, narrow, high aspect ratio keels.

From the above argument it can be seen that the taper ratio of the keel will affect the induced drag, and a more tapered keel should have less drag. This holds up to a point, but if the keel is tapered by too great an amount the vortex

15

forms some distance up from the keel's tip, increasing the drag. The optimum taper is one where the ratio of the tip chord to the root chord is about 40–60%.

The amount of sweepback also affects the water flow, and its effect is tied in with the amount of taper. Although the effect of sweepback is relatively small, a sweepback of 5° gives the least induced drag; however, values ranging from 0–30° will only have a marginal effect on the overall drag. If the keel is given a large amount of taper, or if it gets thicker towards the tip, a greater amount of sweepback is required for minimum drag.

Profile drag is dictated by the foil section used. The major criterion here is the thickness:chord ratio, thick sections resulting in greater drag. In addition, at low speeds fat sections are very prone to separation, as are some of the low drag sections with concave trailing edges developed for use on aircraft. However, thin sections are more prone to stalling when manoeuvring, and their small cross-sectional area means that not as much ballast can be placed in the keel. The optimum thickness:chord ratio is about 8% or 9%, but this is often increased to as much as 15% to incorporate more ballast.

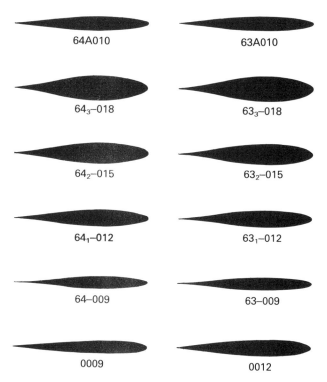

Fig. 1.11(a). A comparison of some NACA foil sections. The last two digits denote the thickness:chord ratio, the first two the foil family. Sections 63A010 and 64A010 do not have a hollow trailing edge, unlike the rest of the 63 and 64 series, and so are considerably easier to fabricate.

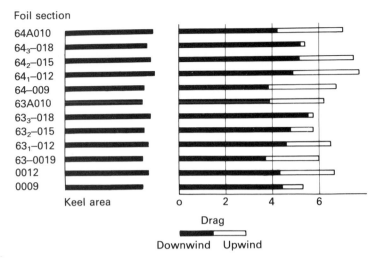

Fig. 1.11(b). Keel section comparison. The areas are calculated to give equal lift at 4° leeway, and then used to determine the drag. The upwind drag is calculated for 4° leeway, the downwind drag assumes zero leeway. The calculations are based upon a 35-foot yacht sailing at 6 knots; as boat speed and keel dimensions are changed, the drag characteristics of the sections also change.

The best sections generally have a fairly full entry, but with the point of maximum thickness about 40% aft of the leading edge, and a fine, straight trailing edge. If the point of maximum thickness is moved forwards the drag is increased, but if it is moved aft the flow is more prone to separation, and stalling occurs at lower angles of incidence.

Keel configurations

The vast majority of boats have a simple fixed keel. It is highly efficient, and needs no adjustment by the crew; its drawbacks are a fixed deep draught, the inability to reduce wetted area when off the wind, and the need for lateral support when drying out. Keels with a large amount of sweepback can present a further problem when drying out as, if the forward end of the keel lies aft of the boat's centre of gravity, the yacht will dry out balanced on the forefoot and the keel.

A trim tab may be fitted in an attempt to improve the keel's efficiency. This is an adjustable flap in the trailing edge of the keel, comprising about 25% of the area. It enables the keel to be given an asymmetric shape, increasing the lift developed. However, the drag is also increased, and it has yet to be proven conclusively that there is an overall improvement in performance. Perhaps its main advantage is that when coupled with the rudder it makes the yacht exceptionally manoevrable.

Some cruising multihulls are designed with no keel whatsoever. Instead, a deep V-shaped hull section is used, acting as a very low aspect ratio keel. This configuration is very inefficient, and the inevitable large angle of leeway is responsible for the poor windward performance of many cruising multihulls. This must be accepted as the price to pay for the benefits of an extremely shallow draught.

Monohulls may be fitted with bilge keels to provide a shallow draught facility, and also to ensure that the yacht remains upright when drying out. The area of the keels has to be considerably greater than normal, due to their low aspect ratio together with the low efficiency of the windward keel when heeled. Even so, leeway may be up to 5° greater than with a conventional fin keel.

Daggerboards offer the advantages of reduced wetted surface area when raised downwind, and a shallow draught. Against this, the board case must be carried right up to the deckhead to ensure the watertight integrity of the hull, and this intrudes upon the interior layout quite considerably. The board and its case are also prone to damage if the yacht runs aground at speed.

On a monohull the board must be able to be locked in place, to prevent it dropping out in the event of a knockdown. If the board is ballasted, it should not be able to be raised to such a height that the boat's large angle stability is impaired; if unballasted, the hull form will have to be more stable to compensate for the higher centre of gravity.

Centreboards offer the same advantages as daggerboards. As the board is pivoted, though, it is unlikely to be damaged by running aground; the case is also much less obtrusive, particularly if set into a stub keel below the hull. Against this, the extra length of the slot causes a considerable amount of turbulence, and thereby drag.

Sailing in waves

Unfortunately the sea is not flat, and boats have to sail through waves. To windward the yacht is sailing into the waves, which results in pitching. This not only causes discomfort to the crew, but also slows the boat. Depending upon the conditions, resistance can be increased by as much as 80%. Off the wind the waves are overtaking the boat, and this can give rise to surfing, broaching, rolling and pooping.

As the boat meets a wave when sailing to windward, the increase in buoyancy forwards causes the bows to rise, and so pitching is initiated. But as the bows rise the stern becomes more deeply immersed, counteracting the pitching moment created at the bows. This suggests that a wedge-shaped hull is best, the bow having fine V-sections with little flare or overhang, and the stern drawn broad and flat with a long, low overhang. Although the V-ed bow sections are ideal for multihulls, they are far from perfect on monohulls when heeled. The buoyancy builds up more rapidly as the bows become immersed, and also the section

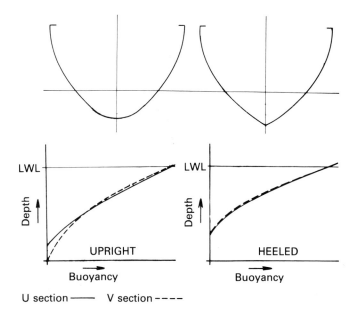

U section ——— V section ----

Fig. 1.12(a). A comparison of U- and V-shaped bow sections. When upright the V section has a more gradual increase in buoyancy with depth, but when heeled the differences are negligible. However, when heeled the V section presents a very flat surface to the waves, resulting in pounding.

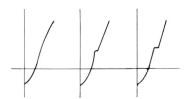

Fig. 1.12(b). Multihull bow sections, showing some of the methods used to increase buoyancy without excessive freeboard or flare.

presents a flat surface to the waves, resulting in pounding.

Another important factor affecting pitching is the weight of the vessel, and its distribution. When the boat pitches it pivots like a seesaw about the centroid of its load waterline, usually just forward of station 6. The amount of energy absorbed in pitching is dependent upon the moment of inertia of the boat. This is the summation of the products of the weight of each element making up the boat, multiplied by the square of its distance from the pivot point, measured in the vertical/fore and aft plane.

From this we can arrive at two conclusions. Firstly, performance can be improved by centralising all the weights, minimising their distances from the pitching centre. This is why some racing boats have ballast ratios of up to 65%, yet carry relatively little of it in the keel. Secondly, light displacement designs will have a relatively small increase in resistance compared to heavier boats. However, the extra stability of heavier boats enables them to carry more than enough sail area to compensate for this, so in practice they perform better than lighter designs. Also, heavier boats have a slower, steadier motion that is less tiring to the crew.

The bows need to have sufficient reserves of buoyancy to prevent the foredeck from plunging under waves. If this were allowed to happen the boat would be slowed, spray created, and working the foredeck would become considerably more hazardous. The greater the moment of inertia of a boat, the greater the reserves of buoyancy required to lift the bows. The best way of providing this is by high freeboard – more flared sections, fuller waterlines or a longer overhang will all increase pitching.

The fine bows of multihulls may require an excessive amount of freeboard, and as an alternative the amount of flare can be increased near the deck edge. Some of the sections used are shown in Fig. 1.12.

A problem peculiar to multihulls is that of keeping the cross-beams or bridge deck clear of the waves. The easiest way of solving this problem is to have plenty of freeboard; alternatively the cross-beams can be kept horizontal for most of their length, and then swoop down to the outriggers. In any event, the bridge deck or cross-beams should be given sharp leading edges to avoid impact damage from waves.

If the boat is designed with a solid bridge deck it should stop some distance short of the bows, to prevent it pounding when the boat pitches. Another problem is that where the bow waves meet under the bridge deck they will combine to create a large crest, which may strike the bridge deck at speed. This wave can be parted by having a vestigial hull underneath the deck, clear of the waterline; this can also improve headroom in the cabin, and increase hull stiffness.

Sailing downwind, a full, flat stern is favoured to promote surfing. The stern must also be sufficiently buoyant so that it can lift to a following sea, and prevent the boat being pooped. Many yachtsmen have extolled the seaworthiness of various designs, particularly the canoe stern; in fact the actual shape is unimportant – it is the amount of buoyancy that matters.

The requirements for the bows are somewhat different from those when sailing to windward. When sailing down the face of a wave the tendency is for the bows to dig in, moving the centre of lateral resistance forwards and increasing the likelihood of a broach. To prevent this the bows must have sufficient fullness in the waterlines. Racing multihulls also need sufficient buoyancy to prevent the bows burying into the face of the next wave, as this may lead to a pitchpole capsize.

All monohulls have a tendency to roll downwind. Although it is impossible to design a hull that will not roll, much can be done to damp it down. One important factor is the lateral area. Small, high aspect ratio keels are notoriously poor when it comes to damping rolling, whilst the large area and low aspect ratio of bilge keels makes them excellent in this respect.

A second factor is the shape of the hull sections. A V-ed hull will roll relatively slowly, but there will be little roll damping; on the other hand a flat, boxy section will seldom roll, but when it does the motion will be very rapid.

Stability

The creation of stability

Designing a hull with low resistance is only half the problem. It must also have good stability, so that it can carry sufficient sail to perform well. No matter what the type of hull, stability is created in the same manner, as shown in Fig. 1.13. In diagram (a) the boat is upright and in stable equilibrium, as the centre of buoyancy, B, and the centre of gravity, G, are both acting in the same vertical plane. Note that the boat is in equilibrium even though the centre of gravity lies above the centre of buoyancy.

In diagram (b) the vessel has now heeled. To windward a portion of the hull has risen out of the water, and to leeward a wedge of equal volume has become immersed. This results in the centre of buoyancy moving to leeward, to B_θ; the centre of gravity has also moved to leeward, but by a lesser amount. This means that a righting lever, GZ, has been set up, and the righting moment is given by $GZ \times \triangle$. Exactly the same principle applies to multihulls, with the lee float becoming increasingly immersed whilst the windward one emerges from the water.

At moderate angles of heel, B_θ can be assumed to lie on the circumference of a circle passing through B, and the centre of this circle is called the metacentre, M. The radius of the circle is given by: $BM = I/\nabla$, where I is the transverse moment of inertia of the load waterline, and is proportional to the waterline length and the cube of the waterline beam. The righting lever is then given by $GZ = GM \times \sin \theta$.

Displacement and ballast ratios

As we have seen, the righting moment is directly proportional to the vessel's weight. It is also dependent upon the height of the centre of gravity, as a lower centre of gravity means a higher value for GZ.

These two factors are very much interrelated. As the minimum hull weight is limited by the need for sufficient structural strength, a heavy displacement design will be able to carry more ballast than a lighter design of the same size, and so the heavier boat will have the lower centre of gravity of the two. Obviously this is an over-simplification as, for example, a heavy displacement design built of steel and

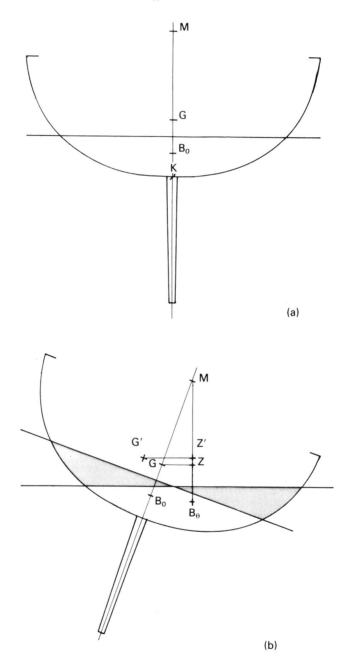

Fig. 1.13. The creation of stability. (a): Upright condition. The boat is in equilibrium, with both B_0 and G lying in the same vertical plane. (b): Heeled to 20°. B_θ is to leeward of G, resulting in the righting lever GZ. If the crew sit on the windward rail G is moved to G', giving an increased righting lever $G'Z'$. For this half tonner, stability is increased by about 50%.

22

with a well appointed interior may carry less ballast than a stripped out racing boat built with lightweight materials. Ballast ratios may vary from as little as 30%, right up to a massive 70% of the displacement; the majority of multihulls carry no ballast though, as they gain sufficient stability from their wide beam.

There are various ways of increasing the effectiveness of ballast. One of the most common is to use a denser material so that the ballast can be placed lower down in the keel, such as a change from iron to lead. Alternatively, the keel design itself can be changed to give more volume, especially lower down; this may include increasing the draught, using a fatter section, or reducing the amount of taper.

Form stability

Form stability can be defined as stability due to the boat's shape. However, it is still related to displacement, as the displacement dictates the immersed volume.

The simplest case to consider is that of the multihull. The small angles of heel mean that we can assume the centre of gravity to remain stationary, and the underwater shape of the hulls to remain constant. This means that stability is entirely due to the transference of buoyancy from the windward to the leeward hull.

Stability increases rapidly until the windward hull lifts clear of the water or, in the case of a trimaran with low buoyancy floats, the leeward float becomes submerged. Once this point is passed, no more buoyancy can be transferred to leeward, and the centre of gravity moves to leeward. Thus the stability rapidly falls off, and a capsize is highly likely. It is worth noting that low buoyancy outriggers reduce the maximum stability of trimarans, as it is not possible to transfer all the buoyancy to leeward.

The form stability of a monohull is not quite so simple. It is highly dependent on the shape of the hull sections, particularly amidships. Figure 1.15 shows a variety of midship sections, together with their stability curves. All sections have the same displacement, and the same position of the centre of gravity.

Sections A, B and C show the effect of changes in the beam:draught ratio, BWL/T_c. The high dependence of stability on beam can be seen, as it varies with the cube of the beam.

Sections A, D and E vary the amount of flare in the topsides. Section D, with a slack bilge and large amount of flare, has a slight advantage in stability at large heel angles; this is due to the flared topsides becoming increasingly immersed as the boat heels. A further advantage in racing yachts is that the crew can sit further outboard, and so their weight has a greater effect on stability. Section E, with little flare and a hard turn of bilge, shows a marked reduction in stability once the bilge has become immersed.

Sections A, F and G show the effects of freeboard and tumblehome. As expected, the low freeboard of section F results in the gunwhale becoming immersed at a lower angle of heel, with a subsequent reduction in stability. If tumblehome is introduced, as in section G, then although the heel angle at which the deck

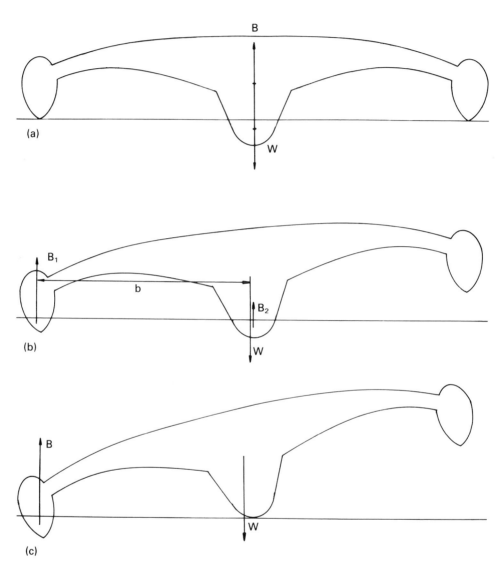

Fig. 1.14. Multihull stability. (a): Upright. The buoyancy B is equal to the weight W. In the case of a catamaran the buoyancy of each hull is equal to $0.5B$. (b): Heeled. The righting moment is approximately given by bB_1, or for a catamaran by $b(B_1 - B_2)$. (c): Maximum stability. Once again, assuming that the angle of heel is small, the righting moment is given by bW.

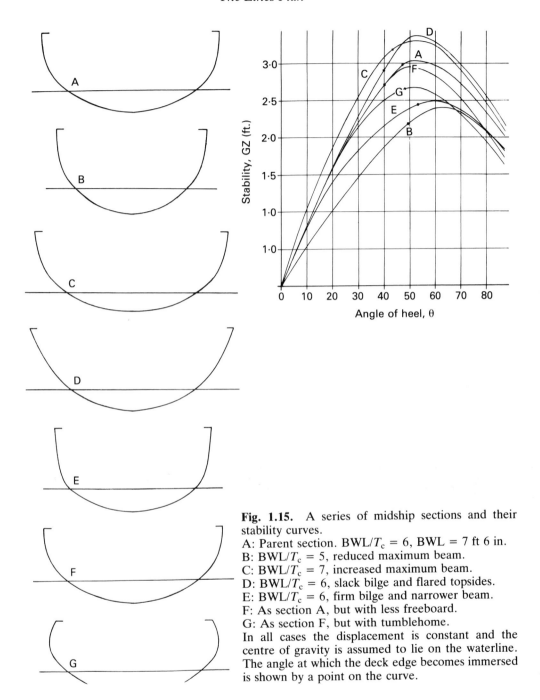

Fig. 1.15. A series of midship sections and their stability curves.
A: Parent section. BWL/T_c = 6, BWL = 7 ft 6 in.
B: BWL/T_c = 5, reduced maximum beam.
C: BWL/T_c = 7, increased maximum beam.
D: BWL/T_c = 6, slack bilge and flared topsides.
E: BWL/T_c = 6, firm bilge and narrower beam.
F: As section A, but with less freeboard.
G: As section F, but with tumblehome.
In all cases the displacement is constant and the centre of gravity is assumed to lie on the waterline. The angle at which the deck edge becomes immersed is shown by a point on the curve.

immerses is increased, stability is decreased. Thus the deck edge becomes immersed in the same strength of wind, but the boat with tumblehome is sailing at a greater heel angle.

Although the midship section makes the greatest contribution to form stability, the shape of the entire hull must be taken into account. This is particularly the case if the boat has a wide, flat stern, which will make a significant contribution to her stability.

Water ballast and hydrofoils

The quest for higher performance has resulted in several methods of increasing stability. One of these is the use of water ballast. Water is pumped into a tank on the weather side, either directly from the sea or from a partner tank on the opposite side. This moves the centre of gravity to windward, and so increases GZ. To date its use has been restricted to monohulls, such as Tabarly's *Pen Duick V* and the Mini-Transat yacht *American Express*. However, the principle could easily be extended to multihulls with good effect.

Another approach uses hydrofoils to stabilise a multihull. This is not the same as designing the boat to fly on foils, with the hulls clear of the water. Flying only becomes advantageous at speeds over about $2.8\sqrt{LWL}$, with a considerable drag penalty at lower speeds unless the foils are retractable.

The foils are set at 40–45° to the waterline, producing a force that counteracts the heeling moment of the rig. If the beam is great enough it is possible to counteract the heeling moment completely. Unfortunately, this requires a beam greater than the boat's length, and structural limitations rule this out. However, a considerable increase in stability can still be achieved with a lesser beam.

Secondary advantages of foils are the use of the lift to prevent the lee bow burying at speed, and a marked reduction in pitching due to the strong damping effect of the canted foils. However, it must be remembered that any increase in stability from foils is dependent upon the boat's speed; if the boat stops, she is no more stable than a conventional multihull.

Ultimate stability – monohulls

Many people assume that a ballasted monohull cannot capsize, but this is not the case. As Fig. 1.15 shows, once a boat heels beyond about 50° her stability drops off quite markedly. Eventually, at an angle of about 120°, a capsize becomes inevitable.

One possible reason for a capsize is a severe knockdown. The risk of this can be reduced by increasing stability at about 90° of heel. As stability depends upon the distance separating the centre of buoyancy and the centre of gravity, this can be achieved by lowering the centre of gravity, or increasing the freeboard or the

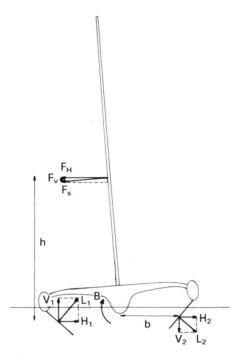

Fig. 1.16. Foil stabilisation of a multihull. The hydrofoils produce lift forces L_1 and L_2. The horizontal components, H_1 and H_2, resist leeway. The moments of the vertical components help resist the heeling moment of the rig, so that in equilibrium: $hF_H = bV_1 + bV_2 + B$ where B is the righting moment produced by the leeward hull. The downward component of the sail force, F_v, is partially counterbalanced by the vertical component produced by the foils, $V_1 - V_2$.

amount of flare in the topsides. Thus yachts with a relatively high centre of gravity should be given a generous amount of freeboard, or a large, high coachroof.

Another reason for a yacht to capsize is a large wave breaking over it; because of the rapidity of this event, dynamic effects come into play. This means that in addition to the need for good static stability, the weight distribution in the transverse plane is also important. A stripped out racing boat, with all her weight concentrated amidships, is more likely to be rolled over than a cruising boat, where the weights are likely to be well distributed through the hull.

If a capsize does occur, the sea conditions will be rough enough for the waves to right the boat quickly. This will be helped by a low centre of gravity, high freeboard and a large coachroof, whilst a large beam will tend to make the yacht more stable.

Ultimate stability – multihulls

It is the risk of capsize that puts most people off sailing multihulls, especially cruising yachtsmen who are more concerned with safety than with speed.

However, the great majority of capsizes occur in racing multihulls, due to the crew pushing the boat right to the limit; capsizes in cruising multihulls are few and far between. Unfortunately, it is the racing capsizes that gain all the publicity.

The problem is that once the weather hull lifts clear of the water stability drops off rapidly, and once the yacht is heeled to about 90° a capsize is inevitable. When capsized, the boat is just as stable as when the right way up, and so there is no possibility of the boat righting herself.

There has been a long running debate about whether trimarans should have high or low buoyancy floats. Low buoyancy floats have a volume less than the boat's displacement, and so when hard pressed the float submerges. Thus the boat capsizes around the main hull, which remains on the water's surface. The advantage of this configuration is that it gives greater warning of a capsize; against this, the yacht's maximum stability is determined by the volume of the outrigger. More importantly, if the lee float becomes submerged when the boat is beam on to a wave a large capsizing moment is set up, due to the high resistance of the float opposing the tendency for the main hull to slide down the wave face. This has resulted in capsizes even when hove to with no sail set.

High buoyancy floats are now much more common than the low buoyancy type. There is no risk of the boat tripping over her leeward outrigger, and the extra stability means that the chances of being capsized by a gust of wind are reduced. The drawbacks are that the crew are not given as dramatic a warning of imminent capsize, and the extra windage of the main hull when well heeled results in a faster capsize.

There are several reasons for a multihull capsize. The most obvious is carrying too much sail; the solution is equally obvious – if in doubt, reef. Particular care should be taken in gusty conditions, as multihulls cannot spill wind by heeling to a gust.

The presence of steep waves increases the risk of a capsize. When the boat heels to a beam wave, the righting lever GZ is reduced. This problem is greatest in trimarans and small catamarans, as the smaller spacing between the immersed hulls means that the vessel contours more closely to the wave shape, and so a larger angle of heel builds up. This is compounded by the capsizing moment due to the boat's tendency to slide down into the trough – though this can be reduced by raising the daggerboard, and so reducing the hull's lateral resistance. In extreme conditions, if all sail is taken off and the daggerboard raised, the risk of capsize is almost zero (except in a trimaran with low buoyancy floats), as the boat behaves just like a raft.

Another method of capsizing is diagonally over the lee bow. This is only likely to occur when sailing fast off the wind in heavy weather. The thrust of the sails tends to depress the lee bow, and this may be exacerbated by the boat surfing down one wave into the back of the next one. The sudden increase in resistance stops the boat, and the driving force of the sails causes her to cartwheel round the lee bow. A capsize over the stern is also possible when sailing to windward over a steep wave with minimal way on. Both of these capsizes can be avoided by providing plenty of buoyancy in the ends of the outboard hulls.

Power to carry sail

After studying the elements of stability, the next step is to see how much sail the boat can carry. Figure 1.17 shows the requirements for equilibrium: the heeling moment of the sails must be balanced by the righting moment of the hull. The centre of effort of the sails and the centre of lateral resistance are assumed to lie at

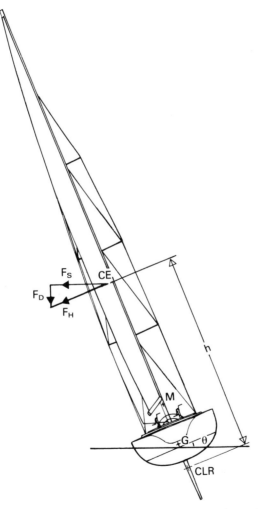

Fig. 1.17. Heeled equilibrium. The righting moment, $\triangle \times GM \sin \theta$, must equal the heeling moment, $F_H \times h \cos^2 \theta$. Note that when heeled there is a downwards component to the sail force, F_D, increasing the boat's displacement.

the centroids of the sail plan and the underwater profile respectively. Expressing the equilibrium condition in a formula gives:

$$F_H \times h \times \cos^2 \theta = \triangle \times GM \times \sin \theta$$

where F_H is the sideways force produced by the sails, and is proportional to the sail area, and h is the heeling arm of the rig.

Whilst this equation gives the equilibrium condition, it is not much use when examining the stiffness or tenderness of a design. For monohulls, the Dellenbaugh Angle (DA) is often used, which is given by:

$$DA = \frac{A_S \times h}{RM_1}$$

where A_S is the sail area, h the heeling arm, and RM_1 the righting moment at one degree of heel. Values range from 7–20°, a large angle implying a generous sail plan. Because of the rapid increase in stability with size, and the lesser contribution of crew weight to stability, large yachts tend to have a smaller Dellenbaugh Angle.

With multihulls the small angle of heel necessitates a different means of comparison; because stability is primarily dependent upon overall beam and displacement, a simpler formula can be used. One of these is a Stability Factor (*SF*), given by:

$$SF = \frac{BMAX \times \triangle}{A_S \times h}$$

where *BMAX* is the overall beam of the vessel, and units are feet and pounds. Values range between 10 and 15, a small value indicating a generous sail plan and low reserves of stability.

If a design has a small Dellenbaugh Angle, or a large multihull Stability Factor, she will be undercanvassed in light airs, and will not need to reef until well up the wind scale. If she carries plenty of sail for her stability, though, this is not necessarily a bad thing. In light airs her performance will be much enhanced, though she will have to reduce sail comparatively early on. This means that in stronger winds the top of the mast will be contributing unnecessary windage, as well as adversely affecting the weight distribution.

Performance parameters

In addition to the waterline length and the displacement:length ratio, designers use a number of ratios to help estimate the performance potential of a design.

The sail area:wetted surface area ratio is a guide to light airs performance, relating the propulsive force to the frictional resistance. A figure of about 2.5 is essential for adequate performance in light airs; a 30-foot racing boat will have a value approaching 3.0, whilst due to scaling factors an 80-footer may have a value slightly under 4.0.

The sail area:displacement ratio (in square feet/ton) compares the propulsive force with the wavemaking resistance. It begins to be significant at speeds of about $0.6\sqrt{LWL}$, and dominates the boat's performance from $1.0\sqrt{LWL}$ until the boat has to reef; beyond this point stability becomes the critical factor. Values for monohulls range from 70 to 180, with larger designs having smaller values. With multihulls values range from 100 for cruising designs, right up to 350 for racing craft.

Two other factors may be used, although not specifically related to performance criteria. One of these is $\sqrt{A_S}/LWL$. A high value tends to indicate a boat designed for light airs, and a low value a bias towards stronger winds. Values range from 0.7 to 1.0.

The other ratio is that of $A_S:\triangle^{2/3}$, sometimes called the Bruce number when calculated in feet and pounds; alternatively, units of feets and tons may be used. Sticking to feet and pounds, yachts with a value below 1.0 are unlikely to perform well; monohulls have values up to around 1.5, but some racing multihulls go as high as 3.3. This ratio is often referred to as the sail area:displacement ratio and used in preference to $A_S:\triangle$ as its value is almost independent of size.

Scaling effects

It is worth looking at how some of the design parameters change with the size of the yacht. If a design is doubled in size, sail area and wetted surface area will increase fourfold; displacement, wavemaking resistance and heeling moment increase eightfold; and stability goes up by a factor of 16. Thus the sail area:wetted surface area remains the same, but the sail area:displacement ratio is halved, and stability has increased by twice as much as the heeling moment.

If the sail area is increased to give a sixteenfold rise in heeling moment, the yacht can carry about 26% more sail. This increases the sail area:wetted surface area ratio by the same amount, enhancing light airs performance. However, the sail area:displacement ratio is still only 63% of its original value, and for this reason small boats find it easier to attain high speed:length ratios than large ones.

Directional control

The rudder

The rudder must fulfill two functions: it makes up part of the lateral area, contributing to lift production and balance; and it is also responsible for steering the boat. Rudder design concentrates on providing good steering characteristics, but this does not significantly mar its efficiency as a creator of lift.

A yacht turns about its keel, and so the rudder needs to be sited well aft to maximise its leverage. For good steering characteristics its area should not be less than about 8% of the total lateral area, with smaller boats needing proportionately larger rudders. If the rudder operates in a region of separated flow, or if it lifts out of the water as the boat heels, a larger area will be required.

The aspect ratio of the rudder varies quite considerably, between 2 and 3.8; shallow draft designs may use even lower aspect ratios so that the blade is not damaged when the boat takes the ground. High aspect ratios give a quick response and low drag, but tend to stall easily if the helm is put hard over. Thus cruising yachts are better off with a lower aspect ratio, giving a slower, steadier response.

The foil section used has a considerable effect on the stall characteristics. A fairly fat section with the fullness well forward will have a large stall angle, and provide gentle stall characteristics. On the other hand a thin section will have a lower stall angle, and although there will be marginally less drag if the fullness is moved aft, there will also be a very sudden stall.

The simplest method of fixing the rudder is to hang it on the transom. However, this is limited to boats with a nearly vertical transom and, in general, to tiller steering. Although cheap and simple, the rudder does lose some efficiency due to being exposed to the water's surface without the end plate effect of the hull.

The most efficient position for the rudder is underneath the hull. The rudder gains in efficiency through being butted up against the hull, and can be controlled by a tiller or a wheel. Generally, some of the rudder area is placed forwards of the stock giving a balanced rudder, which requires less force to operate it. If a long shallow skeg is fitted in front of the blade, the stall angle will be increased, yet the quick response of this type of rudder will not be diminished.

The skeg hung rudder is most common on cruising yachts, particularly in the larger sizes. The skeg may have a chord up to half as long as that of the rudder blade, and it extends to the bottom of the blade. The rudder is attached to the skeg at the tip, and possibly half-way up, protecting it and strengthening it; however, it is essential that the skeg is rigidly connected to the hull structure if it is to withstand the loads placed on it. This configuration gives the rudder a larger stall angle and a slower, steadier rate of response to helm movements, at the expense of increased drag; the larger the skeg in proportion to the rudder, the more marked these characteristics will be.

Directional stability

Boats designed purely for maximum speed tend to be very twitchy to steer, with performance dropping off markedly if the boat leaves its narrow performance groove. Although the crew can maintain the necessary level of concentration over short races, ocean racers and cruising boats should be designed for a much broader performance groove and steadier tracking, at the cost of a marginal drop in maximum speed. Otherwise the crew will tire quickly, and as a result there will be a marked drop in performance.

Keel and rudder design has a marked effect on directional stability. The combination of minimum lateral area and high aspect ratios gives a very rapid rate of response to the helm, together with poor tracking characteristics. To increase the directional stability the lateral area should be increased, the aspect ratios of keel and rudder decreased, and the amount of sweepback and taper increased; also, a skeg rudder should be employed.

The hull has a lesser, but still significant, effect on directional stability. A deep profile will have more grip on the water, and so improve tracking. This is particularly the case forwards, but if taken too far it will also increase the tendency to broach downwind.

Balance

Balance is one of the least well understood areas of yacht design, and designers all work on a rule-of-thumb basis. Several theories have been put forward suggesting what makes a well balanced yacht, most notably Admiral Turner's Metacentric Shelf Theory. Whilst these work for some hull forms, other hulls not conforming to any theory may balance just as well.

The aim is to get the sail plan and the underwater body in correct relation to one another, so that the boat carries only a slight amount of weather helm. The distance by which the centre of effort lies forward of the centre of lateral resistance is called the lead, and is usually expressed as a percentage of the waterline length.

When a monohull heels, the centre of effort moves to leeward of the centre of lateral resistance, and a couple is set up. Thus in the upright position the boat must be given a lead of between 13% and 20% if she is to be balanced when heeled. Beamy hulls, or those with a full bow, need a greater lead than slim boats, or those with a wide, flared stern. On the other hand fractional rigs need a smaller lead than masthead boats, as the large overlapping genoa of the masthead rig moves the centre of effort well aft of its calculated position.

The situation with multihulls is somewhat different. As the lee hull immerses it creates more drag than the windward one, moving the centre of resistance to leeward; at the same time the thrust from the sails depresses the lee bow, moving the centre of lateral resistance forwards. These two factors tend to counteract each other, and so a smaller lead of 5–10% can be used.

Monohull design

The whole art of monohull design boils down to finding the correct balance between an easily driven hull with low stability and low sail area, and a stable hull carrying a cloud of sail but having high resistance.

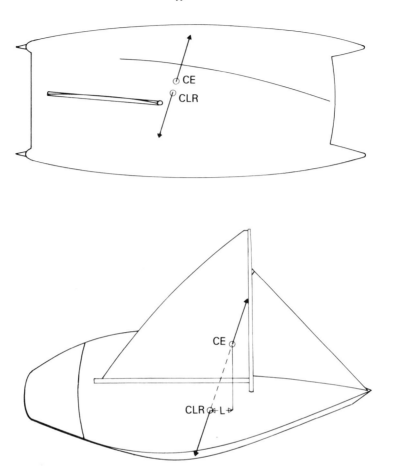

Fig. 1.18. Balance. The catamaran sails almost upright, and the drag moment of the windward hull largely cancels out the moment of the leeward hull, so only a very small lead is required. With a monohull the centre of effort swings out to leeward of the centre of resistance, so a greater lead, L, is required. A trimaran falls midway between a cat and a monohull, as there is no immersed windward hull and the angle of heel is greater than a catamaran's.

Heavy displacement hulls are at their best in light winds, as the deep, rounded sections give a comparatively low wetted area for their displacement, and hence for their stability. Against this the maximum speed is limited to about $1.4\sqrt{\text{LWL}}$. This is no drawback upwind, where speeds are limited to about $1.05\sqrt{\text{LWL}}$, but it does limit performance off the wind. Other advantages are that the extra hull depth increases headroom, and the performance is relatively unaffected by heavy stores.

Lightweight boats come into their own downwind, having a much slower rise in resistance with speed. Against this they have a large wetted surface area for their displacement, and a low ballast ratio. One great advantage is that they are relatively cheap to build, due to the smaller quantity of materials used (unless exotic and expensive materials are used to build an ultra-light hull).

Increasing the beam is in many ways the easiest and most efficient way of increasing stability; it also greatly increases the boat's interior volume. However, the large amount of asymmetry in the heeled waterlines reduces the boat's pointing ability. There is also an increase in wetted surface area, due to the wide, flat hull sections used.

Narrow hulls offer less resistance at low speeds, and also are not tossed around so much by waves. When heeled they are more tolerant of large heel angles, and so less frequent sail changes are required. However, they do suffer from low stability.

We can combine the above characteristics into four hull types: light and narrow, light and beamy, heavy and narrow, and heavy and wide. Obviously these are extremes, and most designs will be more moderate in approach.

A light, narrow hull has the lowest resistance and the lowest stability. She will be relatively undercanvassed, and so a poor performer except downwind in a blow. To avoid this, light designs are drawn with a generous beam to provide adequate stability. In light airs performance is still slightly below par due to the poor sail area:wetted surface area ratio, and to windward the beam detracts from pointing ability. Off the wind, though, performance is excellent, especially in windy conditions.

Heavy, narrow hulls are at their best when light, beamy boats are at their worst. Their strong points are beating and light airs, but off the wind speed is severely restricted by the high displacement:length ratio. If the beam is increased, the resultant increase in sail area improves performance in light airs. However, pointing ability is reduced upwind, and so the boat has to sail faster for the same speed made good; also the maximum speed is still restricted off the wind, and all that the extra sail area will do is increase the tendency to broach.

Multihull design

In some respects multihulls are much easier to design than monohulls. This is because their stability is virtually independent of hull shape, and heel is negligible. Against this, the displacement of each hull varies from virtually zero right up to the full displacement of the vessel, and the hulls must be efficient throughout this entire range.

This is achieved by having a deep forefoot to give a good entry under all load conditions, coupled with sufficient overhang aft to prevent the transom digging in when hard pressed. At present hull shapes tend to be nearly circular amidships to minimise wetted surface area, but it would probably pay to use a flatter section to improve high speed performance, at the expense of a slight increase in wetted area.

As stability is directly proportional both to overall beam and to displacement, wider designs can be built lighter, improving both the sail area:displacement ratio and the sail area:wetted area ratio. If the displacement is increased, the increase in sail area maintains the same sail area:wetted area ratio, but the sail area:displacement ratio drops. For this reason racing multihulls are built as lightly as possible. Cruising multihulls, though, must be comparatively heavy to carry the interior joinery and stores, and to provide a greater margin of safety; this explains the wide gulf between the performance of racing and cruising craft.

The catamaran

Catamarans are favoured by cruising sailors, as in sizes over 30 feet the two hulls and deckhouse combine to give a very spacious interior. This generally results in fairly high freeboard, both to give standing headroom in the hulls and to ensure that there is adequate clearance below the bridge deck.

For the racing yachtsman catamarans are not so popular. Although there is no penalty in the weight and windage of the third hull of a trimaran, both stability and the sail area:wetted area ratio are low. Because of the structural problems involved in supporting a mast between the hulls, the beam is limited to no more than about 60% of the length. In light airs the wetted area of the two hulls may be up to 40% greater than a trimaran carrying almost all her weight on the central hull.

The trimaran

Trimarans offer better racing performance than catamarans, as their overall beam can be as much as 75% of their length, offering 25% more stability than a catamaran. They also have less wetted surface area in light airs, when the leeward hull just skims the water.

For the cruising yachtsman accommodation is restricted to the central hull, and to some extent the solid wings if fitted. The outriggers are too small to be used for anything but stowage until the length exceeds about 50 feet. However, trimarans are favoured for cruising in boats below 30 feet, as the hulls of a catamaran become too small, and a central deckhouse of any useful size cannot be carried.

The main hull is at its greatest displacement in light airs, whilst the outriggers are most heavily loaded at speed. This can be used to advantage in the design: the central hull should have nearly semi-circular sections for minimum wetted area, flattened at the bottom to give a higher beam:draught ratio at speed; to give the outriggers minimum resistance at speed they need to be as long as possible, perhaps longer than the central hull, and with a shallow V-section rounded at the bottom to give a high beam:draught ratio at speed, yet a small wetted area when lightly loaded.

The proa

In the search for speed at any cost, some yachtsmen and designers have pursued a proa configuration. The Atlantic proa is essentially a trimaran without the windward hull; the Pacific proa consists of a main hull with an outrigger to windward, stabilised purely by weight in the windward hull. Luckily, only one or two freak boats have pursued the proa configuration for sailing offshore. The most remarkable feature of the proa is its lack of lateral symmetry, which means that it is unable to tack or gybe in the conventional sense. Instead it is given fore and aft symmetry, and has to shunt round from tack to tack.

The arguments for the Atlantic proa centre on an increase in stability. The beam can be fairly high, and the centre of gravity is moved towards the windward hull, as it carries the rig, crew and stores. Also, the wetted surface area is slightly lower than that of a catamaran, though not as low as a trimaran's.

The need for perfect fore and aft symmetry means that the full performance potential of the proa cannot be realised. As we have seen, a double-ended hull is not the most efficient at high speeds, nor does it perform well in waves. Further complications arise because of the need to reverse the rig, daggerboard and rudder each time the vessel shunts. This creates a very unwieldy craft in confined waters.

The main drawback, though, is the very great risk of a capsize. With the Atlantic proa this will occur if caught aback, but for the Pacific proa it will also occur if there is insufficient weight to windward for the wind strength. The risk is particularly great for single-handed sailors, as it is not possible to stand watch all the time. Designers try to prevent a windward capsize by a prominent bulge on the windward side, which may fulfill its purpose in calm weather but not in a strong wind with rough seas. The safety record of the proa is very poor indeed, and they are now being banned from some races.

Chapter 2

Hull construction

Scantlings Rules

Unlike most other branches of engineering, no direct measurements have been made of the loads to which yacht hulls are subjected. Instead, over the years designers have determined the loads by a process of trial and error. The structural requirements may then be developed into a formal scantlings rule which may be specifically for one material, or in a general form which can accommodate any material.

Some classification societies, notably Lloyd's Register of Shipping and the American Bureau of Shipping (ABS), have developed comprehensive scantlings rules for yachts, which are widely used by designers even if the boat is not intended for classification. In the light of experience designers may modify these rules or develop their own scantlings, especially in areas such as multihull design which are not covered by any published rules.

Lloyd's produces the best known scantlings rule, and have an extensive and rigorous procedure for classifying and surveying boats. Once the plans and the boatbuilder's premises have been approved, the vessel is built under the supervision of a Lloyd's surveyor; finally, when launched it has to prove satisfactory in sea trials.

The classification consists of several parts:

✠	Vessel built under Lloyd's survey.
100	Vessel is suitable for sea-going service.
A	Vessel built to Lloyd's scantlings rules and maintained in class.
or R	Vessel built to Lloyd's scantlings for international classes (e.g. 5.5, 6 and 12 metre classes) and maintained in class.
or R*	Vessel built to R classification, but rating certificate is invalid and vessel is ineligible for 100A1.
1	Anchoring and mooring gear is in accordance with Lloyd's Rules.
or −	Anchoring and mooring gear is in accordance with Lloyd's Rules, but vessel carries only half the regulation length of chain.

To maintain the vessel in class, she has to undergo biennial surveys carried out by a Lloyd's surveyor.

At present, scantlings rules are published covering timber, fibreglass, steel and aluminium; ferro-cement boats can also be classified, but the scantlings are not yet published. The rules also cover ground tackle, the propulsion system, electrical equipment, and the bilge pumping system.

It is widely acknowledged that full classification to Lloyd's is excessive and unnecessary for boats under 45 feet; even in the larger sizes, relatively few boats are classified by Lloyd's.

To encourage more boats to be built under Lloyd's supervision, two more levels of classification have been introduced. The more basic of these is the Lloyd's Register Hull (or Deck) Moulding Certificate, which states that the fibreglass hull or deck has been designed to Lloyd's, and moulded under survey by an approved builder. For complete boats there is the Lloyd's Register Building Certificate, which says that the boat has been built to Lloyd's scantlings under survey, but it is not classified. Sea trials are not carried out, and the machinery installation is not covered.

Lloyd's scantlings are conservative, resulting in an immensely strong but heavy boat; no racing yachtsman would consider having his boat built to Lloyd's. To fill his needs the American Bureau of Shipping, in conjunction with the Offshore Racing Council, has recently introduced a scantlings rule for offshore racing yachts. These result in a strong but lightweight structure.

At present the rule only covers the hull, but it will shortly be extended to cover the rig. The rule is designed so that it can accommodate any building material or framing system. Once the plans have been approved, the boat is built under the supervision of ABS surveyors, and once built, is maintained in class by periodic surveys. There is only one standard of classification, namely ✠ A1 Offshore Racing Yacht.

It is important to realise that any scantlings rule is concerned solely with the structural strength of the vessel. It is not concerned with the seaworthiness of the design, nor with the standard of finish from a cosmetic viewpoint.

Timber Construction

Wood is the oldest and the most aesthetically pleasing boatbuilding material. In a traditional carvel-built yacht a series of closely spaced frames are tied together by the floors and hog on the centreline, and the beam shelf at the gunwhale. The planking is then attached to the frames, using either screws or clenched copper nails, and the planking seams are made waterproof by caulking.

Structurally this is very inefficient. As the planks are not structurally connected to each other the loads cannot be easily distributed through the hull. This means that each component has to be relatively massive to withstand its loads with only

Fig. 2.1. The first skin of western red cedar is being applied to this quarter tonner. The frames will remain in the hull when finished, so the stringers have been notched into them. (*Photo Courtesy of William Payne.*)

minimal support from adjacent members. Also, the hull is not very stiff, so the planks will work, and the seams seep water. As a result of this, and the high cost of construction, hardly any carvel yachts are built nowadays.

The development of resorcinol formaldehyde adhesives marked the beginning of a revolution in construction techniques. These adhesives are highly durable, and the bond is at least as strong as the wood itself; as a result, cold moulded hulls, laminated frames and marine plywood have been developed. By employing these techniques the scantlings used can be much lighter, and yet still produce a much stiffer structure.

A cold moulded hull is basically built by laminating several layers of veneer together over a mould, with transverse and longitudinal framing inside the hull. Some boats, though, have most of the veneers running fore and aft, in which case only transverse framing is required; others have a skin that is sufficiently thick not to require any internal framing at all, though this comes out heavier than a lighter, framed shell.

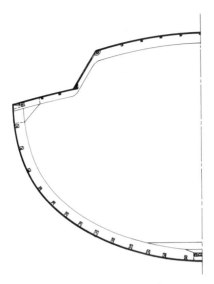

Fig. 2.2. Midship section of a 30-foot cold moulded wooden hull. Scantlings: Frame spacing 18 inches. Hull shell 3 × ⅛ in veneers western red cedar. Frames moulded 3⅜ in, sided 2 in douglas fir. Stringers: above waterline 1 in × 1¼ in douglas fir, below waterline 1 in × 1⅜ in douglas fir. Hog 6 in × 2½ in african mahogany. Beam Shelf 1¼ in × 4 in douglas fir. Deck ⅜ in gaboon plywood. Deck stringers ½ in × ½ in sitka spruce. Deck beams: 1 in × 1⅜ in under sidedeck, 1 in × 1 in on coachroof sides, 1 in × 2⅝ in on coachroof top.

Unless there is a large amount of double curvature in the decks, these will be made of plywood laid over fore and aft or transverse deck beams. Transverse frames may be an extension of the hull frames, the whole unit being laminated up as a ring frame.

The method first developed for building cold moulded hulls consists of moulding the hull over a solid plug, then turning it over and fitting the internal framing. This method is still used for large yachts, or where a run of several boats is required, but the tooling costs are relatively high.

Alternatively the plug can be dispensed with entirely, and the hull built inside out. The frames and bulkheads are set up, and then covered with a closely spaced set of longitudinal stringers; finally, the shell is laminated directly onto these stringers.

If it is important to keep the costs low, a chined plywood hull can be built. This method is also ideally suited to amateur builders. First of all, the frames are set up, and then fairly heavy stringers are laid up along the chines. The hull is then planked with panels of plywood scarfed to length. The hull shape must be carefully designed so that it does not have too much double curvature, and also to ensure that the run of the chines conforms as closely as possible to the water flow.

Fig. 2.3(a). Hard chine plywood construction. This Wharram catamaran has the backbone and stringers in place, and is now being covered in plywood. (*Courtesy J. Wharram.*)

Fig. 2.3(b). The hull has now been turned over. Much of the internal woodwork is complete, as all the stringers and frames are already in place. (*Courtesy J. Wharram.*)

Although the chines do inflict a slight drag penalty, it is not as great as many people imagine.

Amongst racing yachts there has been a small revival of interest in wood sandwich techniques, used so successfully in the Mosquito aircraft. The veneers, often of thin ply, are laid up each side of a lightweight core, such as foam or balsa planking running fore and aft. Wood sandwich techniques are perfectly capable of producing a hull at least as good as one using Kevlar and epoxy, despite the lack of exotic appeal, especially in sizes over about 35 feet.

A traditional laid deck can be applied on top of the structural deck, giving a pleasing appearance with no leaks. Planks about ¼ inch or ⅜ inch thick are glued and screwed into place, and the seams 'caulked' with a black epoxy resin or butyl rubber composition. Teak is usually used, though other species such as agba or pitch pine can be used to good effect. Motor boats usually have the planks running fore and aft, rabbeted into the sheer planks, whilst sailing yachts traditionally have swept planks, following the sheer line and rabbeted into the king plank.

Both the strength and stiffness characteristics of wood increase with the density of the species, but on a weight for weight basis the ligher species are superior. Thus, whilst the heavy species such as teak, mahogany, iroko and afrormosia may be used throughout the yacht, the lighter softwoods such as sitka spruce, douglas fir and western red cedar are not suitable for highly stressed areas. Strength is also highly dependent upon the moisture content of the wood, a lower moisture content giving increased strength.

Marine plywood is available in two grades. The best grade is to BS1088; here the species of timber used are all highly durable hardwoods, and only the highest grade of veneer is permitted. The plies are bonded with a marine grade adhesive, and no gaps are permitted where the veneers join in a ply. The lower grade is to BS3842. This is similar to BS1088, except that less durable species can be used, impregnated with a preservative. As it is not quite so durable as plywood made to BS1088, its use should be restricted to the interior.

Adhesives fall into two categories, the formaldehydes and the epoxy resins. Two types of formaldehyde are used, urea formaldehydes and resorcinol formaldehydes. The urea formaldehydes are not fully weatherproof, and so are only suitable for the interior; however, the resorcinol formaldehydes are fully waterproof, and so can be used throughout the vessel. Although under laboratory conditions they have a higher bond strength than the epoxies, the conditions needed to achieve this are fairly stringent. The timber must have a moisture content between 12% and 18%, and gaps along the glue line must not exceed 1 mm. The joint must be held with cramps or staples whilst the glue cures, and warm temperatures are required. Also, the bond is relatively brittle, and so may fail if it flexes.

Epoxies have slightly lower strength, but the less stringent application requirements result in a more reliable bond. Also, a wide range of additives are available that permit the properties to be tailored to suit the job. Gaps of up to ⅜ inch present no problems, and the joint does not need to be kept under pressure whilst curing. Temperature is not too critical, and the moisture content may be anywhere between 7% and 18%. This has the further advantage of permitting the use of drier, stronger wood.

An extension of the use of epoxy resin as an adhesive is the fillet joint. A lightweight filler is mixed into the resin to form a paste, and this is used as a filler where one panel butts up against another. For extra strength the joint may then be glassed over. This joint is considerably easier and quicker to form than using a length of stripwood, especially where curves are involved.

Where mechanical fastenings are required, they should be of aluminium bronze, silicon bronze or copper. The bronzes are to be preferred due to their high strength and durability. If brass fastenings are used, electrolytic action will remove all the zinc from the metal, destroying its strength. The wood itself may be affected by electrolysis, for example mahogany rots if left in contact with iron or mild steel, due to the iron salts given off; conversely, the acid chemicals given off by wet oak may attack aluminium and other alloys.

Timber is susceptible to marine borers and rot. There are two species of borer, the gribble worm and the teredo worm. The gribble is about ⅛ inch long, and it burrows short tunnels in and out of the wood; however, it cannot penetrate a properly maintained paint finish.

The teredo worm presents a more serious problem. It enters the woodwork as a tiny creature through a crack in the pain, and then tunnels along the wood. In Britain it grows to about 8 inches long, but in the tropics it can grow to lengths over 6 feet, forming tunnels in excess of 1 inch in diameter. Because it stays in the woodwork it may cause extensive damage before being discovered. Sheathing the hull below the waterline makes it proof against borers, and this is virtually essential in the tropics.

Rot, whether wet or dry, is a fungus which attacks the wood when its moisture content exceeds 30%. Softwoods are particularly prone to attack, and also absorb water readily. For this reason they should not be used on the outer veneer of the hull unless it is sheathed below the waterline.

With the great dimensional stability of cold moulded hulls, and the high performance finishes available, rot is unlikely to occur in a properly built and maintained vessel. However, care must be taken to ensure that there are plenty of large limber holes, and all lockers and enclosed spaces have proper drain holes. Also, no end grain should be left exposed, as this soaks up water like a sponge.

If the hull is sheathed, maintenance is greatly reduced, and durability increased. This is without doubt the best finish for a wooden hull. The two sheathing systems in common use both perform well, one using a glass cloth with an epoxy resin and the other a nylon cloth with a vinyl resin.

Fibreglass Construction

Almost all production built boats are now made from fibreglass or, more accurately nowadays, fibre reinforced plastic. The construction techniques are ideally suited to production runs, though the cost of the moulds is fairly high. As the material is created *in situ* there are no difficulties in forming complex shapes – shapes which would either be prohibitively expensive or impossible in most other materials.

Fibre reinforced plastic consists of a matrix of high strength fibres, bonded together by a comparatively weak and brittle resin. Thus to obtain the best possible strength properties the resin content should be kept to the minimum required to impregnate the fibres thoroughly. However, a more resin rich laminate has better weathering properties, and so may be used for the outermost laminate.

Originally only glass fibres and polyester resins were available, and they are still used for the majority of boats, but a much wider variety of materials are now available. At first, orthophthalic polyester resins were used exclusively, but isophthalic resins are becoming increasingly common, either in just the gel coat or the whole laminate, offering much better water resistance and slightly better strength characteristics. Racing boats may be built from a vinyl ester or epoxy resin to achieve better structural properties. These resins have a greater shear strength between the plies of the laminate, and also extend by a greater amount before failing. This means that whereas with a glass/polyester laminate the resin fails first, due to its greater brittleness, with an epoxy or vinyl ester/glass laminate both the resin and the fibres fail simultaneously, as the more elastic resin enables the fibres to use their full strength. However, kevlar and carbon fibres extend much less than glass at failure, and so a polyester resin can be used.

A further advantage of epoxy resins is that they do not emit any vapours upon curing, whereas the styrene fumes emitted by polyester and vinyl ester resins whilst curing can result in the resin shrinking by as much as 6% of its volume, introducing stresses to the laminate. Against this, epoxy resins are considerably more expensive than either polyester or vinyl ester resins.

The fibre reinforcement is available in several materials and constructions. The most basic construction is chopped strand mat, which is a thin blanket of fibres about 2 inches long, all randomly orientated, held together with a binder that is soluble in the resin. It is very easy to work with, conforms to curves well, and is cheap; however, it does need a lot of resin to wet it out, and this, combined with the lack of continuity of the fibres, makes it the weakest form of reinforcement.

Woven fabrics offer superior performance due to the continuity of the fibres, and their greater orderliness means that less resin is required to wet them out. For boatbuilding purposes woven rovings are used; the rovings consist of broad, thin bundles of fibres, which are woven into a loose fabric. A cloth may be used for lightweight fabrics; this is slightly stronger, but does not conform to curves nearly as well. A laminate using a fabric is about twice as strong as, and one and a half times stiffer than, one using chopped strand mat of the same thickness.

The problem with fabric reinforcements is that the bond strength between the laminates is relatively poor, and in time this may lead to delamination. The superior properties of epoxy resin can be used to avoid this, but different measures must be taken if a polyester or vinyl ester resin is being used. The simplest solution is to alternate between layers of woven rovings and mat, using the mat to ensure a good interlaminar bond; obviously this method incurs a considerable weight penalty. Alternatively, milled glass fibres can be added to the resin applied between laminations, but this mixture is more difficult to work with.

Unidirectional rovings form the strongest and most versatile form of reinforcement. The resin content is very low, and no stiffness is lost in trying to straighten out the weave of the cloth. Comparing two layers of unidirectional rovings laid at 90° to each other against woven rovings, both the strength and the stiffness are increased by about 50%. Where strength is needed in only one direction, for example on frames, the strength and stiffness characteristics are some three times greater than a woven roving reinforcement.

Almost all production boats use a reinforcement made from low alkali E glass, this material offering the best ratio of strength to unit cost. However, a higher grade of glass may be used for racing boats, designated S glass in the USA and R glass in Europe. It is about 30% stronger than E glass, but offers no improvement in stiffness, the weak point with all glassfibre laminates.

Kevlar is an aramid fibre developed by Du Pont. It has excellent properties when in tension, being about 60% stronger and stiffer than E glass. However, when in compression its stiffness drops to 90%, and its strength to only 60% of that of glass. This means that in laminates subjected to bending loads (the normal situation in a boat's hull), the stiffness is 75% greater than glass, but the strength is slightly less for a given thickness. As Kevlar is considerably lighter than glass, though, a considerable weight reduction can be achieved, particularly where stiffness is the main design criterion. Kevlar also has excellent impact resistance, failing more like a metal than brittle glass fibre, and therefore resulting in a much tougher boat.

Finally, there is carbon fibre. Its high cost means that it is almost always used to reinforce a glass or Kevlar laminate at present, although carbon fibre spars are becoming more common. There are two types of fibre available, one with high strength and the other with high stiffness. The high strength type is almost three times stronger, and nine times stiffer, then E glass; the high stiffness type is just under twice as strong as glass, but eleven times stiffer. The very stiff, brittle nature of the fibre causes its own problems, though. It has very poor impact resistance, and in a mixed laminate at least 5% of the laminate needs to be carbon fibre if it is

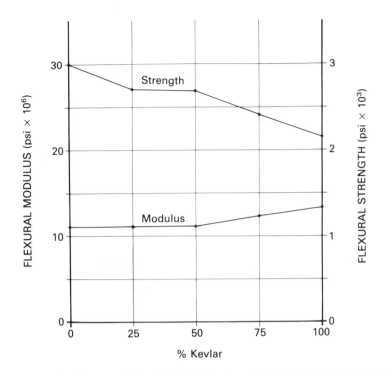

Fig. 2.4. The characteristics of Kevlar/E glass hybrid cloth. Hybrid cloths enable both the cost and the properties of a laminate to be tailored as required. (*Courtesy Fothergill and Harvey.*)

not to take an excessive proportion of the load, and fail prematurely. However, the impact resistance can be improved significantly by adding about 10% of Kevlar or glass to an all-carbon layup.

There are several ways of building a fibreglass boat, but for production work only a female mould is economical. The standard of finish of the mould must be near perfect, as any imperfections will be transferred directly to the finished hull.

First of all, a release agent is applied to the hull mould, followed by the gel coat. This is a thin layer of resin intended to protect the laminate from water absorption. The laminate is then built up with several layers of reinforcement, each layer being fully wetted out before the next one is applied. Stiffening members are glassed in as required, normally formed round a foam or balsa core.

Many yachts use sandwich techniques, particularly in the deck, as a means of reducing the weight of laminate required. Panels of foam or end grain balsa are laid onto the wet glass, and then further laminates are laid up over the core. As each panel consists of many small individual blocks of balsa or foam, held together by a light glass cloth on one face, it can easily conform to the shape of the hull without the need for external pressure.

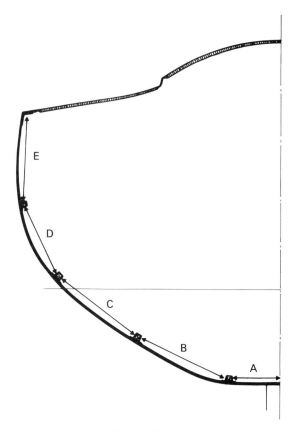

Fig. 2.5. Midship section of a 35-foot fibreglass cruiser-racer. Using alternate plies of mat and woven rovings of equal weight, and a polyester resin, the following laminate weights were used: A 6700 g/m^2; B, C 5500 g/m^2; D 5000 g/m^2; E 4000 g/m^2. Deck 1100 g/m^2 each side of a $5/8$ in balsa core. Coachroof 600 g/m^2 each side of a $5/8$ in balsa core. Longitudinal stringers 1½ in square, laminate 1000 g/m^2. Transverse frames 3 in square, laminate 2000 g/m^2 below waterline, 1000 g/m^2 above waterline. Note the marked reduction in laminate weight where sandwich construction is used. Using a solid laminate with a single longitudinal stringer, the laminate would have been 4000 g/m^2 on the deck, and 5000 g/m^2 on the coachroof.

Once the hull is completed, it is released from the mould and fitting out can begin. However, even if kept indoors the hull will not achieve full strength until about two weeks after it was moulded.

Usually, one mould is used for the hull and another for the deck, though some larger boats have the hull mould split into two along the centreline. The mouldings are joined by a combination of bolting and bonding with fibreglass; to ensure a good bond, this must be carried out before the moulding has attained its full strength, particularly if a polyester or vinyl ester resin is used.

Throughout the whole moulding process it is essential that both the temperature and the relative humidity are controlled. The temperature must remain between 16 and 25°C, and the relative humidity must not exceed 70%. If this is not done, not only will the laminate be weaker than the designer intended, but there will also be a greater chance of osmosis developing.

Almost all one-off fibreglass boats use sandwich construction, both for economic reasons and to compensate for the material's low stiffness characteristics. The simplest technique uses a male mould finished with closely spaced longitudinal battens. This is covered with pre-shaped sheets of foam, which are simply wired in place. The outer laminate is laid up onto the foam, and the surface filled and faired; then the hull is broken off the mould, turned over and placed in a supporting cradle before the inner skin is laid up.

Fig. 2.6. The outer skin is being laminated on this three-quarter tonner.

Now the trend is to cover the mould with sheets of ply, or, where cost is important, with several layers of strong adhesive tape, and laminate the inner skin onto the mould. The core is then laid onto a mix of resin and filler, often in conjunction with a vacuum bag to ensure a good bond. Finally, the outer skin is laid up over the core, filled and faired before the hull is broken off the mould.

This method avoids any risk of distorting the hull when it is turned over, as it is extremely stiff when it comes off the mould; it also makes it easier for the laminators to keep the amount of resin used to a minimum. It is particularly recommended where Kevlar is used, as draping the cloth over a convex mould helps ensure that none of the fibres are moulded up under compression.

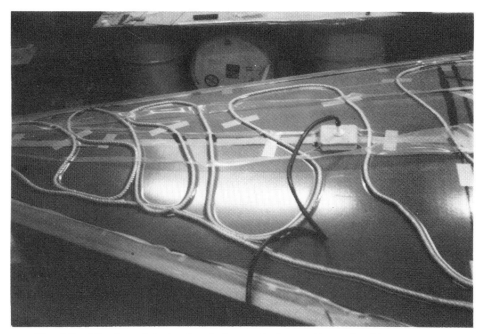

Fig. 2.7. The foam is being bonded onto the inner skin, assisted by a vacuum bag. The rope underneath the bag gives a route for air to escape; the dark patches are where excess resin has squeezed up between the slabs of foam.

End grain balsa is by far the cheapest core material, and is also immensely strong. Its chief drawback is that if the outer skin is punctured the balsa soaks up water like a sponge, and so it is best not to use it below the waterline. Racing boats, though, will tend to use one of the foam cores available, as their density is about half that of balsa; also, their closed cell construction means they do not soak up water, and so can be used with safety below the waterline. Most sailing boats to date have used PVC based foams, but other types such as the urethanes are just as suitable. Sometimes a paper honeycomb core is used, but it is ridiculously expensive for the possible weight saving, and it is difficult to ensure a good bond with the laminate due to the low gluing area available.

Where the hull is subjected to highly concentrated loads, such as under the keel bolts and deck fittings, a sandwich construction cannot withstand the loads. Thus the moulding must be reinforced by removing the core and laying up a thickness of glass, or the core must be replaced with a stronger material, usually plywood. Naturally, the degree of reinforcement required is closely related to the expected loadings.

At one stage it was believed that fibreglass was maintenance-free. Although maintenance is low, the real threat is osmosis. Polyester resin is not totally impervious to water, and the laminate inevitably contains minute air-filled voids. The water works its way into these voids and dissolves the soluble residues of the curing process, resulting in a highly acidic solution. An osmotic pressure is thus created, causing more sea water to be absorbed in an attempt to neutralise the acidity of the solution. Very high pressures can be built up in the voids, up to four times atmospheric pressure, resulting ultimately in tell-tale blistering of the gel coat. If left unattended this will weaken the laminate by destroying the bond between the fibres and the resin, as well as removing the protective gel coat when the blister bursts, and so letting more water be absorbed.

Some surveys estimate that as many as one third of all fibreglass boats suffer from osmosis to a greater or lesser extent. In many cases, though, it does not become severe enough to warrant attention, or does not break out until the boat is over 10 years old. Obviously, though, it is worth doing as much as possible to prevent the problem. Good control of temperature and humidity during construction, together with a high standard of workmanship and the use of good materials, can go a long way towards this.

The gelcoat is also very important, and should preferably be of an isophthalic resin – these absorb about half as much water as the orthophthalics. The pigment may promote osmosis, and it is best omitted below the waterline, painting the hull with an epoxy or two-part polyurethane paint. It is also worth painting the bilges, as bilge water is just as likely to cause osmosis as sea water, and there is no protective gelcoat present.

Many builders use fibreglass mouldings for the interior of the yacht. Although they help keep the cost down, and are easy to clean, they can present problems if not well designed. The main problem is that they can make areas of the hull and deck inaccessible; this can make repairs very difficult, and might endanger the boat if she is holed behind an inner moulding. It may also be impossible to get to the fastenings or fittings, or plumbing or wiring which runs behind a moulding. They are only really acceptable if they give full access to the hull and deck, or if the space behind the moulding is completely sealed off with a closed cell foam, with no systems or fastenings present. This latter solution has the great advantage that by adding sufficient foam the boat can be made unsinkable even if flooded.

Steel Construction

Steel is in many ways the ideal material for cruising boats, especially in the larger sizes. It is immensely strong, tough, and cheap – some 20% cheaper than fibreglass. Also, there are very few parts of the world where repairs are not possible. The two drawbacks are weight and corrosion. Not much can be done to reduce the weight, but as the size of vessel increases the weight penalty becomes less. Corrosion need not be as much of a problem as it used to be, though, thanks to the development of high performance, durable finishes in the shipping and offshore industries.

Mild (or low carbon) steel is normally used, with a carbon content below 0.3%. Although a higher carbon content increases the strength, it also makes welding with electric arc equipment considerably more difficult.

Some people favour the use of low alloy steels, such as Cor-Ten, as they are about 40% stronger, and have greater corrosion resistance above the waterline. However, they cost about 40% more than mild steel, and also need to be welded by the argon arc process, which is more costly and beyond the capabilities of the amateur. Their use is only really justified in the larger sizes of yacht, as only then can a weight reduction be achieved by reducing the plating thickness.

Whichever grade of material is used, the metal thickness should not be less than ⅛ inch. Below this there is insufficient allowance for corrosion, and welding distortion becomes considerable.

The first stage in construction is to build a jig to take the frames and stringers, which are temporarily attached to it by tack welds. Round rod or tube is used for the stem, gunwhale and chines, whilst flat bar, angle or T-section may be used for the stringers and frames. The plating is then cut to shape, and if the hull is round bilged it is curved by rolling equipment. It is then tack welded to the framing.

Now comes the most critical stage, when the welding is completed. It is essential that the final welding sequence is carefully planned to minimise distortion. At best, a distorted hull will require a large amount of filler between the frames to fair up the hull; at worst, the whole hull may be twisted out of true. Once all the joins have been fully welded, the hull is broken out of the jig and decked.

A simple way of reducing the weight is to use a plywood deck and coachroof, usually bolted onto steel deck beams. A secondary advantage is that it will provide some sound insulation between the deck and the cabin.

An exposed lead keel should not be fitted, due to electrolytic action with the steel, though a cast iron keel is perfectly acceptable. Alternatively, a hollow steel keel can be fabricated, filled with molten lead, lead pigs bedded on a bitumastic compound, or steel punchings cast in with resin or cement. To avoid internal corrosion, the keel should be sealed either by welding on a covering plate, or covering it with cement.

It is the fear of rust that puts most people off a steel boat. However, rust almost always looks worse than it actually is – if a ⅛ inch plate were to become fully rusted it would become over 1 inch thick.

Corrosion is at least as likely to occur inside the hull as outside, and so the whole hull needs to be adequately protected. Rusting is likely to be most severe near the water's surface, so the waterline and the bilges warrant particular attention. The other major starting point for rust is weld metal, due to the metallurgical changes that take place during the welding process.

The first step in preventing corrosion comes when ordering the steel; it should be delivered de-scaled and coated with an anti-corrosion primer. This will prevent rust from getting a foothold during construction. Once the hull has been welded up, the welds must be ground smooth, and studs welded on to take the sacrificial anodes. These are essential in controlling corrosion, and are discussed in detail later in the chapter.

Before the hull can be painted all traces of rust must be removed. This can only be satisfactorily achieved by grit blasting. Immediately afterwards, preferably within half an hour but definitely the same day, the first protective coating should be applied. The greater the interval before the hull is protected, the greater the chance of minute patches of rust forming, which will in time undermine the paintwork.

The next decision is whether or not to metallise the hull. This consists of spraying it, inside and out, with molten zinc. It has the same effect as galvanising and, although it slightly increases the cost of the boat, it also increases the boat's life span considerably. The zinc virtually prevents rusting so long as it is intact, and even if scratched it will inhibit corrosion on scratches up to $\frac{1}{4}$ inch across. As the zinc coating is slightly porous, though, it still needs painting for maximum protection. If the hull is not metallised, some cathodic protection can be given by using a zinc chromate or zinc phosphate paint for the primer.

The final stage in corrosion protection is the painting of the hull. Two paint systems are recommended, based upon an epoxy tar resin or on a chlorinated rubber composition. Pure epoxy paints do not perform any better than the epoxy tar paints, and are considerably more expensive. The epoxy tar paints produce a very hard finish, but the chlorinated rubber paints are better able to withstand abrasion, originally being developed for use on the inside of sewer pipes. There is not a lot to choose between them, but the chlorinated rubber paints are probably better below the waterline if the boat takes to the bottom, whilst the epoxy tar paints give a better finish cosmetically.

Inside the yacht the framing and stringers tend to produce water traps. These can be avoided by the use of limber holes, or by filling up the water trap with cement. The alkalinity of cement makes it an excellent rust inhibitor, and the bilges can be cemented to avoid corrosion.

Although a metal hull will not overheat in hot weather, it will become cold and suffer from condensation when the temperature drops. Insulation can do a lot to overcome this, as well as acting as a noise dampener. The best option is to have foam sprayed directly onto the hull, to give a thickness of about 1 inch. Sheets of foam can also be used, glued to the hull. Another possibility is to use a paint containing cork granules, but this is not nearly as effective.

As all mild steel is magnetic, compass deviation can be a problem. Nothing can be done to prevent this, but with a well sited and properly adjusted compass there should be few problems. This is discussed further in Chapter 9.

Aluminium Construction

Aluminium is probably the most maintenance-free boatbuilding material available, so long as care is taken to avoid electrolysis. It is also very strong and light, being popular in racing boats over 40 feet in length. Against this it is relatively expensive, costing about 20% more than fibreglass.

Aluminium alloys can be divided into two categories. The non heat-treated alloys are strengthened by cold working, and can be welded with a relatively low loss of strength at the weld, in the order of 15%. The heat-treated alloys are strengthened by various methods of heat treatment. The high heat input of the welding process destroys the heat treatment, and the strength is reduced to less than half of its original value. Small items can have the strength restored by postweld heat treatment, but this is not possible on larger items.

Welded aluminium boats are built in almost exactly the same way as steel boats. However, distortion is a much greater problem, as aluminium expands about three times as much as steel when heated. This makes it impractical to use plating less than 0.1 inch thick, thus preventing aluminium from being used in lightweight craft below about 40 feet long.

Aluminium may be welded by either the MIG or the TIG (argon arc) process. MIG welding produces less distortion, and in its pulsed arc form can be used on metal as thin as 16 s.w.g. (0.046 inch). However, TIG welding is generally used, as it is easier to work with in the confined spaces often encountered in boatbuilding, and it produces a neater weld.

Obviously only non heat-treated alloys are suitable for welded construction. 5083 alloy is the most commonly used, but other suitable grades include 5056A, 5154A and 5251. Although not as strong, these grades offer better corrosion resistance.

The incessant search for lighter construction techniques has led to the adoption of epoxy bonded aluminium construction, originally developed in the aerospace industry. At present the joints are reinforced with countersunk rivets, but as confidence in the system increases, the amount of rivetting will probably decrease. Not only does this system allow thin plating to be used without distortion, but also the metal's full strength is retained due to the absence of welding. The heat-treated alloys can be used, such as 6061 or 6082 grade, with a further increase in strength. For the most exotic craft, very high strength grades such as 7035 or 7039 could be used so long as they are clad with a corrosion resistant alloy.

The keel can be bolted directly to the hull with no great risk of electrolysis, so long as both it and the keel bolts are electrically insulated from the hull. However, if the ballast is placed inside a prefabricated aluminium shell there will be no risk of electrolysis. As with steel boats, a top plate is required to protect the lead from bilge water.

Unlike steel, aluminium will not corrode if left on its own. However, if electrolysis occurs it will be attacked by most other metals, and this must be borne in mind throughout the boat's life. This is discussed in detail later in this chapter.

If wet wood, or any other damp absorbent material for that matter, is left in

Fig. 2.8(a). The tubular chines of this aluminium Extrovert 22 are laid on the jig, ready for plating. A solid jig is essential to control distortion in the thin hull plating. (*Courtesy Linkleters Ltd.*)

Fig. 2.8(b). The hull is now complete. Note the hard chine deck used for ease of construction. Also items such as the toe-rail, genoa tracks and chainplates have been built into the structure. (*Courtesy Linkleters Ltd.*)

contact with aluminium, corrosion can occur. To prevent this, the aluminium must always be given a generous coating of zinc chromate primer.

Ferro-cement Construction

Ferro-cement consists of a steel framework (or armature) encased in cement; the steel takes the tensile loads, whilst the cement takes the compressive loads. It is a very tough form of construction, and withstands knocks well. Although the density of the material is similar to that of aluminium, its strength is considerably lower, and it cannot be applied in thicknesses less than ⅝ inch. This makes it relatively heavy in small boats, though the weight penalty has virtually disappeared on boats over 50 feet long.

As the materials required are cheap, and the level of skill demanded is low, it is an ideal method for home construction. If built professionally, the large number of man hours required does tend to put up the price, but it is still comparatively cheap.

To construct the armature, frames of 1 inch diameter steel pipe are set up at about 30 inch centres. These are frequently made into web frames, thus allowing a thinner shell to be used. Longitudinal stringers of ¼ inch rod are then welded on at 2 or 3 inch centres. On yachts over 40 feet long, a second set of rods running diagonally may be used to take the torsion loads.

This basic framework is then covered with the required number of layers of welded wire mesh, normally a ½ inch mesh of 22 s.w.g. wire. Chicken wire may be used for this but as one third more layers are required the tendency is to use it only where the curves are too tight for the welded mesh. The mesh is tied into place at 2 inch centres, welding not being used as it can distort the hull. High tensile steel should be used for the same reason, as it bends without kinking.

Ferro-cement may be used for the deck, in which case the armature is built in one piece for the hull and deck, though the plastering is normally completed in two stages. Alternatively, plywood can be used over wood deck beams; in this case the armature ends in a flange at the gunwhale.

The next stage is the plastering of the hull. A dry mix of Portland cement and sharp sand is used. Although the standard Portland cement is perfectly adequate in temperate waters, in the tropics the higher temperatures make it possible for the magnesium sulphate in sea water to attack the cement. To avoid this, the sulphate-resisting grade of Portland cement should be used. In any case the mix must be dry, both to make handling easier and to reduce shrinkage as the cement dries.

The plastering is usually carried out in two sessions, one for the hull and one for the deck. Once the armature has been fully filled and covered, the excess cement is removed, and a ⅛ inch thick finishing coat is applied to the outside of the hull. If there are any thin patches in this coat streaks of rust will appear, showing where water has seeped through to the armature. This is the only stage that is best left to the professionals.

The cement is now allowed to set. If left to its own devices the water will evaporate before it has had time to react with the cement; this will reduce the strength of the hull, and cracks will appear due to the large amount of shrinkage. Thus the rate of evaporation must be carefully controlled, and this is achieved by using a sprinkler system to keep the hull wet. Within limits, the slower the rate of drying, the stronger the hull will be.

On the first day all the excess water is allowed to evaporate off. On the second day the sprinkler system is switched on, wetting both the inside and the outside of the hull for at least 10 days, and preferably for 3 weeks. Only at the end of this period is evaporation allowed to take place, by switching off the sprinkler on the inside of the hull. This allows slow drying from the inside, and after about 4 weeks the hull will be fully cured.

Fig. 2.9. Ferro-cement construction. Cement has been applied from the inside of the hull, and is now being applied to the outside. (*Courtesy of Practical Boat Owner.*)

Corrosion presents no problem with ferro-cement. The finishing coat prevents water from reaching the armature, and even if this should occur, the cement's alkalinity will inhibit corrosion. The only point to note is that no metal fittings should be allowed to come into contact with the armature, as this will result in electrolysis.

If the hull is damaged, all that is normally required is to make good the surface with new cement. If the armature is rusted, though, the cement must be cut back to an unaffected area and the rust removed before new cement is applied.

Corrosion and its prevention

If a metal comes into contact with sea water, electrolysis will occur. Positively charged ions leave the metal and dissolve in the water, leaving their electrons on the metal and giving it a negative charge. This attracts the positive hydrogen atoms in the water, and they deposit themselves onto the metal. To complete the reaction, oxygen dissolved in the water reacts with the electrons and the hydrogen atoms, forming water; alternatively, with steel the iron ions react with the oxygen to form rust.

The region where the metal is dissolved (i.e. corroded) is known as the anode, whilst the region where water is formed is called the cathode. Electrolysis can only occur if the anode and cathode are electrically connected. This will be the case if both regions occur on the same piece of metal, or if two pieces of metal are joined without an insulator between them. Even if an insulating gasket is placed between the two pieces of metal some electrolysis will occur, because of the conductivity of sea water; however, its rate will be greatly reduced.

Obviously the rate of reaction is highly dependent upon the amount of oxygen available. This means that corrosion will be most severe at the waterline and in the bilges, where plenty of oxygen is dissolved in the sea water; it also means that if two zones on one piece of metal have different oxygen concentrations, the zone with the lower oxygen concentration will be corroded. This can result in severe pitting where the propeller shaft or rudder stock passes through a bearing, or under the heads of fastenings used below the waterline.

If two different metals are present, the one with the lower electrode potential will tend to be corroded, whilst the other (more noble) metal will act as the cathode. Figure 2.10 lists the electrode potentials of a variety of metals. Where possible, metals with a potential difference of more than 0.2 volts should not be used together. The greater the difference in potentials, the greater the corrosion rate.

The ratio of the areas of the cathode and anode can have a marked effect on the rate of corrosion. If the anode is relatively small, the corrosion rate will be considerably greater than expected. If, on the other hand, the anode is very large in relation to the cathode, the rate of corrosion may be so low as to be insignificant.

Any highly stressed area will tend to form an anode, and so be corroded. Thus rivet heads, and the area each side of a weld, will tend to be corroded more easily than might first be expected.

Sacrificial zinc anodes are the chief means of preventing corrosion below the waterline. They are electrically bonded to the items that are to be protected, and are preferentially corroded. Once 80% of the anode is corroded away, it needs to be replaced. On wood, fibreglass and ferro-cement hulls one anode is used to protect fittings made from stainless steel, manganese bronze and other metals of similar potential, and another anode is used for mild steel fittings. Each anode must be sited where it can 'see' the fittings it is protecting, and so more than one anode may be required in each system.

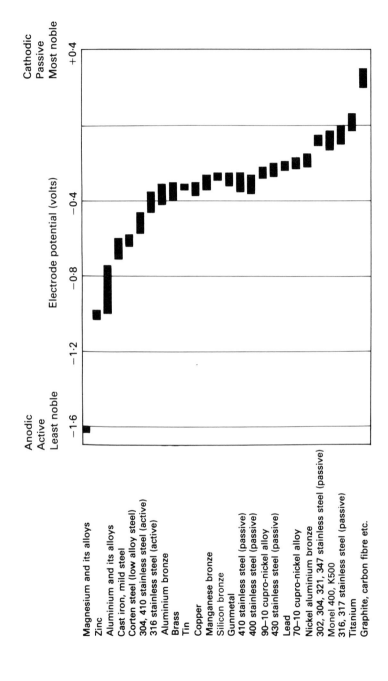

Fig. 2.10 The galvanic series for metals in sea water. When two metals are immersed in sea water, and electrically connected, the one with the lower potential will tend to be corroded. The greater the difference in potentials, the faster the rate of corrosion.

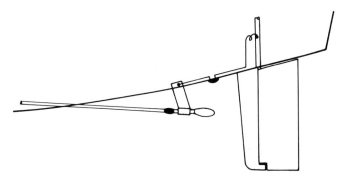

Fig. 2.11. The installation of an anode system. One anode on the propeller shaft protects the shaft and propeller. A second anode mounted on the hull protects the P bracket and rudder stock – it must be connected to any item it protects by heavy gauge wire. If the hull is metal, all fittings below the waterline should be electrically insulated from the hull, and either be of the same or a slightly higher potential compared to the hull.

The anodes are electrically bonded to the fittings they protect by a copper strip or wire. If several items are bonded in series, the wires should enter and leave each fitting at the same point, so no current flows through the fitting.

The rotating propeller shaft is best protected by an anode bolted directly onto the shaft, close to the P-bracket. It can be bonded to an anode on the hull through the engine, but this means bridging the flexible coupling, and there is no guarantee that the engine will provide a low resistance path for the current, due to insulating films of lubricating oil.

Steel hulls, or aluminium hulls where metals with a higher electrode potential are present, have the anodes bolted directly to the hull. Several anodes are fitted, the number depending on the hull's surface area. For steel hulls it is simply the weight of the anodes that is important, whilst for aluminium hulls the area of exposed anode assumes greater importance.

A good, waterproof paint finish can go a long way towards preventing corrosion – for example, an unpainted steel hull needs four times the weight of anodes compared to a similar hull with a good paint finish. All protected parts should be painted, except for stainless steel components, as in this case the painting may result in pitting corrosion. Obviously, the sacrificial anodes must never be painted. Paints containing any of the heavy metals, namely copper, tin or mercury, must not be used on an aluminium hull, as this will result in corrosion; neither should they be used on a boat protected with zinc anodes, as they will cause the anodes to be eaten away more quickly.

Aluminium forms an inert oxide layer on its surface, which prevents it from corroding through simple oxidation. However, in places where this oxide layer is damaged a small amount of corrosion may occur, forming a white deposit. This is seldom serious, provided that marine grade alloys have been used. It can easily be prevented by painting or anodising.

Unfortunately the oxide layer does not prevent bimetallic corrosion; as anodising merely increases the thickness of the oxide layer, it is of no use either. Thus direct contact with metals other than zinc, cast iron, or steel in its galvanized, cadmium plated, or stainless forms, is to be avoided. With other metals, a gasket of neoprene, PVC, or Tufnol is required as an insulator, in addition to zinc anodes.

Marine grade aluminium alloys contain magnesium and silicon. Suitable grades are 3103, 5056A, 5083, 5154A, or 5251. Of the non heat-treatable alloys, grades 6061, 6063, or 6082 may be used. For castings, LM5, 6, 10, 18 or 25 are acceptable.

Unlike aluminium, mild steel forms no protective layer, and so rusts; thus it

Alloy Grade	UK Grade	Ultimate tensile stress (p.s.i. × 10³)	Elongation at failure (%)	Welded UTS (p.s.i. × 10³)
		Non heat-treated alloys		
3103	N3	25–29	4	13–19
5056A	N6	45	5	37
5083	N8	39–50	8	40–51
5154A	N5	40–47	6	31–40
5251	N4	33–40	5	23–29
		Heat-treated alloys		
2014A	H15	64	7	34
2031	H12	56	6	
2618A	H16	62	5	
6061	H20	43	7	27
6063	H9	29	8	22
6082	H30	43	8	
		Aircraft grade alloys		
7039		65	13	NOT WELDABLE
7075		83	11	
7079		78	12	
7178		88	10	

Fig. 2.12. The properties of aluminium alloys. The British classification system is being replaced by an international one, based upon the American system. The properties quoted are for the highest strength grade of alloy. Some variation will occur according to the amount of heat treatment or cold working to which the alloy has been subjected. The aircraft grade alloys must be used with care, due to their high susceptibility to corrosion – their welds corrode so rapidly that they must not be welded if used in a marine environment.

must always be protected. There are three levels of defence. Firstly, there is the paint system; secondly, the hull may be metallised; finally, there are the zinc sacrificial anodes.

To prevent corrosion, mild steel should not be allowed to come into contact with materials other than zinc, cast iron, or galvanized, cadmium plated, or stainless steel, without an insulating gasket between the two materials. Whilst metallising is the best way of protecting the hull and other major items, small fittings can be protected by hot dip galvanizing, and fastenings and chain can be spun galvanized.

Stainless steel is normally protected by an inert chrome oxide that forms as a film on the surface. This makes it less likely to attack, or be attacked by, other metals than would be expected by its electrode potential. With the film present it is in its passive state. The thickness of the oxide film can be increased by giving the surface a bright, polished finish; however, if little or no oxygen is present the film degenerates, and the metal assumes its active form. In this state it is highly likely to be attacked by pitting corrosion. Thus, whilst 304 grade is perfectly satisfactory for use above the waterline, where there is plenty of oxygen available, only 316 grade should be used below the waterline because of its higher resistance to pitting. Alloys such as Monel, titanium and the bronzes are to be preferred below the waterline, as they do not suffer from pitting corrosion.

A further problem concerning stainless steel is that of corrosion occuring at welds. This can be avoided by using the low carbon grades of 304 S12 and 316 S12, as opposed to the slightly higher strength 304 S15 and 316 S16 grades, in conjunction with TIG welding. Alternatively, grades 321 S12, 321 S20, or 347 S17 can be used where strength is an important consideration.

There are two common problem areas that merit special attention. The first of these is the stern gear and propeller installation. Figure 2.14 tabulates which materials are compatible with the hull material. The second problem area is that of fastenings. Figure 2.15 shows which fastenings are compatible with which metals; the recommended fastenings should present no corrosion problems whatsoever, but there may be problems with other materials, and these should only be used if absolutely necessary. If two different metals are being joined the fastenings clearly need to be compatible with both of them.

Finally, all fastenings should be removable so that repairs can be made if necessary. A particularly bad area here is the keel, with some builders glassing over the keel bolts in the hull, and some keels being built in such a way that the bolts cannot be removed. If the keel bolts should need replacing, the only way of doing this may be to melt down and recast the entire keel!

Paint Systems

Paint is primarily a protective coating, and its decorative effect should be only a

Grade	Ultimate tensile stress (p.s.i. $\times 10^3$)	0.2% proof stress (p.s.i. $\times 10^3$)
302 S17	73.9	30.5
302 S25	78.3	31.2
303 S21	73.9	30.2
303 S41	73.9	30.2
304 S12	71.1	28.3
304 S15	74.0	30.5
310 S24	78.3	31.2
315 S16	78.3	30.5
316 S12	71.1	28.3
316 S16	78.3	30.5
317 S12	71.1	28.3
317 S16	78.3	30.5
320 S17	78.3	30.5
321 S12	74.0	28.0
321 S20	73.9	30.2
325 S21	73.9	30.2
326 S36	73.9	30.2
347 S17	74.0	30.5

Fig. 2.13. The strengths of marine stainless steels. The elongation at failure is 40% for all grades. The last two figures of the grade indicate the carbon content. Low carbon grades have slightly lower strength properties, but their welds are more resistant to corrosion. The ultimate tensile stress is the load at which the specimen fails; the proof stress is the load required to give an extension of 0.2%.

	316 stainless steel	304 stainless steel	Monel	Manganese bronze	Silicon bronze	Aluminium bronze	Nickel aluminium bronze	Gunmetal	Aluminium alloy
Propeller shaft	C	×	✓	C	✓	✓	✓	✓	
Propeller	C	×		C			✓		C
Sterntube, P-bracket	C	×		C				✓	
Seacocks	C	×		C	✓	✓	✓	✓	C
Rudder stock, pintels	C	×	✓	C	✓	✓	✓		C

Fig. 2.14. Sterngear compatibility chart. A tick signifies that the material is perfectly satisfactory. A C means that it must be given cathodic protection, unless the boat has a steel hull. A cross means that the material should not be used. Where a space has been left, the material is not generally used for that application, usually due either to poor physical properties or high cost.

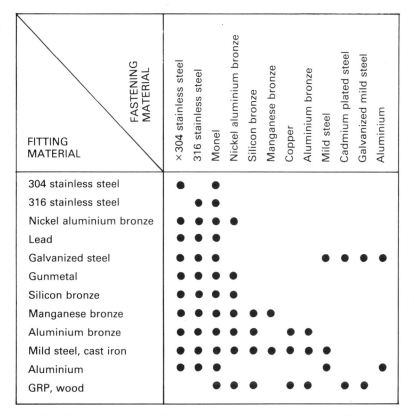

FITTING MATERIAL \ FASTENING MATERIAL	×304 stainless steel	316 stainless steel	Monel	Nickel aluminium bronze	Silicon bronze	Manganese bronze	Copper	Aluminium bronze	Mild steel	Cadmium plated steel	Galvanized mild steel	Aluminium
304 stainless steel	●	●										
316 stainless steel		●	●									
Nickel aluminium bronze	●	●	●	●								
Lead	●	●	●									
Galvanized steel	●	●	●						●	●	●	●
Gunmetal	●	●	●	●								
Silicon bronze	●	●	●	●								
Manganese bronze	●	●	●	●	●	●						
Aluminium bronze	●	●	●	●	●		●	●				
Mild steel, cast iron	●	●	●	●	●	●	●	●	●			
Aluminium	●	●	●					●				●
GRP, wood			●	●	●		●	●		●	●	

Fig. 2.15. Fastenings compatibility chart, for use below the waterline. The aim is to have the fastening slightly cathodic with respect to the fitting, but not so much that the fitting will corrode.

secondary consideration. However, one or two points concerning colour schemes do merit attention. At one stage, all wooden yachts were painted white. This was necessary because of the poor dimensional stability of traditional construction methods, as light colours have a low rate of heat absorption, and so help minimise movement of the planking. This is not necessary with the high stability of cold moulded hulls. Light colours can also have the effect of making the yacht look larger than she actually is.

Dark colours are to be favoured for steel and aluminium hulls, as the extra heat absorbed helps to reduce the amount of condensation. Dark colours visually reduce the boat's size, and also tend to show up imperfections in hull finish.

With the high freeboard found on many modern designs, the traditional cove line is often replaced with a broad band of one or more horizontal stripes. These emphasise the boat's length, and draw attention away from her high freeboard. To a lesser extent the same effect can be achieved by painting the boot top in a colour that contrasts with the antifouling and the topsides.

Any paint system consists of a primer suited to the material being painted, followed by an undercoat which is filled and sanded until fair, and finally a topcoat. The type of primer is largely dictated by the material being painted, but a wide range of undercoat/topcoat paint systems are available.

The cheapest form of paint is the well tried yacht enamel. It is very flexible, and so ideal for traditional wooden boats. However, it does need regular repainting, and is not a very tough paint.

Next up in the performance league come the one-pot polyurethanes. These can be divided into two groups: the urethane modified alkyds and the isocyanates. The modified alkyds offer better chemical resistance than the enamels, and good abrasion resistance; they dry by oxidation. The isocyanates are moisture cured, and slightly more costly. However, they offer better gloss retention, durability and chemical resistance, and are also less permeable to water. The finish will last for at least 2 years before needing repainting.

The two-pot polyurethanes also come in two varieties, but both types perform better than the one-pot polyurethanes. Those using an aromatic hardening system have a first class finish, but on exposure to sunlight the surface will yellow and look chalky after about 3 years. Also, the paint is very brittle, and so is likely to crack if the hull flexes. Those employing an aliphatic hardening system produce the best and most durable finish – it should last for at least 5 years. The paint has excellent heat, abrasion and chemical resistance, is very hard, and provides a first class barrier to water. The surface retains a good gloss finish, and does not pick up dirt easily. As this paint is more flexible than the aromatic type it is less likely to crack, though it is not as flexible as a one-pot polyurethane or an enamel paint.

Finally there are the epoxy paints. These are extremely durable, and provide the highest resistance to abrasion, water, heat and chemicals. Unfortunately, they are susceptible to degradation by the ultraviolet component of sunlight, and as a result have poor gloss retention. For this reason they are normally overcoated with an aliphatic polyurethane. This combination should last for 8 to 10 years before needing repainting.

Varnish is essentially a paint without the pigment. This means that the coats are considerably thinner, and so a greater number are needed for the same degree of protection. In addition, the lack of pigment results in increased susceptibility to ultraviolet light. The deep, lustrous brightwork seen on some boats can only be achieved in one way – a large number of coats, with plenty of rubbing down.

The bottom of the boat must be protected with an antifouling paint if it is not to become overgrown with weed and barnacles; this should extend up the topsides for a couple of inches to allow for variations in trim. The boot top is often curved in sympathy with the sheer, being higher at the bow and stern. Once again, a variety of types of paint are available.

Soft antifoulings are seldom used on yachts nowadays. If the yacht is allowed to dry out, a new coat of antifouling needs to be applied; also, its soft composition means that it is very easily damaged, and cannot be scrubbed down.

The semi-hard types are very popular. They are easy to apply, can be easily sanded smooth or scrubbed down, and are not affected by drying out. As they are free of heavy metals they can be used on aluminium hulls.

The hard, or racing, antifoulings provide a hard, durable finish that can be sanded and polished to give a very smooth surface. Unfortunately many of these paints contain copper or mercury, and this can cause corrosion problems.

International Yacht Paints' *Micron* is one of the latest developments in antifoulings. Like the hard antifoulings, it can be given an extremely smooth finish. However, this paint is free of heavy metals, and once launched it slowly dissolves away, ensuring that fresh antifouling is always exposed, and avoiding a thick build-up of paint over the years.

The Forces Acting on a Hull

There are two main groups of forces acting on the hull: those due to the motion of the boat through the sea, and those due to rigging loads. As the hull moves through the water it is subjected to localised loads from the water pressure, from waves hitting the hull, and from the hull slamming due to pitching. It is also subjected to bending loads due to unequal support from the waves. For monohulls under about 100 feet in length the hogging and sagging forces due to unequal support from the waves are small enough to be ignored. However, in multihulls, quite high torsional loads can be created when, for example, the bow of one hull and the stern of another are supported by wave crests, with the rest of the boat lying in a trough. These forces are concentrated where the cross beams join the hulls, and this is a common area of failure.

The localised water forces are greatest below the waterline and in the forward third of the boat. However, the topsides and deck need to be sufficiently strong to withstand green water coming on board. It is important that the hull is locally stiff as well as strong, as any flexing or panting will result in increased frictional resistance. As the slamming forces are of very short duration, an average force is used when designing the structure. Within limits, the larger the panel, the lower the figure used for the average load; this is because at any one instant the hull is only subjected to high loads in a few places.

Loads from the rig are very rarely high enough to cause a structural failure in the hull, except at local stress points where the rig meets the hull, but the hull needs to be as stiff as possible to minimise forestay sag. An important factor here is structural continuity, that is, minimising the hinge effect found at the ends of the coachroof and cockpit, and other places where sudden changes in shape occur.

Otherwise the main deflections occur in the bow, as the hull sections are relatively small in this region and so contribute little to the overall stiffness.

There are two approaches to hull design. The more traditional approach consists of a skin reinforced with a system of stringers and frames. This approach achieves its greatest weight efficiency with a thin skin and a closely spaced grid of stringers and frames dividing the hull up into square panels. The deeper and thinner the frames, the greater their efficiency; with aluminium or steel, depth:thickness ratios of up to 30 can be used without risk of permanent buckling. Their efficiency can be further increased by using angle or T-section framing, or by taking advantage of the directional properties of wood and fibreglass.

Several factors tend to prevent this approach from achieving its full efficiency. Firstly, the relatively small panel size demands a relatively high design pressure to be used. Secondly, building such an intricate framing system is expensive – many boats are built with relatively thick skins and purely longitudinal or transverse framing, longitudinal framing being preferred because it increases overall stiffness and is easier to fair. The thin materials required may prove impossible to build due to limitations in building techniques, for example because of excessive weld distortion; also, the thin skin may have insufficient impact resistance. All these problems tend to be greatest with small boats, and where relatively dense materials are being used.

The other approach is to design the hull as a monocoque structure, with little if any framing. In its most basic form, this can be achieved simply by using a much thicker shell weight; this approach is often used with steel or fibreglass boats so long as weight is not too important a factor. However, this does result in a relatively heavy structure, with fairly high material costs.

If a sandwich form of construction is used, though, the hull can be considerably lighter than the best framed hull, with equal local strength and improved local stiffness. This is all achieved by moving the two skins away from the centre of the shell, so that for a given deflection the skins are subjected to a higher stress than would be the case if there were a single skin of equal weight. However, there is a limit to how far this principle may be taken, as thicker cores require stronger materials to transfer the increased loads between the skins, and this can result in a significant weight increase. Also, if the skins are too thin they will have insufficient puncture resistance. However, the main problem is once again that of building techniques; sandwich construction is best suited to fibreglass, and could also be used much more widely with wood, but can only be used in flat panels with other materials.

The rig loads try to bend the entire hull, and so longitudinal stiffness is essential. This is primarily dependent upon the amount of material in the skins and the longitudinal stringers; transverse frames make virtually no contribution to the fore and aft stiffness of the hull, and only help the deck slightly by preventing buckling. Once again, sandwich construction is the most efficient way of

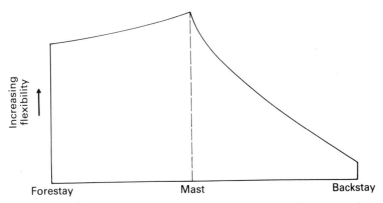

Fig. 2.16. Hull stiffness under rig loads. Note the lack of stiffness in the bows, due to the narrow sections reducing the amount of material present. The calculations assumed that a space frame was not fitted; also, deflections due to discontinuities at the ends of the cockpit and coachroof were ignored.

preventing buckling, followed by a grid of longitudinal and transverse frames. Then there are marked reductions in efficiency in using longitudinal stringers, transverse frames, or an unstiffened plate.

As the loads are almost all in a fore and aft direction, the directional properties of wood and fibreglass may be put to good effect. Also, materials with good local stiffness characteristics are at an advantage, as they can be designed to make a contribution to the overall stiffness whilst still retaining sufficient local stiffness, for example by using fewer transverse frames.

The weight reduction achieved by a sandwich construction is due to reducing the thickness of the skins, which also results in a large reduction in overall stiffness. Thus the hull needs to be stiffened up by having an internal framework linking together the mast and rigging; due to scaling effects this problem is most severe on larger boats. The framework can consist of having the bunk fronts of heavy ply running continuously from the stem to the stern, or a proper aluminium framework. This is most efficient if designed as a space frame, that is, as a framework where all the members are either in tension or in compression, with no bending forces involved.

The mast and windward shrouds produce predominantly vertical forces, with a smaller compressive load across the deck. These forces need to be tied together and distributed throughout the boat. This can either be achieved by a structural bulkhead, or by a metal floor connected to the chainplates by tie rods. If the mast is deck stepped its supporting structure may spread the loads sufficiently into the hull so that no further reinforcement is required, otherwise a strong centreline structure is needed to distribute the loads to frames fore and aft of the mast.

Supporting the mast is a problem on catamarans, as they have no central hull on which it can be stepped. If the design has a bridge deck, though, this is sufficiently strong so long as a transverse frame is fitted. On designs where the hulls are

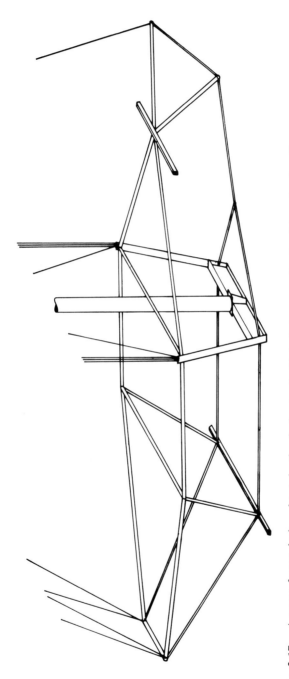

Fig. 2.17. A space-frame designed to take the rigging loads. Note that no member is subjected to bending loads, except the *I* beam under the mast. The tension members along the hull are flat bar, whilst the compression members under the deck are tubular to prevent buckling. As allowance must be made for the crew's accommodation, a perfect space-frame is not possible in most boats. Thus each node (where the members join) is bonded to a frame to relieve the space-frame of some loads and increase torsional rigidity.

connected by cross-beams there are basically two options. The shrouds and split backstay can be taken out to the hulls, and the mast and forestay supported by cross-beams; these need to be fairly massive to take the large, concentrated loads in mid span. They must also be designed to be very stiff, so that the rig is stable. However, the large shroud angle reduces the compressive loads on the mast, permitting a smaller section to be used. For this reason, some trimarans also take the shrouds out to the outriggers.

Alternatively, a central nacelle can be used, with the shrouds coming down to it inboard of the genoa. Although the narrow shroud base means higher shroud loads, the forces can easily be triangulated to provide a more stable rig. Also, lighter, less rigid cross-beams can be used, and the boat's overall beam increased.

Ballasted keels give rise to two sets of forces. First, there is the simple downwards load due to the keel's weight. Second, when heeled, the keel tries to hinge round the hull, putting a torsional load on the centreline structure. These forces are resisted by a reinforced centreline structure tying in to the mast step at the forward end and a series of keel floors along the length of the keel, or alternatively by a considerable increase in shell thickness. The loads are greatest on narrow keels, as these have only a small bearing surface against the hull.

The inter-hull structure of multihulls has three sets of forces acting on it, in addition to any loads from the rigging. Firstly, there is the bending load due to the righting moment being transmitted by the cross-beams. The weight efficiency of the beams increases by making them as deep as possible when combatting this set of forces. Secondly, there are the torsional forces created by waves. These forces can be reduced by positioning the cross-beams well into the ends of the hulls, and using a closed section such as a cylinder or an ellipse. Finally, there may be a tensile or compressive loading due to the hulls resisting leeway. This is relatively small, and presents no problems structurally.

Problems tend to occur not in the cross-beams themselves, but where they are attached to the hulls. The torsional loads in particular can be difficult to transfer from the cross-beams into the hulls. This is especially so when a lightweight hull construction has been used, as it is unable to take high local loads without extensive reinforcement. Difficulties can be avoided by ensuring that the beams have as large a bearing surface on the hulls as is possible, and turning the beam through 90° so that it meets the hull from above. The hull needs reinforcing with frames each side of the beams to prevent distortion. Using three or four beams reduces the loads in each beam, but also results in a significant weight penalty.

Solid bridge decks are much stronger than cross-beams due to their large size, and the extensive contact they have with the hulls. Thus they seldom have any structural problems. For racing boats, though, they are seldom used because of the extra weight and windage.

Material	MATERIAL PROPERTIES			EQUAL WEIGHT COMPARISON			EQUAL LOCAL STRENGTH			EQUAL OVERALL STRENGTH	
	Specific gravity	Flexural strength σ_f(p.s.i. $\times 10^3$)	Young's Modulus E(p.s.i. $\times 10^6$)	Local stiffness ($\times 10^6$)	Local strength ($\times 10^3$)	Overall stiffness ($\times 10^6$)	Weight ($\times 10^{-3}$)	Local stiffness	Overall stiffness ($\times 10^{-4}$)	Weight ($\times 10^{-4}$)	Overall stiffness
Western red cedar	0.32	1.65	0.55	17.3	16.1	1.73	7.93	8.20	13.6	1.94	333
African mahogany	0.50	2.55	0.75	6.04	10.2	1.51	9.90	5.87	14.9	1.96	296
Teak	0.63	2.82	0.90	3.60	7.12	1.43	11.8	6.01	17.0	2.23	319
Chopped strand glass/ polyester	1.54	19.4	0.66	0.19	8.18	0.44	10.9	0.75	0.47	0.79	34

E-glass woven rovings/vinyl ester	1.70	29.1	1.37	0.28	10.1	0.1	9.95	0.77	0.80	0.58	47.1
Kevlar woven rovings/epoxy	1.30	26.5	2.44	1.11	15.7	1.88	7.98	0.74	1.50	0.49	82.1
Carbon fibre cloth/epoxy	1.70	77.7	17.2	3.50	26.8	10.1	6.11	0.77	6.17	0.22	221
Mild steel	7.80	70.0	29.0	0.0612	1.15	3.72	32.5	1.57	11.3	1.11	414
5083 welded aluminium	2.70	22.0	11.0	0.56	3.01	4.07	18.2	1.06	7.41	1.23	500
6082 glued aluminium	2.70	36.7	18.3	0.93	5.04	6.78	14.1	2.32	9.55	0.74	499
7075 glued aluminium	2.70	73.0	36.5	1.85	10.0	13.5	10.0	1.84	13.5	0.37	500
Ferro-cement	2.69	10.0	1.90	0.1	1.38	0.71	26.9	3.62	1.90	2.69	190

Fig. 2.18. A comparison of various boatbuilding materials. The derivations of the comparison factors are given in Appendix B. Please note that figures in different columns are not directly comparable. The local strength comparison applies to a single skin laminate, the overall strength comparison to a sandwich structure.

73

Lightweight Materials

As has been discussed in Chapter 1, a lightweight hull is of considerable benefit to monohulls, and is essential for racing multihulls. This section studies the weight efficiency that is possible with various materials, but it must be emphasised that good structural design is at least as important as using lightweight materials.

The most obvious requirement of any structure is that it has sufficient strength, and in the case of hull design it is the local strength that is the important factor. However, the hull must also have sufficient local stiffness, and overall stiffness against rigging loads.

Figure 2.18 lists the density, ρ, strength, σ_f, and stiffness, E of a variety of boatbuilding materials. These figures are then used to produce the strength and stiffness characteristics on a basis of equal weight, and then equal local strength. Finally, the weight and overall stiffness characteristics are given on the basis of equal overall strength, so that the efficiency of materials in sandwich construction can be compared. Please note that the figures in different columns cannot be compared directly. The derivation of the factors used is given in Appendix B.

Comparing these figures, we see that wood has excellent local stiffness and strength for a given weight, due to its low density. Similarly, on the basis of equal local strength it compares well with a metal or single skin fibreglass hull, and its exceptional overall stiffness means that a space frame is not necessary on any but the largest of vessels.

On a weight for weight basis fibreglass has quite good local strength, but its stiffness characteristics are poor. The situation becomes much worse when looked at on the basis of equal strength, and in fact most single skin hulls have to be designed on the basis of stiffness, not strength. This results in a considerable weight penalty unless the framing is spaced very closely. Also, the abysmally low overall stiffness means that an aluminium space frame is essential on any racing yacht, and of course this increases the weight of the hull. However, on the basis of equal overall strength fibreglass is the lightest material available, due to its high ratio of strength to density. Although the overall stiffness figures seem low, a sandwich structure is so stiff that this is not important. Note that these overall stiffness figures relate to the local stiffness of a sandwich structure, and not the overall stiffness of the hull.

Whilst aluminium comes out poorly on a weight-for-weight basis, when compared on the basis of equal local strength its high overall stiffness becomes apparent, second only to timber. However, it suffers from poor local stiffness characteristics, as its high density results in relatively thin plating. Thus it is essential for an aluminium hull to have as thin a shell as possible, with numerous closely spaced stringers. When used in sandwich construction, only the highest grades of alloy are competitive with fibreglass, and in any case the thin skins have very low puncture resistance. Throughout the table the superior performance of glued construction is apparent. Aluminium can still be competitive with fibreglass on large boats, as the weight of the space frame required by the fibreglass boat becomes increasingly significant.

Neither steel nor ferro-cement offer any potential for lightweight construction, as is immediately obvious from the table. The only reason why steel was once used in racing craft is that it was awarded a considerable allowance under the scantlings rule incorporated in the RORC rule, the predecessor to the IOR.

It is not possible to choose the lightest material purely on its structural efficiency, though. Leaving aside economic factors, the limitations of construction techniques must also be taken into account. Because of its low density there is no real restriction on the minimum weight of timber structures, plywood being available in thicknesses down to 0.6 mm. Bonded aluminium and fibreglass are also available in very light weights, but because of their greater density, impact resistance and puncture resistance might be unacceptably low. On the other hand, ferro-cement cannot be made less than ⅝ inch thick, and welded steel and aluminium are limited to thicknesses of ⅛ and ⅒ inch respectively. This results in minimum unstiffened skin weights of 8.8, 5.1 and 1.4 lbs/sq ft respectively.

Chapter 3

The Sail Plan

Aerodynamic Considerations

The rig's function is to propel the yacht. The way in which this is achieved varies according to whether the yacht is beating, reaching or running. Each of these points of sail has different optimum design characteristics, and the sail plan must be a compromise between these conflicting requirements.

Looking at the close hauled condition first, Fig. 3.1 shows that the total force F_T developed by the sails is angled well away from the direction of travel. In fact, when it is resolved into a driving component F_R and a sideways component F_H, F_H is found to be three or four times greater than F_R. This large sideways force is harmful on two counts: firstly, it means that a large heeling moment will be generated, so the amount of sail that can be carried is limited by the stability of the yacht; and secondly, the yacht will sail at an angle of leeway, λ, to develop a side force to counteract F_H, which results in a considerable increase in hull drag.

All this means that we cannot expect much improvement in performance by simply increasing F_T, as this will result in a commensurate increase in F_H. Instead, we need to improve the angle that F_T makes with the yacht. This angle is expressed as the lift:drag ratio, $F_L : F_D$, where F_L is the component of F_T perpendicular to the wind, and F_D is the parallel component. This ratio is used in preference to $F_R : F_H$ as it is independent of the yacht's course, and so enables the efficiency of the rig to be evaluated independently of the hull. A good rig has a lift:drag ratio of about 6.

One method of improving the lift:drag ratio is to use high aspect ratio sails. On any sail, air leaks around the head and the foot from the high pressure windward side to the low pressure leeward side. As a result of this, strong vortices are formed at the head and foot, which greatly increase the drag force. A high aspect ratio sail clearly has much smaller ends than a low aspect ratio sail, so less air flows around the ends, the vortices are less powerful, and less drag is created. However,

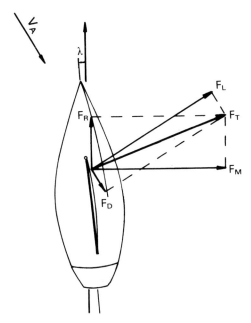

Fig. 3.1. Forces developed by the rig when sailing to windward.
Lift:drag ratio = 5.5.

aspect ratio is limited both by the increase in heeling moment due to the higher centre of effort of the sails, and also by the detrimental effects which the necessarily larger, heavier mast section has on both the airflow over the mainsail, and on the weight distribution of the yacht.

The other method of improving the lift:drag ratio is to reduce the number of sails to a minimum. Because each sail is working in the air deflected by the sail immediately in front of it, it will have to be sheeted closer to the centreline to be at the same angle to the airflow. Thus the sails at the rear end of the series will be developing almost no driving force, whilst the wider sheeting angle of the leading sail will require the boat to sail at a greater angle to the wind. This explains the poor performance of ketches and schooners to windward. However, the sloop is generally preferred to the una rig because of the lower centre of effort of the sail plan, and also because the slot greatly improves the stability of the airflow over the mainsail.

When the boat is reaching, F_R is about three times greater than F_H (Fig. 3.4). Because of the much lower side force, stability requirements and hull drag due to leeway are of much less significance. Thus the aim is simply to maximise the drive produced by the sails, even if this does result in a lower lift: drag ratio. As the force developed by a sail is proportional to the angle it makes with the wind, this is simply achieved by increasing this angle. However, if this angle becomes too large, the pressure drop on the lee side of the sail becomes too great, and the

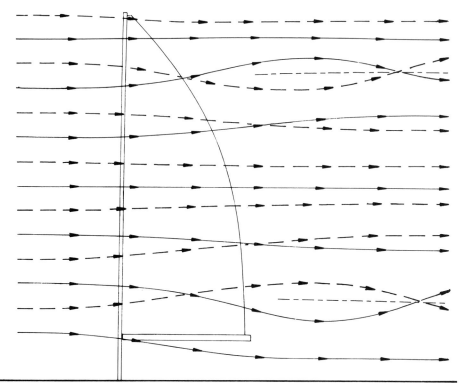

Fig. 3.2. A sketch of the airflow over a sail, showing the tip vortices.
——————→—————— Flow over windward side of sail
— — →— — — Flow over leeward side of sail
— · — · — · — · Centre of vortex

airflow degenerates from stable, laminar flow to a broad band of turbulent eddies. This first occurs at the leach, but quickly progresses to the luff. As soon as this stalling commences, there is a marked reduction in the lift produced.

The angle at which stalling occurs can be increased by introducing more air to the lee side of the sail, reducing the pressure drop and preventing the airflow from becoming turbulent. This air is introduced from the windward side of the sail by two possible routes. Firstly, it may flow around the ends of the sail. Low aspect ratio sails are now at an advantage, as they allow a greater amount of air to transfer to the leeward side. Secondly, several sails may be used in series, each slot transferring air from the windward side of the forward sail to the lee side of the after sail. The greater the number of sails, the more the airflow can be deflected, and so the greater the resultant driving force.

On a run, the driving force is derived entirely from the drag of the stalled sails. The main factor governing performance is the ability to set a large amount of sail in clear air. This obviously puts two-masted rigs at a disadvantage, as the sails set on the forward mast will be partially blanketed by those on the after mast.

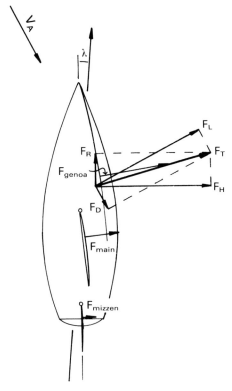

Fig. 3.3. Forces developed by a ketch when sailing to windward, showing the forces developed by each sail. Overall lift:drag ratio = 4.5.

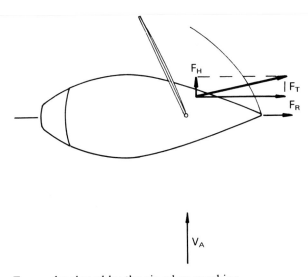

Fig. 3.4. Forces developed by the rig when reaching.

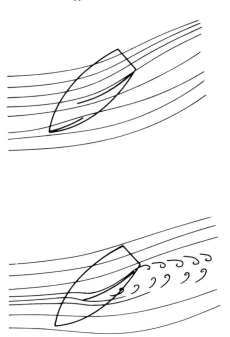

Fig. 3.5. The slot effect. The mainsail is stalled without the jib, but the addition of the jib means that the direction of the airflow is changed more gradually, and so a stall is avoided. Note that the streamlines converge in the slot, indicating that the velocity is reduced.

High aspect ratio sails show a slight performance advantage, as low aspect ratio sails tend to form an area of dead, stationary air in the centre of the sail. However, this is largely offset by the difficulty of controlling high aspect ratio spinnakers in a blow, and also the greater likelihood of downwind rolling occurring in monohulls.

Practical Considerations

Whilst it is obviously important that the rig is aerodynamically efficient, it is at least equally important that the crew are able to handle the sails. This is particularly the case with short-handed or cruising yachts, where ease of handling may well be the most important factor.

It is generally agreed that the maximum sail area one man can handle is about 500 square feet, though it is hard work changing a headsail much over 400 square feet. It is largely in changing sails that lack of manpower is apparent; thus mainsails and roller reefing headsails are considerably easier to manage, and can exceed the 500 square feet limit without being excessively difficult to handle. However, all sails need to be sheeted in, and even with the powerful winches available this can still be hard work. Thus cutters, ketches and schooners, with their smaller sails, are favoured by many cruising yachtsmen.

Ketches and schooners have a significantly lower centre of effort than a sloop or cutter, and this can be an advantage where a high reserve of stability is required. An example of this is the cruising multihull, where a two-masted rig can be used to reduce the likelihood of a capsize due to carrying an excessive amount of sail.

If a second mast is being considered, it must be borne in mind that it will add a significant amount to the cost of the yacht. In addition, it will reduce the amount of uncluttered deck space, as well as having a strong influence on the interior layout. Because of this, it is seldom worth considering on yachts below 40 feet in length.

The Masthead Sloop

This rig is very popular on yachts of all sizes because of its good sailing performance, and the simplicity of its rigging. With the shrouds, forestay and backstay all meeting at one point, the mast is purely in compression. The shrouds take all the sideways loads of the rig, whilst the forestay and backstay take the fore and aft loads.

It has been found that the most efficient configuration to windward is that of a large genoa with an aspect ratio (foretriangle height I: foretriangle base J) of about 3.0 to 3.5, and a small mainsail with an aspect ratio (luff P: foot E) of up to 3.6. Some boats are now carrying larger mainsails, though, to improve reaching performance. Most of the drive comes from the large headsail, the mainsail being there principally to stabilise the airflow and improve reaching performance.

Windward performance is good, though in strong winds some efficiency is lost due to the slot becoming excessively wide when reefed. Close reaching tends to be a weakness, again due to the wide slot, though performance can be improved on larger yachts by setting a staysail, and thereby creating an extra slot. Once the spinnaker is set there is no shortage of sail area, especially on the run with the blooper set. This sail has the additional advantage of helping to balance out the forces on each side of the yacht, reducing any tendency for the yacht to broach.

The disadvantages of the masthead sloop are a direct result of the large foretriangle. Upwind the sheet loads are high, and the headsails need frequent changing to suit the wind strength. This means not only hard work for the crew, but also a fairly extensive sail wardrobe. Downwind the large, high aspect ratio spinnaker can be tricky to control in a blow, and may try to take charge of the boat.

The Fractional Sloop

With this rig the forestay joins the mast at about 75% to 85% of its height, resulting in a large mainsail and small foretriangle. To prevent the centre of effort from becoming too high, the mainsail has a low aspect ratio of 2.5 to 3.0, giving a

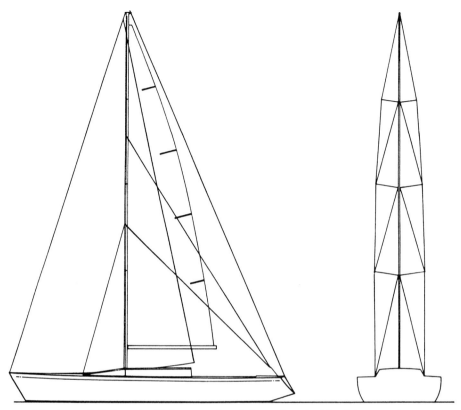

Fig. 3.6. Sailplan of a 47-foot masthead sloop rigged with triple spreader mast, baby stay and twin checkstays. Sail areas: Mainsail 447 sq ft; No. 1 genoa 867 sq ft; Total 1314 sq ft. (Note that all the sailplans up to Fig. 3.12 are based on a 47-foot hull, and the areas are calculated to give the same heeling moment.)

foretriangle aspect ratio of 3.0 to 3.4. Even so, it does have a higher centre of effort than a masthead rig, and so must carry slightly less sail area.

The small headsails make the rig considerably easier to handle. More emphasis is laid on depowering the mainsail, so less frequent sail changes are needed, together with a smaller sail wardrobe. Sheet loads are also lower, so tacking is easier and smaller winches are required. Upwind the rig is efficient throughout the wind range, as a narrow slot is maintained. Off the wind the smaller spinnaker is considerably easier to control, though it is not easy to set a blooper efficiently, and staysails are not as effective as on a masthead rig. The smaller sail area off the wind also causes a slight reduction in performance in light airs; in stronger winds an excessively large mainsail will increase the tendency for the boat to broach in the gusts.

The fractional rig is almost mandatory on racing yachts up to about 40 feet, because of the ease of tuning the rig to suit a wide range of wind conditions, and the greater upwind sail area permitted under the IOR compared with the

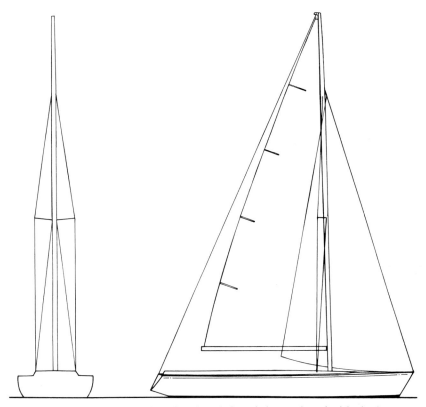

Fig. 3.7. Sail plan of a 47-foot fractional rigged sloop, rigged with single swept spreaders. Sail areas: Mainsail 690 sq ft; No. 1 genoa 517 sq ft; Total 1207 sq ft.

masthead rig. It is also growing in popularity on large boats because of the easier handling of the large spinnakers, though gybing the large mainsail can be a problem.

The drawbacks are found in the staying of the mast. Obviously it is not possible to have a permanent backstay to the top of the foretriangle, and this can be solved in one of two ways. Either the shrouds are swept back by about 20 or 30°, or runners are used. The absence of runners makes life easier for the crew, but the lack of control of forestay sag does reduce performance to windward, and in a breeze there is little control of sideways mast bend. Even if runners are fitted, some sweepback may be maintained in case the boat tacks or gybes without having the runners made up.

Racing yachts will take the runners right to the transom to minimise the sideways loading on the mast, but cruising yachts will site them further forward. This should make it possible to sail to windward with both runners made up, the lee runner only needing to be cast off when sailing off the wind.

A backstay is still taken to the masthead both to provide additional support to the masthead, and also as a means of inducing mast bend. Racing yachts may

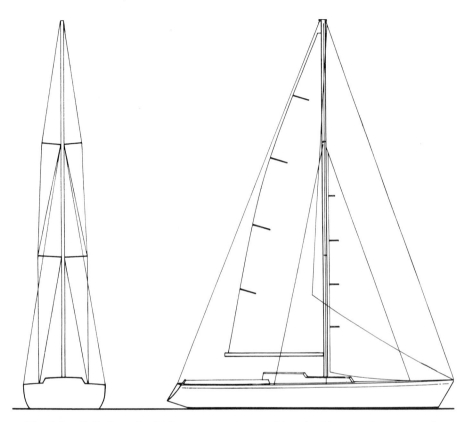

Fig. 3.8. Sail plan of a 47-foot cutter, rigged with a double spreader mast and lower runners. Sail areas: High-clewed jib 515 sq ft; Staysail 230 sq ft; Mainsail 479 sq ft; Total 1224 sq ft.

require the addition of jumpers to prevent excessive mast bend above the hounds if the mast is severely tapered.

The Cutter

The cutter provides the simplest way of dividing the sails into more manageable sizes. The large genoa of the masthead sloop is split up into a jib set on the forestay, and a staysail on the inner forestay. The mast does need some additional support at the inner forestay. This is normally achieved by having the inner forestay coincide with a spreader to provide athwartships support, and a set of runners for fore and aft control; these are normally sited so that both can be left made up when beating.

Upwind, the rig performs at its best if neither jib nor staysail have any significant overlap; this results in the characteristic high clewed yankee jib. With this sail combination, windward performance is only slightly inferior to the sloop rig. In strong winds sail can be reduced by lowering the jib. This is very efficient, as the staysail maintains a narrow, efficient slot.

Off the wind, sail area can be increased and efficiency improved by replacing the jib with a reaching genoa. Unfortunately, the large masthead spinnaker is still part of the rig. However, for the cruising yachtsman good performance can be achieved by setting the jib and staysail wing and wing.

The Ketch

The ketch rig consists of a smaller mizzen mast set aft of the mainmast. The sail area is thus divided into three sails, two of which are set on masts. This gives easy sail handling, and in addition permits staysails to be set between the masts when off the wind. The mizzen can also be effective in adjusting the balance of the yacht, being set well aft of the centre of lateral resistance.

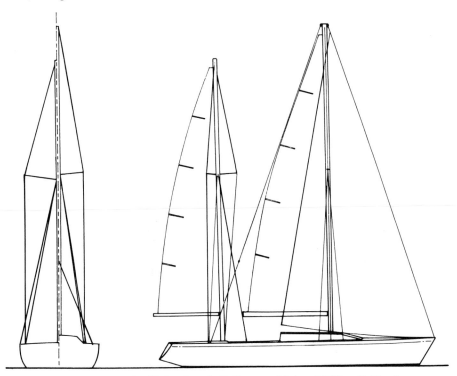

Fig. 3.9. Sail plan of a 47-foot ketch. Sail areas: Mainsail 388 sq ft; No. 1 genoa 647 sq ft; Mizzen 280 sq ft; Total 1315 sq ft.

Offset against this, the mizzen is often a very small sail, in which case it will contribute only minimally to the yacht's performance. This is particularly the case when sailing to windward as, in addition to the poor aerodynamic performance, the presence of a heavy mast right at the end of the yacht will significantly increase pitching. If the mizzen is relatively large it will be more efficient aerodynamically, as well as improving the weight distribution, although if sited too close to the mainsail the poor slot shape will reduce windward performance.

On a run the mizzen and mizzen staysail will tend to blanket the mainsail and spinnaker, reducing performance. This is compensated for by good reaching performance, as the rig can set a large sail area in a highly efficient configuration.

The staying of the mizzen mast deserves some consideration, particularly in a force and aft direction, due to the limited deck space available. On almost all ketches there is insufficient space for a normal masthead forestay. If there is space for a permanent mizzen backstay, the mizzen forestay and main backstay can be combined into a triatic stay joining the two mastheads. The problem with this is that if one mast should fail, it will probably bring the other one down with it.

Many yachts lack space for either a permanent backstay or a forestay taken to the mizzen masthead. Various solutions may be found, but the best arrangement is to have aft swept shrouds taken to the masthead, and a fractional split forestay. If necessary, the top of the mast can be further supported by jumpers. Running backstays are sometimes used, but they are to be avoided if possible as they increase the crew's workload. The main backstay may have to be split and led each side of the mizzen, to ensure that it will clear the leach of the mainsail.

The Schooner

With this rig the mainmast is set abaft the shorter foremast. As may be expected, this rig is basically similar to the ketch. As the masts are of more equal size, the genoas and spinnakers are smaller, and the weight distribution of the spars is better. The strong point of the schooner is reaching, when the gollywobbler can be set. This large, powerful sail makes the schooner unbeatable on a reach. However, when running the mainsail will have a large blanketing effect on the foresail.

The staying of the masts is also similar to the ketch, although the mainmast, with its greater height, will need more support than the mizzen. If a permanent single or split backstay is not feasible, the shrouds should be swept aft. There is greater justification in using a triatic stay instead of a fractional forestay and jumpers, because of the greater distances involved. Alternatively, a split forestay can be used in conjunction with spreaders and a split lower forestay.

Cat and Junk Rigs

Over the last few years cruising yachtsmen have become increasingly interested in cat and junk rigs. This is because of the ease of handling which they offer, with no need for sail changes, nor for a variety of sails to be accommodated below decks. The use of an unstayed, keel stepped mast is also an advantage, as it does permit

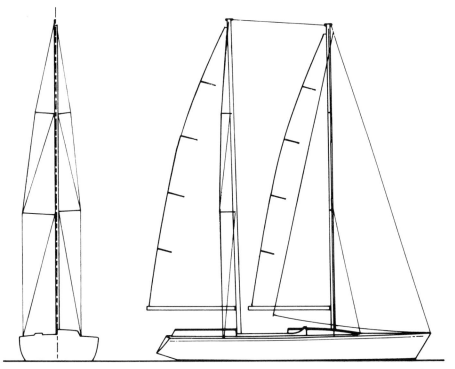

Fig. 3.10. Sail plan of a 47-foot schooner. Sail areas: Mainsail 438 sq ft; Foresail 382 sq ft; No. 1 genoa 648 sq ft; Total 1468 sq ft.

the sails to be hoisted or lowered on any point of sail. However, because it lacks the support of standing rigging, the mast is unable to support the same sail area as one that is stayed, and it must of necessity be both larger and heavier. As a result the sail plan tends to be of moderate aspect ratio, and two-masted rigs are seen on comparatively small boats.

The penalty to pay for the ease of handling afforded by these rigs is a below-par performance. Upwind, the low aspect ratio sails, and the inefficient shape of the slot in two-masted rigs, results in poor performance. Off the wind, the sail area needs to be increased by setting a staysail if the boat is to perform well.

Junk rig. The junk rig has been imported from China, where many regional variations exist, all working on the same basic principles. The sail sets like a fully battened balanced lugsail, the battens dividing the sail up into a series of panels. Each batten is attached to the mast by a rope retaining loop, and has its own sheet at the after end. There is also the usual halyard fastened to the yard, which forms the top batten; and a topping lift supporting the boom, arranged so that it contains the sail and battens when lowered.

To reef the sail one simply lowers the desired number of panels, and then adjusts the sheets. Because of the low loads, tackles are generally used instead of winches; as a result, long lines are required, and chafe can be a problem.

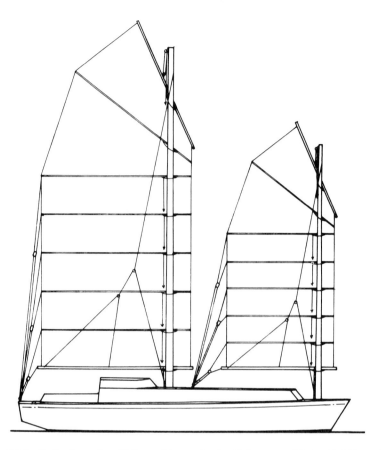

Fig. 3.11 Sail plan of a 47-foot chinese junk. Sail areas: Mainsail 841 sq ft; Foresail 419 sq ft; Total 1260 sq ft.

Cat rig. The cat rig revival has centred round the Freedom rig designed by Gary Hoyt. This uses a sleeve luffed sail, set well forward due to the lack of a headsail, combined with a wishbone boom; the area of sail below the boom acts as a kicking strap. Sail area is reduced by slab reefing of the sail above the boom. By using a reef pendant on the luff as well as the leach, this can be carried out entirely from the cockpit.

Staying the Mast

The mast and rigging have to provide support for the sails, and also transfer the forces developed by the sails from the rig to the hull. This is achieved by a simple braced framework, with the mast and spreaders in compression, and the shrouds and stays in tension. The bending forces on the mast are comparatively small,

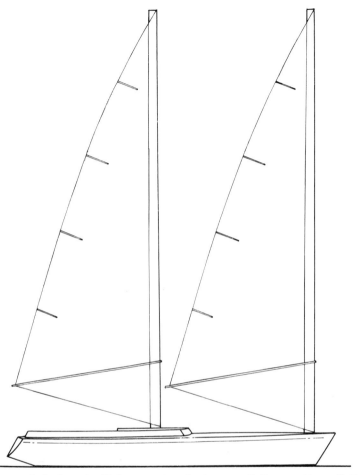

Fig. 3.12. Sail plan of a 47-foot cat rigged schooner. Sail areas: Foresail 693 sq ft; Mainsail 693 sq ft; Total 1386 sq ft.

except in the cases of unstayed masts and the upper part of fractional rigs. In both these cases, the mast behaves as a cantilever.

The compressive loading on the mast depends on several factors. The most obvious of these is the size of the sail plan, as this will govern both the forces developed by the rig, and the length of mast requiring support. Closely related to this is the stability of the yacht. Each time a gust hits the boat, the force produced by the sails suddenly increases. Whilst a tender monohull absorbs a large proportion of this shock load by heeling, and so presenting less sail area to the wind, a stable multihull will not heel, and so the rig must be considerably stronger to absorb this shock loading.

Other factors are dependent on the geometry of the rig. The mast is divided into a series of panels by the standing rigging, in both the athwartships and the fore and aft planes. The shorter the length of a panel, the greater its resistance to buckling.

Fig. 3.13 A cat rigged Freedom 40, with its light weather staysail set.

Therefore, the greater the number of panels, the smaller the section that can be used. Also, the greater the angle made between the rigging and the mast, the smaller the loads developed in supporting the same sail force. As can be seen in

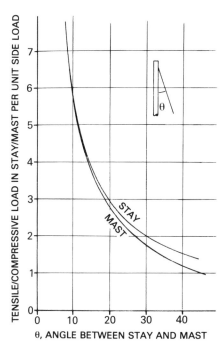

Fig. 3.14(a). Graph of mast and stay loads *vs* angle made between stay and mast.

Fig. 3.14, the loads rise very rapidly at small angles. An angle of 8° is regarded as the absolute minimum, and where possible it is increased to 10° or more.

The width of the staying base for the shrouds is limited in most cases by the overlap of the genoa, or otherwise by the beam of the boat. If the genoa is to be sheeted at its most efficient angle, the chain plates should be at no more than 12° or 13° to the centreline at the stem. To enable the shrouds to make a reasonable angle with the mast, they are held out by spreaders. The thrust of the spreaders on the mast is then taken by lower shrouds attached close to the spreader root. Between one and four sets of spreaders may be used, each set not only reducing the size of the panel, but also increasing the angle made between the shroud and mast. However, the more sets of spreaders used, the more difficult the mast is to tune. Thus racing yachts may use three, or occasionally four, sets of spreaders, whilst cruising yachts generally limit themselves to one or two. Multihulls have sufficient beam to take the cap shrouds outside of the genoa to the outer hulls, reducing compression loads on the mast at the expense of increased loading on the cross-beams.

In the fore and aft plane, the presence of the sails makes it more difficult to support the mast, hence it is deeper in section than it is wide. The basic support comes from the forestay and backstay in a masthead rig, or forestay and runners or

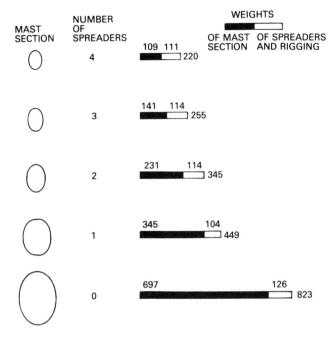

Fig. 3.14(b). A comparison of masts rigged with zero, 1, 2, 3 and 4 sets of spreaders.

aft swept shrouds in a fractional rig. However, most masts will require additional support. This is normally supplied by twin lower shrouds or a baby stay. A baby stay or inner forestay makes tacking more difficult, particularly if it is led well forwards. Also, unless it can be cast off, it means using a twin pole spinnaker gybe.

Lightweight racing spars may also require intermediate runners to prevent the mast bowing forward excessively. This is particularly the case if a considerable amount of mast bend is induced by the backstay and baby stay as a means of controlling the shape of the mainsail.

Stepping the Mast

The mast may be either deck or keel stepped. Unstayed masts clearly need to be keel stepped, as the mast receives all its support from being held rigidly at the deck and the heel. Keel stepped masts which are stayed also benefit from this support, and are able to have a taller lower panel. To gain this extra support, the mast must be firmly held at deck level.

The great advantage of a deck stepped mast is that it allows much greater freedom of layout inside the yacht. The support for the mast heel can easily be incorporated into a bulkhead, or a much more slender, less obtrusive strut can be

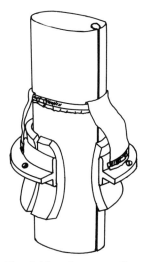

Fig. 3.15. A mast collar.

used. In addition, a keel stepped mast may allow water to enter the interior in bad weather; an effective mast collar is essential, as shown in Fig. 3.15.

The Standing Rigging

Standing rigging is now almost universally stainless steel, as it normally lasts at least ten years before requiring replacement. 1 × 19 construction is generally used because of its low stretch characteristics, but a more flexible construction such as 7 × 7 may be used for runners. Any wire rigging should be replaced as soon as one strand fails, as the others are likely to fail in the near future. This normally occurs at a stress point, such as where the wire emerges from a terminal, or passes over a spreader tip.

Many racing boats use rod rigging, because of its lower stretch and windage. Unfortunately, it does have a short life span. This is because the wind sets up vibrations in the rigging, resulting in fatigue failure. Rod rigging is also severely weakened by any hard spots; because of this, it is best to use linked rigging. Another drawback is that rod rigging is unable to give any advance warning of failure by stranding. Although perfectly satisfactory for use on inshore races, it should only be used on long distance races if it is replaced regularly, and the crew are prepared to accept the increased possibility of losing the mast.

Wire rigging is terminated either by a swage, applied by a special press, or by a swageless patent terminal. Although the swage terminal is neater and lighter, the big advantage of the swageless type is that it can easily be fitted by the crew without any special tools.

Rod rigging may be terminated in several ways. The easiest method is to cut a thread directly onto the rod, with a screw fitting. However, this results in a

Fig. 3.16. Linked rigging. To avoid bending rod rigging over the spreader tip, all three members are terminated at the spreader, with a small bottlescrew adjusting the diagonal member.

considerable reduction in strength, and so is seldom used. Normal practice is to fit a swage terminal, similar to that used on wire rigging. Where maximum strength is required the end of the rod is belled out, and the upper half of the terminal is seated on this. The lower half is then screwed on from underneath.

The commonest way of attaching rigging to the mast is the T terminal. The terminal ends in a T bar, and is swaged to the stay. It then slots into the mast, which is locally reinforced by a backing plate. There should also be a retaining plate to prevent the terminal from jumping out of the mast. This system is both easy to fit, and aerodynamically clean.

Racing yachts may use an internal tang arrangement. The stay enters the mast through a stainless steel bearing plate, and is then fastened either to the headbox or the spreader bracket. Although very clean aerodynamically, access is relatively poor.

External tangs are preferred by cruising yachtsmen, and they are essential for runners, as they can swivel to allow for the varying lead angles that will be encountered. The stay ends in an eye, which is held between the plates of the tang by a clevis pin. The tang is then fastened to the mast wall.

Turning now to the lower end of the rigging, some form of adjustment is required to permit tuning and allow for stretch in the rigging. Turnbuckles, or bottlescrews are used for this, except on the forestay where a pair of link plates

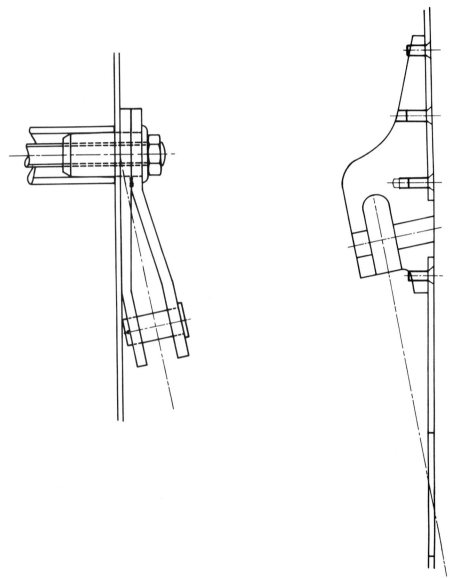

Fig. 3.17. Sections through an internal and an external rigging tang. In each case the shroud ends in an eye, which is pinned or bolted to the fitting. (*Courtesy Proctor Masts.*)

may be used instead. The turnbuckle should be able to be locked either by split pins, or by lock nuts secured with Loctite.

Every stay must have a toggle between the turnbuckle and the chain plate, so that it is able to align itself with the direction of load. In addition, any stay that has a sail set on it must have an additional toggle at the upper end, to allow for the sag that will occur.

Runners may end in an eye which carries a block for the rope tail, or they may simply have the rope tail spliced on. When cast off, the runners should be led forwards of the boom – if pulled up to the backstay they will rapidly chafe the leach of the mainsail. Systems for tensioning the runners are discussed in Chapter 4.

Whilst most boats lead all the shrouds down to the deck, the cluster of rigging running between the spreader tips and the deck does offer considerable windage. The racing boat may avoid this by linking the rigging at the spreader tips, so that there is one common vertical member of increasing diameter. This arrangement is to be preferred for rod rigging, as it avoids the formation of stress points at the spreader tips. The drawbacks obviously lie in maintaining and adjusting the rig, as each component member will require its own turnbuckle, many of which will be high up off the deck.

The Mast

Almost all spars are now made of 6082 or 6061 grade aluminium alloy; 6061 grade has slightly higher stiffness. The only exception to this is that some unstayed masts are made of glass fibre. This material is able to withstand much greater deflections before failure, and has a much greater reserve of strength than an unstayed aluminium spar. Carbon fibre is often incorporated to keep mast bend within tolerable limits, and allow a lighter section to be used. Unstayed masts, and the upper part of fractionally rigged masts, are normally tapered. This reduces both weight and windage from the area where they do most harm.

Because of the need for greater stiffness in the fore and aft plane than in the athwartships plane, most mast sections are based on an elliptical section. A development of this is the 'delta' type section, with a much squarer rear half. By moving material away from the centre of the spar, strength is greatly increased, yet the airflow is not adversely affected. In addition to deciding on the shape of the section, spar makers will decide on whether to go for a large, thin walled section, or a heavier, smaller section – race results show that a relatively small section performs best.

Many racing spars need additional stiffening at local stress points, or need a greater wall thickness, and this is achieved by internal sleeving. This should be both bonded and riveted to the spar; if it is just riveted, the rivet holes will eventually elongate under the combination of corrosion and stress, and ultimately the rivet heads will shear off. The sleeve should end in a gradual taper to prevent failure at the ends. This is particularly common on booms where hydraulic kicking straps are used.

It is important that the spreaders are strongly fastened to the spar, as they are subjected to large fore and aft loads when the mast bends. This is particularly the case with the smaller, more flexible sections used on racing yachts.

An aluminium tube is an excellent carrier of sound, and the noise made by halyards rattling against the mast is quite considerable. The sound can be deadened by filling the mast with a lightweight foam, though room needs to be left for internal halyards and electric cables.

Without going into the detail design of mast fittings, it is worth considering the effect that they have on the strength of the spar. This is particularly important in highly stressed areas such as the gooseneck, or where a keel stepped mast goes through the deck.

Fastenings should be as widely spaced as possible – a horizontal row of fastenings weakens the spar much more than a vertical row. Cut-outs in the spar should be as small as possible, with well rounded corners. Once again, vertical cut-outs are to be preferred to horizontal ones.

Tuning the Rig

Tuning commences with the stepping of the mast. The mast heel should initially be located in the middle of the step, and then the cap shrouds should be adjusted so that the mast is vertical, checking this by hoisting a tape measure on the main halyard and measuring to the gunwhale abreast of the mast on each side of the boat. The tape is then replaced by a plumb bob, and the rake measured between the bob and the aft face of the mast at deck level. It is normally expressed as a percentage of the mast height. On a masthead rig, a rake of 1% or 2% is normal, though some fractional rigs seem to perform better with a larger rake, of about 2% or 3%. With two-masted rigs, the after mast usually carries more rake than the forward mast.

The rest of the rigging can now be tightened up. It is essential that the mast remains straight both fore and aft and athwartships – this can easily be checked by sighting up the mast from the deck. An over-tight inner forestay or baby stay will bow the mast forwards, whilst if one shroud has more tension than its opposite partner the mast will be pulled towards the shroud with the greater tension. Once adjusted, all the rigging should have approximately the same tension.

The next stage is to take the boat out in about 15 or 20 knots of wind, so that she can just carry her largest headsail when close hauled. The first thing to do is to adjust the backstay tension on a masthead rig, or the forestay on a fractional rig without runners. It should be tightened until sag in the forestay is minimised. If the backstay is adjustable, the turnbuckle should be tightened until it is just possible to apply maximum tension with the adjusting mechanism. The rest of the fore and aft rigging can now be adjusted so that the mast is straight. This includes any lower shrouds if they are led fore or aft of the mast.

Now the athwartships rigging can be adjusted. Firstly, tension the cap shrouds until the leeward one is just slack. Next, the lower and intermediate shrouds should be adjusted so that the mast is straight athwartships.

Only now that the rigging tension is correct is it possible to adjust the balance of the yacht. Sailing close hauled, with the sails correctly set, there should be between 2° and 4° of weather helm. This means a tiller deflection of somewhere between ¾ inch and 1½ inches, measured 24 inches from the rudder head. The amount of weather helm is decreased by moving the centre of effort forwards, either by moving the mast forwards or by decreasing the amount of mast rake. To increase the amount of weather helm, the centre of effort is moved aft by using the opposite techniques. Once the mast has been moved, the rigging will need to be readjusted.

A final point is that once in harbour any adjustable standing rigging should be slackened off. If the hull is continually subjected to high rigging loads it will quickly lose some of its stiffness, and the rig tension will bend the hull up at the ends instead of keeping the forestay tight.

Flexible Masts

Flexible masts are used throughout the racing fleet. Their major advantage is the great control of mainsail shape that can be achieved.

With a masthead rig, tensioning the backstay increases forestay tension and induces mast bend. A baby stay is also frequently used in the larger sizes to induce mast bend low down. One or two check stays may be used to prevent the mast from pumping in a seaway, and to keep mast bend within safe limits. These are particularly important in slender, multi-panel spars.

There are many more possibilities with a fractional rig. The simplest system uses aft-swept shrouds and an untapered mast. The stiff topmast means that backstay tension has the dual effect of tensioning the forestay and bending the mast. This system is particularly suitable for small cruisers. However, it is not possible to achieve sufficient forestay tension in stronger winds, and the large topmast section is detrimental to airflow over the mainsail. Also, there is little control over sideways bend in the mast.

To overcome these disadvantages, runners are fitted to control the forestay tension, whilst the backstay controls mast bend. This enables a tight forestay to be maintained, and the topmast can be tapered. If the shrouds are not swept aft, the mainsail can be let right out on the run. Also, the mast can be raked forwards by easing off the backstay and runners, reducing the amount of weather helm on spinnaker reaches. A large amount of forestay tension will increase the compression loads on the mast, and so increase any bend already present. Thus boats fitted with lightweight mast sections will require one or two check stays to limit mast bend.

In boats over about 40 feet, a baby stay may be fitted to enable mast bend low down to be controlled independently of backstay and forestay tension. Also, a topmast with a large amount of taper may be used, supported by jumpers; these may be led down to the deck to enable the flexibility of the topmast to be controlled.

There is no simple guideline concerning how far a mast may be bent without failing. For masts without check stays, a bend of two mast diameters is generally perfectly safe, but a bend of more than three diameters is not recommended. Masts fitted with check stays can be bent to a far greater extent, the exact limit depending upon the design parameters of the rig.

The best way of determining the amount of mast bend is by having a series of stripes on the mainsail at about mid height, parallel to the mast. These are spaced at about half the mast's diameter, and so the amount of bend can be found by simply sighting up the mast from deck level.

The Mainsail

Because the mainsail is not changed but reefed to suit the wind conditions, it must be able to be well reefed to cope with gale conditions. The deepest reef should be at least 60% up the luff if the mainsail is not to be replaced by the trysail in bad weather.

There are basically three methods of reefing: slab reefing, roller reefing round the foot, or furling round the luff. Here we shall look at their pros and cons, and the next chapter will deal with the layout of their controls.

Slab reefing is by far the most popular system. Sail area is reduced in a series of slabs by easing the halyard, dropping an eye in the luff over a hook at the gooseneck, and pulling down the leach with a rope pendant. Although sail area can only be reduced by relatively large amounts, this is more than compensated for by the ease of handling, and by the excellent shape of the reefed sail.

Roller reefing is seen on many smaller boats, especially those designed along more traditional lines. The boom is rotated, and the sail wrapped round it, by turning a handle at the gooseneck. It allows any amount of sail to be set, and it is a fairly simple system to use. Disadvantages are that the reefed sail is too full for efficient windward work, and the end of the boom drops as the sail is reefed. Both these effects can be prevented to some extent by having a flattener reef in the leach. The main drawback with roller reefing is that the poor sail shape makes it necessary to lower the mainsail and replace it with the trysail when beating in heavy weather.

A furling mainsail is loose footed and without any battens. It is rolled around a spar, either inside the mast or immediately behind it, by easing off the clew outhaul and hauling in on the reefing line. It is particularly suited to large cruising boats where slab reefing can be hard work, especially if short-handed. Although some deterioration of sail shape does occur, it is not nearly as great as with a roller reefing sail.

The trysail is purely a storm sail, and so its area should be no more than one third that of the mainsail. As the boom will have the mainsail furled around it, the sail should be set without the boom. This sail is only used regularly when roller reefing is fitted, slab reefing or furling mainsails only needing the trysail as an emergency sail.

Jibs and Genoas

The number of headsails carried depends primarily on whether the boat is going cruising or racing. The cruising yachtsman need only carry a reefing genoa with an overlap of about 40% for light airs, a working jib that fills the foretriangle, a heavy weather jib of about two thirds this area, and a storm jib (Fig. 3.18).

Racing boats will carry a considerably larger wardrobe, the aim being to have a sail to suit every wind condition. A large, well equipped boat may carry three No. 1 genoas with a 50% overlap: a drifter, a light, and a heavy No. 1, each with a different cloth weight and sail shape. Next comes the No. 2, with an overlap of about 30%. Two No. 3 genoas may be carried, a high aspect ratio sail with a full

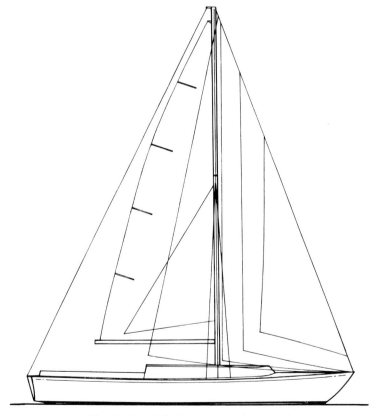

Fig. 3.18. Sail plan of a cruising yacht.

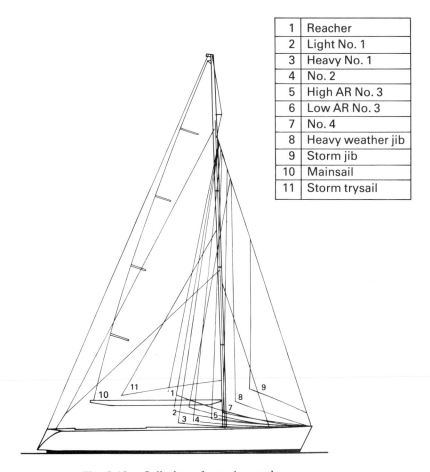

1	Reacher
2	Light No. 1
3	Heavy No. 1
4	No. 2
5	High AR No. 3
6	Low AR No. 3
7	No. 4
8	Heavy weather jib
9	Storm jib
10	Mainsail
11	Storm trysail

Fig. 3.19.   Sail plan of a racing yacht.

hoist luff and little or no overlap for general use, and a low aspect ratio sail with more overlap for use off the wind, or to windward when there is a heavy sea running. Then comes the No. 4 genoa, with a 90% luff and 85% foot, before we come to the heavy weather and storm jibs. The Offshore Racing Council rules that the heavy weather jib shall have a maximum area of $0.135 \times IG$. The area of the storm jib is limited to $0.05 \times IG$, with a maximum luff length of $0.65 \times IG$, where IG is the height of the foretriangle.

Roller reefing has become very popular amongst cruising and short-handed yachtsmen, as it can virtually eliminate sail changing; unfortunately, there are drawbacks to the system which must be considered. As the sail is reefed it becomes increasingly full, especially in the middle third of the sail. This is particularly apparent if a low aspect ratio sail is being reefed, such as the No. 1 genoa. In addition to this the sail maintains the same aspect ratio as it is reefed.

Thus when sail is reduced by roller reefing one has a low aspect ratio sail, much less efficient to windward than a high aspect ratio No. 3. Both of these factors are particularly detrimental when sailing to windward.

There are two ways of getting round these problems. The first is to use roller reefing only on the working jib, using normal sail changes for the genoas. Alternatively, a cutter rig can be used, with roller reefing on both the jib and the staysail.

A final point is that to avoid having to adjust the sheet lead whenever the sail is reefed, the clew should be cut considerably higher than usual, so that the sheet lead is approximately perpendicular to the luff. If a normal low clewed sail is used, a very long genoa track will be required.

If roller reefing is not to be fitted, the choice lies between a luff groove system or hanks. A luff groove stabilises the airflow over the sail, and for the racing man it means that there is no need for bare headed sail changes. However, when the sail is lowered it does not remain attached to the forestay, so there is a greater possibility of the sail blowing over the side. Because of this, most cruising and short-handed sailors prefer hanks.

The number of headsails required can be reduced by fitting reef points along the foot of the sail, enabling each sail to cover a wider range of wind speeds. However, this should not be used on heavy weather or storm jibs, because the reef points do weaken the sail.

Downwind Sails

The traditional downwind rig for the cruising yachtsman consists of twin boomed out headsails, using either the yacht's working sails, or special lightweight running sails. Alternatively, a single poled out genoa may be used.

However, the cruising chute is becoming increasingly popular, offering easier handling together with improved performance. It is not a new development, though, but simply a rebirth of the balloon jib. With the luff set up tight it acts as a reaching genoa, but when the wind is abaft the beam the sheet and halyard are eased, making it a running sail almost as efficient as a spinnaker. On a run it can be set without a pole, but performs best if poled out to windward. Multihulls can tack the sail down on the windward hull to ensure that it is in clear air. The only drawback to the sail is that in light airs with a swell running it is prone to wrapping itself round the forestay.

The downwind sail for racing boats is still the spinnaker, as the area is about 20% greater than a cruising chute, which is in any case banned under the IOR. Spinnakers vary quite considerably in size and shape according to their intended use, and several spinnakers may be carried to cover the wind spectrum.

Running spinnakers are cut with broad shoulders and a fairly full shape, except if intended for very light or very strong winds. In drifting conditions there is insufficient wind to support a large head, and so the sail is cut with narrower shoulders. In strong winds a smaller, flatter sail with narrower shoulders is used, resulting in a more stable shape that is easier to control. Reaching sails are also cut flat and with narrow shoulders, as the leach of a full sail would hook up to windward and act as a brake. Heavy weather spinnakers will be shorter on the luff and foot, but the foot will be reduced by a proportionately greater amount than the luff to keep the spinnaker pole at a reasonable height.

Racing boats may carry a variety of other sails for use when the wind is free, especially in the larger sizes. Firstly, when the boat is just too close to the wind to set a spinnaker, a reaching genoa may be set. This is a high clewed sail sheeted well aft, resulting in a leach that will not hook up to windward, and a foot that will not drag in the water. This may be supplemented by a staysail set on the inner forestay, a high aspect ratio sail with a small overlap that converts one excessively wide slot into two highly efficient ones, as well as adding extra sail area.

Secondly, on the run a masthead rigged boat may well set a blooper, or big boy. This is set flying, with a strop at the tack and the luff slack, so that it can blow out to leeward of the mainsail and find clear air. It not only increases the sail area, but also makes the boat easier to control by balancing out the forces on each side of the yacht.

Finally, a variety of spinnaker staysails may be carried. They perform best in medium airs with an apparent wind angle of 60° to 90°, but may also prove effective on a broad reach. Many different proportions have been tried, but only two are currently in vogue. The tall spinnaker staysail has a full hoist with a slight overlap, sheeted to the lee rail or boom end. The Dazy staysail, so called after its use on *Golden Dazy*, is cut shorter on the foot and sheeted to the main boom; although it is smaller, it is also considerably easier to set effectively. It is also a useful sail to windward in zero wind conditions, as it cannot snag on spreaders and is of very light cloth. The staysail is tacked down to a short track along the centreline, normally as far aft as is permitted under the IOR.

Ketches and Schooners

The foresail of a schooner and the mizzen of a ketch are basically similar to the mainsail in setting and reefing. In addition, staysails can be set between the masts when sailing off the wind. These may vary from spinnaker staysails, looking just like a spinnaker but set without a pole, used on the run and tacked down on the weather rail, right down to close reaching genoa staysails tacked down on the centreline, which can be used with an apparent wind angle of only 60°.

Schooners have the option of setting a gollywobbler, the large quadrilateral sail set in lieu of the foresail, that totally fills the area between the masts. As mentioned earlier, this sail greatly enhances a schooner's reaching performance.

Fig. 3.20. Here it can be seen how the blooper balances out the spinnaker on a run. Note how far the halyard has to be eased on this maxi rater to make the sail set — on smaller fractional boats this makes it impossible to have a blooper of any reasonable size. (*Photo courtesy of William Payne.*)

Fig. 3.21. An Ocean 60 with gollywobbler set. The luff may be set flying, as in this case, or it may have a bolt rope and be hoisted up the mast track. (*Photo courtesy of William Payne.*)

The Cut and Design of Sails

Whilst the cutting and shaping of sails is outside the scope of this book, there are some points regarding sail cloth and sail construction that are worth looking at.

Beginning with the choice of sail cloth, Terylene (or Dacron) is now used almost universally for all mainsails, and most genoas and jibs. This is because of its low stretch, which is essential if a stable sail shape is to be maintained. On the other hand, downwind sails need to be light, so nylon is used. Its elasticity enables it to absorb the shock of a gust of wind without becoming permanently distorted. A grid of heavier threads is often incorporated to improve tear resistance.

It is in the finish of the cloth that the major differences occur. This is because most cloths are impregnated with a resin to improve the stability of the cloth, particularly if intended for use on racing sails. Unfortunately, highly resinated sails are very stiff, and therefore bulky to stow and hard to handle. In addition, the resin will eventually break down, resulting in the cloth losing much of its stability. Because of this, cruising yachtsmen are better off with a soft, unresinated cloth. Although not quite as stable, it will have a longer useful life, stow into a smaller space, and be kinder on the hands.

In the search for ever greater stability, racing yachtsmen are using sails made from Mylar (Melinex). Mylar is polyester in the form of a film, instead of woven into a Terylene cloth. As a result it is extremely stable, especially to loads that do not run along the warp or weft. It does have poor tear resistance, and to improve this it is bonded to a light Terylene or Kevlar cloth. Its chief use is in genoas, where it gives a very stable sail that needs little adjustment of halyard tension. Another use is reinforcing the leach of the mainsail. Kevlar may also be used, though it has a short life for a sailcloth. Because of this, coupled with its high cost, its use is restricted in IOR boats.

Ultra-violet light degrades any sail, and after a few years the cloth will become brittle and tear easily. Dark coloured cloths are slightly more resistant to this, as the dye helps filter out the light. Some sail makers have now developed an unresinated cloth with improved ultra-violet resistance, specifically intended for cruising sails.

Chafe is the other destroyer of sails, both chafe of the sailcloth and of the stitching. Stitching does need regular inspection if seams are not to fail; however, if the seams are triple stitched instead of the normal two rows there is obviously less risk of this occurring.

The best way to minimise chafe is to ensure that wherever possible the sail does not bear on any surface, and where this is inevitable, to ensure that there are no rough areas left exposed. To this end, turnbuckles and spreader tips should be taped over, and on cruising yachts the tack of headsails can be raised level with the guardrail by means of a strop. Also, sacrificial chafe patches should be sewn or glued onto the sails where necessary, particularly where sails touch the spreader tips. These can then be periodically replaced, with no damage to the fabric of the sail.

The main stress points on the mainsail are the head and clew. These should be attached to the spars by slides, even if a bolt rope is used on the sail. A bolt rope is aerodynamically more efficient than slides, and there is no need to feed slides into the mast track. Against this, when the sail is lowered, slides help keep the sail under control. If roller reefing is fitted, the luff should have a luff tape and slides, so as to reduce the bulk of cloth at the gooseneck when the sail is reefed. If slab reefing is used, there should be a row of eyelets between the reef points so that the reefed part of the sail can be tied up around the boom.

Jibs and genoas will be fitted with either a bolt rope or with piston hanks. If hanks are fitted, there should be a plastic disc between the hank and the sail to prevent chafe, and the hanks should extend right up to the head of the sail, to keep the head close to the forestay. If a luff groove system is being used, a bolt rope incorporating PTFE in the outer cover helps reduce friction when hoisting the sail.

Roller reefing headsails need to have a lightweight sacrificial strip along the leach and foot, to prevent ultra-violet degradation when the sail is furled. The leach of high aspect ratio, non-overlapping sails may have short battens fitted to advantage as a means of controlling leach flutter.

Spinnakers employ a variety of cuts designed to distribute the forces in the sail with a minimum of distortion. The simplest is the cross cut, with the panels running across the full width of the sail. Unfortunately, although cheap to produce, it is very prone to distortion, particularly in the head. Because of this, it is only used for cruising spinnakers nowadays.

The problem of distortion is solved by having the panels radiating from the corner of the sail, so that the loads run parallel to the threads in the cloth. This the basis of most spinnaker cuts. The simplest of these is the radial head, combining a cross cut lower portion with a radial cut head. This prevents distortion of the head, and is used on many running sails.

When reaching, or running in strong winds, the clews are prone to distortion. The tri-radial cut now comes to the fore, with all three corners cut radially, and a cross cut central portion. Because of its stability, this cut is used for almost all racing sails. In the strongest winds a star-cut spinnaker may be flown, with the three radial cut corners meeting in the centre of the sail.

Chapter 4

The Deck Layout

The design of an efficient deck layout is largely determined by the intended use of the boat. A fully crewed racing boat does not require much shelter for the crew, and there is plenty of manpower available so leads can be spread about the boat, enabling several operations to be carried out simultaneously. A family cruising boat or a short-handed ocean racer must have all the gear operable by one or two crew members, with safety and shelter both coming high up in the order of priorities. The chief differences here are that the ocean racer will require heavier gear, and the rig will have more controls so that the best performance can be extracted from it.

When planning a deck one must consider every evolution that is likely to be carried out, and the number of crew available. Using this analysis, the various possibilities can easily be compared to find the one that best meets the requirements.

Another aspect to be considered is the possibility of combining systems, so that the amount of deck gear can be minimised – both reducing cost and, if well designed, resulting in a simpler and more efficient layout.

The Cockpit and Coachroof

The position and dimensions of the coachroof and cockpit are largely dictated by the interior layout on cruising boats, whilst on racing boats it is the deck plan that determines the interior.

The height and breadth of the coachroof is dictated by the headroom requirements below deck, and the amount of camber in the deck. As far as ease of working is concerned, the coachroof sides and forward end may either make a shallow angle with the deck so that they can be walked upon in safety, or they can be made nearly vertical to provide a foot stop for the crew.

Fig. 4.1. This ketch has a deep, roomy centre cockpit and an aft cabin. The mizzen mast has a pair of runners instead of a fixed forestay.

The cockpit forms the heart of any deck plan; nowadays most controls are adjusted from the cockpit, and it also provides shelter and security for the crew. In most boats it is placed right aft, leaving the maximum possible amount of space for the accommodation. Alternatively, a centre cockpit may be designed, in conjunction with an aft cabin. This arrangement is best suited to larger, two-masted boats.

Racing yachtsmen will go for a large, shallow cockpit giving plenty of space to work in, as the interior layout is of secondary importance. The cockpit will be shallow to keep the winches at the correct height for maximum efficiency, with the top of the winch about 28 inches off the cockpit sole.

The cruising yacht will have a smaller, deeper cockpit, with coamings along the sides to provide more shelter. If the width between the seats does not exceed 2 foot 3 inches, the crew will be able to brace themselves against the leeward seats; otherwise a central footrest will be needed. Although deep seats provide more shelter, they must not be so low relative to the coachroof that the helmsman's view is impaired.

Winches on cruising boats are often placed on top of the cockpit coamings, too far away from the crew for efficient operation. This can be overcome by having a winch platform immediately aft of the coachroof coming well into the cockpit; below decks the extra space can be used for a hanging locker, or to give better access to a quarter berth.

Fig. 4.2. Twenty-six-foot Super Seal fast cruiser. The line emerging through the deck forward of the mast raises the centreboard which is unballasted, all the ballast being kept in the bilges. Also note the outboard well at the aft end of the cockpit, and the large anchor well on the foredeck.

On tiller steered boats the helm gets a much better view sitting outboard, using a tiller extension. To make this comfortable the coaming needs to be wide, and sloped outboard to give a more level platform when heeled. Also, the inboard edge of the cockpit seat will require a lip or recess moulded in, or a bar incorporated, to act as a foot brace.

To provide a comfortable backrest, the coamings need to be at least 11 inches high and angled well outboard. The top of the coaming is often used as a stepping point when entering or leaving the cockpit, and so for safety should be at least 8 inches wide to provide a secure foothold. However, the coamings must not extend outboard to such an extent that the sidedecks become too narrow – these need to be 10 inches wide as a minimum, and preferably at least 15 inches wide. In cases where the sidedecks would be too narrow, it is better to extend the coaming right outboard to the gunwhale.

Many cruising boats have a sprayhood over the hatchway to prevent rain and spray going down below, and to provide additional shelter for the crew. Usually these are of the folding variety, a PVC cloth stretched over a hingeing alloy frame. These are easily damaged in extreme weather conditions, even if folded down; also, they often interfere with the helmsman's view, and render inoperative

Fig. 4.3. The size of equipment needed on a maxi rater is clearly visible here, with twin coffee grinders for the sheets. The coaming and shallow cockpit ensure that there is full standing headroom below. (*Photo courtesy of William Payne.*)

winches mounted close to the hatch. A much better option, though for some reason not as popular, is a rigid sprayhood over the hatch. This can often be made into an attractive feature, with plenty of windows for good visibility, and sufficient room to operate winches; it will also be proof against the crew standing on it or green water landing on it. On bigger boats it can be enlarged to provide a doghouse or an interior steering position.

Steering Systems

In deciding upon a steering system the racing yachtsman is looking for maximum sensitivity, so that the helm gets as much feedback as possible through the rudder. However, this sensitivity makes helming tiring over long periods, and so the cruising man requires a less sensitive system that damps out some of the loads on the helm.

A tiller provides the simplest, cheapest and most sensitive form of steering. For this reason it is almost standard on boats up to about 35 feet in length, and is often used on larger racing yachts. On larger boats, though, the length of tiller needed to obtain sufficient leverage takes up an excessive amount of space in the cockpit, and the helm has to move the tiller through an increasingly large distance for a given rudder angle.

Wheel steering basically consists of a wheel mounted on a pedestal, linked to a quadrant or short tiller arm mounted on the rudder stock. The linkage may be hydraulic, wire cables, or torsion rods; other systems such as rack and pinion or worm drive are seldom used nowadays. The wheel is usually about 3 feet in diameter, but some racing boats use a very large wheel recessed into the cockpit floor, or a pair of smaller wheels mounted well outboard, to enable the helmsman to sit well outboard and obtain a better view.

The commonest, cheapest and most sensitive form of wheel steering uses a pair of wires to link the wheel to a quadrant on the rudder stock. The wires are connected to the wheel by a roller chain passing over a sprocket, and are then led over sheaves to the quadrant.

To reduce friction the number of sheaves should be kept to a minimum; they must be at least sixteen times the diameter of the wire, and turn the wire through as small an angle as possible. Racing boats may use an A-shaped pedestal and roller bearing sheaves to have as little friction as possible.

The system will have some means of tensioning the steering cables; any slack will result in sloppy steering, and also make it possible for the wires to jump off the sheaves. The steering cables are subjected to heavy loads, which are directly transmitted to the sheaves and the steering pedestal, and so it is imperative that these are attached to strong members.

A variation on cable steering, best suited to small boats, has the wires running inside a sheath, similar to engine control cables. This system is easy to install, as

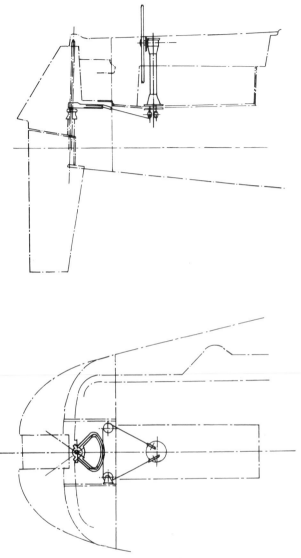

Fig. 4.4. A typical wire steering installation. (*Courtesy Simpson-Lawrence.*)

there is no need to fit and align sheaves. However, it suffers from a considerable amount of friction, particularly when the cables are turned through a tight radius.

Rod steering is ideal for cruising boats as, although slightly less sensitive than wire steering, most of the equipment is virtually maintenance-free. It is also less obtrusive, not requiring a bulky quadrant, and is suitable for use with twin steering positions, or on the twin rudders of a catamaran.

The rotational motion of the wheel is transmitted to the rudder by a series of torque tubes and bevel boxes, finally coming to a reduction box, which is

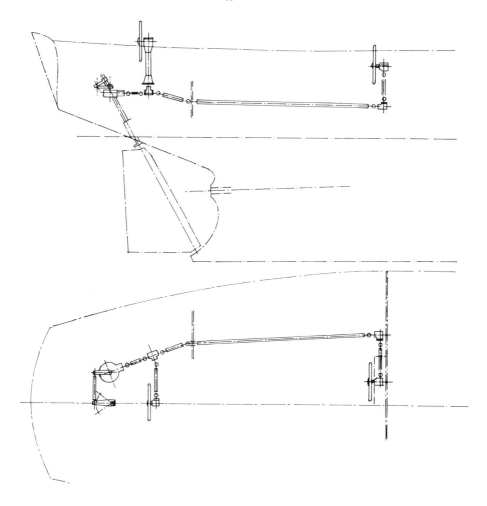

Fig. 4.5. A twin wheel rod steering installation. (*Courtesy Simpson-Lawrence.*)

connected to the tiller arm by a drag link. Universal joints may be incorporated in the torque tubes for small changes in direction, up to about 18°; if used for larger angles, hard spots will develop in the steering.

Hydraulic steering is best suited to larger boats. It eliminates all feel to the rudder, which makes steering very light work. It has all the versatility of rod steering, but in addition the hose can be taken along any route, and there is virtually no wear in the system.

The steering wheel is linked to a hydraulic pump, and hydraulic hoses are taken to each side of a double-acting hydraulic cylinder connected to the tiller arm. The stroke of the cylinder and the mechanical advantage of the system can be varied to suit most rudder installations.

No matter what form of steering is fitted, the stock should be taken up the deckhead and designed to take an emergency tiller. This may have to be cranked to clear the steering pedestal.

The rudder stock needs to be supported by bearings that take the weight of the rudder and also the steering loads. The bearings may be of nylon, duratron, bronze or tufnol; racing yachts may use roller bearings to minimise friction. However, the most important aspect of reducing friction is ensuring that the bearings are aligned absolutely accurately, irrespective of the material used.

On a tiller steered boat the stock can simply run up a fibreglass or aluminium tube to the deck, with the top bearing taking the weight of the rudder. Where wheel steering is fitted, the tiller arm or quadrant will be below the deck. Thus a watertight gland will be needed, as fitted to the propeller shaft. The actual quadrant or tiller arm must be keyed to the stock, or the stock squared off to take it, as simple clamping is not strong enough under the high loads imposed on the system.

Sail Controls

Mainsail

Controls for the mainsail can be split up into two groups: sail trimming controls such as the mainsheet, kicking strap and cunningham hole; and sail setting controls which include the halyard and reefing gear.

Many different mainsheet configurations have been dreamt up, but the simplest has the mainsheet coming off the boom and leading directly to the centreline or the traveller car. The further aft the sheet can be sited, the greater the leverage it exerts; thus a lower purchase can be used, and less rope is required. Racing boats may have a secondary mainsheet, attached to the standing part of the mainsheet with a two-part purchase, to permit fine tuning under load. Some large boats may use a hydraulic ram for this purpose, though some speed of operation is lost.

When a traveller is fitted, the mainsheet should be arranged so that the sheet tension does not vary as the traveller is moved. On most boats this simply means having the mainsheet cleating off on the traveller car, but on larger boats where a winch is required the mainsheet will probably be taken out to the sidedecks, with a single central winch or one on each side.

Upwind the mainsheet is best used to control leach tension, and thereby the amount of twist in the sail; the traveller should be used to control the lateral trim of the sail. Here boats with centre sheeting are at an advantage, as for a given length of track the traveller can control the main over a greater arc. Plenty of power must be available in the traveller control lines to allow easy adjustment, so that the traveller can be controlled just as easily as the sheet. The lines may be cleated on the sidedeck or, for a better lead, on the car; larger boats will require

Fig. 4.6. This rudder stock is made from 6082 grade aluminium alloy. Thus to avoid weakening it with welding, the tangs are bonded into holes drilled through the stock. It will be covered by the foam core visible on the right, before being glassed over.

Fig. 4.7. To give independent control of the mainsheet and the traveller, the mainsheet is cleated on the traveller car. This boat has a 4:1 primary purchase on the mainsheet, with a 3:1 'fine tune' to give a total purchase of 12:1. Also worth noting are the measures taken to make the helm secure and comfortable.

winches. It must be possible to haul the car up to windward in light airs, so that the main can be trimmed with minimal leach tension. Thus a single control line pulling the car into the centreline is not sufficient.

Off the wind it is the mainsheet that controls the position of the boom, whilst the kicking strap or vang determines the amount of sail twist. Unfortunately the three or four-part purchase fitted to many cruising boats is totally inadequate for this – a purchase of at least six to one is required on even the smallest of boats, whilst larger boats will need to lead the kicker to a winch or use a hydraulic ram to obtain sufficient power. A powerful kicking strap does, however, impose large loads on the boom, and so the boom may need to be reinforced round the attachment point.

Instead of the normal rope purchase, a rigid kicker may be used. This doubles as a topping lift, and relieves the sail of the weight of the boom in light airs. A rope or wire purchase pulls the boom down, whilst when not under load it is supported by shock cord, a spring, or an air cylinder.

The vang is best led back to the cockpit for ease of control. This is particularly important on racing boats, as, when reaching under spinnaker, releasing the vang depowers the main, and so helps avoid broaching.

The cunningham hole, clew outhaul and flattener (or leach cunningham) are used to control the actual shape of the sail. On cruising boats these controls may be regarded as superfluous, but on racing craft they are a necessity, and once again are best led aft for ease of control.

Rope purchases are generally adequate for these controls, led to a small winch on larger craft. A hydraulic ram may be used for the flattener on boats over 40 feet, and possibly for the clew outhaul on the largest boats. The clew outhaul and flattener are sometimes linked together for operation by the same control line, which simplifies the deck layout but prevents individual adjustment.

As halyard and reefing systems are generally used together, they must be considered in conjunction. On short-handed boats all the controls are best grouped round the mast, where they can be operated by one person. On a fully crewed boat they can be led aft, so that most of the work can be carried out from the safety and shelter of the cockpit, only one man needing to go forwards to the mast.

Where roller reefing is fitted, the actual reefing gear must be sited at the gooseneck, though the halyard can be led aft. Although normally only fitted to racing boats, a leach cunningham is worth having as it flattens the sail before reefing, and also prevents the boom drooping as the sail is rolled up.

With slab reefing one crew member must be at the mast to drop the luff eye over the tack hook. He may also deal with reef pennants, in which case they will probably pass through stoppers built into the boom at the gooseneck, and lead down to a winch on the aft face of the mast. Alternatively, the winch may be placed on the boom, but this arrangement is not as easy to operate, as the boom may be swinging about whilst the reef pennant is being taken up. The halyard is led aft, and on larger boats the reef pennants will also be taken aft for quicker reefing.

If the sail is furled round the luff, the whole operation can be carried out from the cockpit. Reefing is achieved by easing off the clew outhaul, and then winching in on the reefing line. Both controls are led aft from the base of the mast. With this system it is important that the mast does not bend, and so particular attention must be paid to the staying arrangements, especially with a cutter rig.

Headsails

Headsail controls are relatively simple, consisting of a halyard, luff groove or forestay, and sheets.

The tack of the sail is attached to the stem fitting by a carbine hook sewn into the sail, fastening to an eye on the stem, or an eye in the tack of the sail attaching to a snap shackle, an open hook with retaining clip, or a ram's horn on the boat. The positive systems of a carbine hook or snap shackle are best, as there is no possibility of the tack coming adrift when the sail is lying on the deck or being hoisted.

Headfoils are fitted with twin grooves to prevent bare-headed sail changes; these may be side by side or on opposite sides of the extrusion. If placed on opposite sides, the crew must be careful not to twist the halyards round the forestay as the headfoil is turned for successive sail changes. Plastic extrusions are lighter than alloy ones, but are subject to ultra-violet degradation in sunlight, and are less likely to withstand the spinnaker pole hitting the forestay. Some aluminium sections replace the forestay completely, offering lower stretch under load, but also a possible weight penalty.

Twin headsail halyards should always be fitted, both to avoid bare-headed sail changes and to leave a spare halyard if one should fail. On fully crewed boats the halyards are best led aft to the cockpit via turning blocks at the base of the mast, with the halyard emerging from the mast about 8 feet above the deck so that the crew can haul down on it directly. For short-handed crews, though, the halyards are best left at the mast so that the crew are closer to the sails, making hoisting and lowering easier. Winches should be placed on the sides of the mast, as they will catch sheets when tacking if located on the forward face. Placing the winches fairly high up makes them easy to wind, but also means that the mainsail may make the leeward winch inoperative when sailing off the wind.

The genoa sheets are led to one or more tracks; the greater the overlap of the sail, the narrower the sheeting angle it requires. Thus a 150% genoa will have its innermost tract at about 7.5° to the centreline, whilst non-overlapping headsails will be sheeted on an 8.5° track. In rough water, tracks placed further outboard may increase these angles by about 2.5°, and when reaching the sails are best sheeted to the rail.

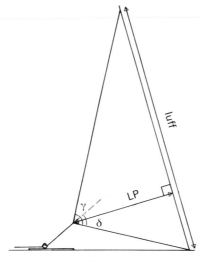

Fig. 4.8. Jib ana genoa sheeting angles. The angle between the sheet lead and the foot of the sail is given by: $\delta = \gamma(1 - LP/\text{luff})$ where γ is the clew angle, and *LP* is measured perpendicular to the luff. (*Courtesy Horizon Sails.*)

Tracks running fore and aft are most common, twin sheets being used to obtain sheeting angles between the tracks. Alternatively, athwartships tracks may be fitted, lying vertically beneath the clew of the sail, fitted with barber haulers so that both the fore and aft and the athwartships setting angles may be adjusted at

119

Fig. 4.9.   Here a large diameter wheel is used so that the helmsman can sit well outboard. The mainsheet track is unobtrusively placed on the cockpit floor; the sheet has a 4:1 purchase for coarse control, with the wire pennant led to a hydraulic ram for fine control. (*Photo courtesy of William Payne.*)

will. However, this does result in a considerable increase in complexity, especially as the barber hauler position must be independent of the athwartships track position.

The genoa cars may be located by a simple spring plunger, but this makes it difficult to adjust the sheeting position under load, and at least one crew member must go down to leeward to move the car. Instead, free running cars, possibly using ball bearings, may be fitted, with a control line led aft to pull the car forward or inboard. The actual sheaves should be well rounded and free to pivot, to minimise chafe; wide sheaves that can accept two sheets are useful when changing between sails that use the same car.

The simplest sheeting arrangement has the sheet running directly from the track to the winch, but on most boats this is not possible as the sheet will not lead fair from all sheeting positions; it also makes it impossible to take the sheet up to weather. Thus most boats have a turning block sited abreast the cockpit; this is subjected to very high loads, up to twice the load in the sheet.

Headsail reefing gear is normally fitted as an afterthought, but can be designed into the boat. This may include features such as recessing the drum into a well to

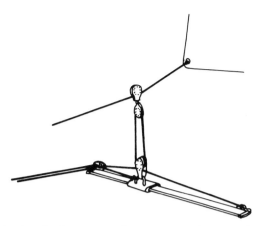

Fig. 4.10. A barber hauler system for genoas, using an athwartships track. (*Courtesy Rob Humphreys.*)

keep the tack of the sail low, having a high-clewed sail so that the track position does not need changing as the sail is furled, and designing a lead for the reefing line that the crew are not going to trip over.

As with headfoils, the luff spar may fit over an existing forestay or replace it completely. With the first system there is considerable friction due to the section rubbing on the forestay; although the second system avoids this, thrust bearings are required top and bottom to take the rigging loads, which introduces friction from another source. Some sections may be designed with twin grooves, permitting twin headsails to be set when running, or allowing the system to be used as a headfoil when racing.

The headsail halyard may still be led down the mast, by incorporating a swivel at the head of the sail; alternatively, it may be led down the outside of the luff spar, cleated off at the base, and have the tail removed. The latter solution is cheaper, but the halyard tension increases forestay sag, sail changing is less easy, and there is no means of adjusting luff tension whilst sailing.

Finally, some points concerning the drum and reefing line. A wire line has less stretch and, being thinner, permits a smaller drum to be used; with a rope tail spliced on, it need be no more difficult to handle than an all-rope line. Despite what some manufacturers say, a winch is essential, as the sail reefs best if some sheet tension is maintained whilst reefing – a self-tailing winch is ideal for this purpose. The drum must be fitted with a fairlead and a guard to prevent tangles, yet still permit access if a tangle should occur – unfortunately, the more extensive and effective the guard, the poorer the access to the drum.

Spinnakers

Spinnakers require fairly complex equipment as the sail is not attached to a spar,

121

and so all three corners of the sail have to be controlled with ropes; in addition, the sail has to be held clear of the mainsail by a spinnaker pole running between the mast and the tack.

Beginning with the halyard, this is basically set up in the same way as a genoa halyard at deck level. The only addition worth considering is a rope stopper or clutch; this prevents the crew losing control of the halyard if the sail should fill before the halyard is made fast. It may be positioned at the halyard winch or, if the crew haul on the halyard at the mast, just behind the turning block at the base of the mast.

At the masthead, the sideways pull on the halyard makes chafe a problem. The best solution is to have the spinnaker halyards separate from the genoa halyards, passing over a free-swinging block to relieve the halyard sheave of the sideways loads and prevent the halyard chafing against the mast wall. Alternatively, the halyard sheave, and if necessary the forestay, can be protected with well rounded stainless steel chafing plates.

The shackle used to attach the spinnaker to the halyard must incorporate a swivel, to prevent the rope twisting as the spinnaker swings round. A small disc may also be required to prevent the halyard being pulled up so far that it jams in the sheave cage.

Boats up to about 35 feet in length will gybe the spinnaker pole end-for-end, with the sheet doubling as the guy. A lazy guy may be fitted in large boats to make gybing easier. This system is simple, but care needs to be taken with the way the sheet and guy are arranged. On a reach, the guy needs to be sheeted down at the point of maximum beam, so that it makes the maximum possible angle with the pole; the sheet must be led well aft to prevent the leach of the sail from becoming too closed. On a run, though, the sheet can be brought forward to create a fuller sail, and also to make the sail more stable in strong winds.

The simplest way of meeting these requirements is to have a snatch block on the toe-rail to take the sheet or guy when necessary, but the rope can only be put into the block when the loads are low. A better solution, though slightly more complex, is to have a pair of barber haulers on the sheets passing through a block at the maximum beam position; these should be led back to the cockpit for ease of adjustment.

Larger boats will use a dip pole or twin pole gybing system, with twin sheets and guys on the sail; as the guy is taken down to the point of maximum beam, and the sheet led aft, the leeward guy can be used in lieu of the sheet when running.

Both sheets and guys need to be taken back to winches in the cockpit via turning blocks, which should be free to swivel and provide a fair lead. The sheet should be able to be taken up to windward, so that the sail trimmer can obtain a good view of the luff of the sail; however, when to windward it must not cross the mainsheet, as this will lead to problems when gybing.

The spinnaker pole is essentially a compression strut hinged at the mast, keeping the spinnaker clear of the mainsail and allowing it to be swung into undisturbed air on a run. It is subjected to the highest loadings when reaching, due to the very shallow angle between the pole and the guy. The height of the pole has a considerable effect on the fullness of the sail, and so this is adjusted by a track on the mast and an uphaul/downhaul on the pole. The aim is to keep the pole horizontal, and so minimise the interference between the mainsail and the spinnaker.

On smaller boats the crew can easily slide the pole up and down the mast track, and so all that is required is a spring-loaded plunger on the slide to lock it in position. On boats over about 35 feet, though, the large forces on the pole result in a large amount of friction, and the pole height is best adjusted by a rope purchase, or, on the largest boats, a chain drive winch.

The pole end fittings and uphaul/downhaul arrangements are largely dictated by the gybing method used. Where end-for-end gybing is used, the pole must have a piston fitting at each end, attaching to an eye on the mast track. The uphaul and downhaul will be attached to bridles, preferably adjusted so that the inboard part of the bridle is just slack, and the downhaul will usually come down to the deck at, or close to, the mast.

If the uphaul and downhaul were attached directly to the middle of the pole, bending forces would be introduced, and a considerably larger pole required. Taking the downhaul to the base of the mast means that it does not need adjusting whenever the guy is trimmed, and so there is one less task for the crew; however, it does increase the loads on the pole when it tries to sky, and doesn't hold the pole as rigidly in light airs with a sloppy sea.

On boats using a dip pole or twin pole system, the inboard end of the pole will be a bayonet fitting, locating into a cup on the mast; two cups will be required for twin pole gybes. Both the uphaul and the downhaul are attached to the outboard end of the pole, the downhaul leading down to a block in the bows. The plunger fitting in the outboard end of the pole may be designed so that it remains locked open until the guy bears down on a trigger in the mouth of the fitting.

When reaching, a jockey pole may be used to lead the guy outboard of the hull, and so increase the angle it makes with the pole. This has the effect of reducing the loads in both the guy and the spinnaker pole. The guy runs over a sheave located in a deep groove at the end of the pole, whilst the inboard end attaches to an eye a couple of feet off the deck; the pole also needs to be tied to the shrouds, preventing it from swinging fore and aft.

Many boats simply lower the spinnaker pole to the deck when not in use, to obtain quicker sets and drops; the uphaul is simply cast off, with the slack secured by a clip at the base of the mast. The only disadvantages to this arrangement are that a trough may be required in the forward end of the coachroof, and hatches fitted on the centreline cannot be used.

Multihulls do not need to use a spinnaker pole at all. Instead, the position of the tack can be controlled by three lines: a guy leading to the stern, a downhaul leading to the bows on the centreline, and an outhaul leading to the forward end of the windward float. Although this simplifies the gear required, it also means that the tack of the sail is not held rigidly unless the sail is drawing and all three control lines are tight.

For cruising and short-handed yachtsmen, one of the most difficult aspects of spinnaker handling is setting and dropping the sail. A spinnaker sock can make both these operations considerably easier. The spinnaker is hoisted in its sock which, when all is ready, is pulled up over the sail to the masthead, thus breaking out the spinnaker. To lower the spinnaker, the sheet is eased off and the sock is hauled down over the sail. Now that the sail is totally under control, it is lowered to the deck in its sock.

Bloopers and cruising chutes

Although used in very different ways, the gear required to handle these sails is essentially the same. This is because they are both free flying sails, controlled as much by luff tension as by the sheet.

At the masthead, the halyard requirements are identical to those for a spinnaker. However, if the luff tension is adjusted by the halyard, it must be led back to the cockpit. The alternative is to have an adjustable tack tackle led aft, but this is not really feasible under the limitations of the IOR as the tack strop may not be more than 2.5 feet long. The sheet is simply led to the cockpit via a turning block on the quarter.

On a run the cruising chute is blanketed by the mainsail, and should be goosewinged. Although this can be done without a pole, the sail is considerably more powerful and stable when poled out – as is a goosewinged genoa. To be really effective, the pole needs to be considerably longer than a spinnaker pole – ideally about half as long again as the base of the foretriangle. This length presents a considerable stowage problem, and a telescopic pole offers a much more compact unit.

Staysails

Many different sails are covered by the term staysail, and the deck gear required depends upon exactly what sail is being referred to by this somewhat vague term.

The classical staysail is the inner headsail of a cutter rig. This is set up in exactly the same way as any other headsail, except that the sail is best sheeted to a narrower angle of 6° or 7° to the centreline.

Another well established staysail is the mizzen staysail. When reaching, a sail cut like a genoa is set, tacked down on the centreline just aft of the mainmast; the

Fig. 4.11. This foredeck has a staysail track, blocks for the spinnaker pole downhauls, and an eye to take the headsail tack. The pulpit has a fairlead built into the forward leg, and a rod protecting the navigation light from stray lines.

close-windedness of this sail is largely limited by the breadth of the mizzen's staying base. Off the wind a sail cut like a spinnaker is set, but because of the racing rules this is tacked down to windward rather than poled out; the mizzen is often lowered to give the staysail clear air. These sails are set like a genoa and a cruising chute respectively.

In the racing fleet a staysail usually refers to a sail set under the spinnaker. The sail is hoisted on a genoa halyard, and tacked down at about the midpoint of the foretriangle base – generally as far aft as is permitted under the IOR. The sheet is normally taken to the end of the main boom, or may be taken to the lee rail.

Standing Rigging

With the advent of flexible masts, adjustable standing rigging has become a necessity on racing boats. Athwartships standing rigging is not normally adjustable whilst sailing. Fore and aft rigging may be adjusted for two reasons: to control forestay sag, or to control the shape of the mainsail through mast bend.

With a masthead rig the amount of forestay sag is controlled directly by the amount of backstay tension. Thus on a racing boat a hydraulic backstay will be fitted, whilst on a cruising boat the backstay will be controlled by a screw adjuster or, on smaller boats, a bridle across a split backstay.

Fig. 4.12. The hatch in the cockpit floor gives good access for the navigator, but if used in bad weather could let water down below. (*Photo courtesy of William Payne.*)

On a fractional rig forestay tension is controlled by the runners – the only exception to this is where the shrouds are swept aft and no runners fitted, in which case the rig relies on the stiffness of the topmast to transfer backstay tension to the forestay. The runners normally terminate in a two part rope purchase, the tail of which is led to a winch that is often sited behind the helmsman. To ensure that the same runner tension is applied on each tack the forestay may be fitted with a small hydraulic or electronic load cell, with a dial in the cockpit displaying the forestay tension.

Mast bend is controlled by lower runners (or check stays) meeting the mast below the forestay, by the baby stay and the backstay. On a fractional rig the check stay usually ends in a rope purchase attached to the runners, so that both are tensioned simultaneously.

The backstay is only lightly loaded on a fractional rig fitted with runners, and a multi-part purchase can be used on boats up to about 35 feet perfectly satisfactorily, but above this size a winch is required.

The baby stay can be subjected to surprisingly high loads, due to the shallow angle it makes with the mast. In the size of boat requiring a baby stay, this makes a hydraulic ram essential, and this is often concealed below decks. A removable baby stay is well worth having, as it allows easier tacking and dip pole gybes when released. A highfield lever set into the deck can be used for this if the stay is not adjustable, or a simple snap shackle if it is.

Mooring Gear

When mooring alongside, the basic requirements are for robust cleats and fairleads in the bow and stern; larger boats will also have cleats amidships to take the spring lines. Open fairleads are the easiest to use, but the rope may jump out if subjected to an upwards load.

When anchoring, a strong cleat and a stemhead roller are required. Where a nylon warp is used a windlass is not strictly essential on boats under about 40 feet in length – it can still be dispensed with on larger boats if the warp can be led aft to a sheet winch. However, the warp is very bulky, and a bow well large enough to take the main anchor and the coiled warp is very useful on cruising boats.

Where chain is used, boats as small as 30 feet will benefit from a chain windlass. The chain will be led to a chain locker in the bilge (preferably sited close to amidships) by a navel pipe, and the anchor will stow on deck or in an anchor well. To protect the deck, it is well worth fitting a stainless steel chafing plate along the route followed by the chain; also, the stem roller must be of stainless steel or bronze, as nylon and plastic rollers are not tough enough. A cleat or chain stopper will also be required, as the windlass is only designed to haul in the chain, and not to hold it securely.

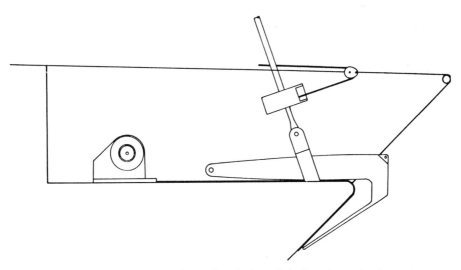

Fig. 4.13. This cruiser has a large foredeck well designed to take the anchor, windlass, and roller reefing drum. Instead of having a roller, the anchor and chain runs out over a stainless steel chafing plate.

On most boats a single or two speed hand operated windlass is perfectly satisfactory, but on larger sizes a powered winch may be desirable. Electric windlasses are the most common, but their high power requirement makes heavy demands on the batteries, and water may get into the electrics; a better option is a hydraulic windlass run off the engine. Where a powered winch is fitted, it must also be capable of manual operation in the event of a power failure.

Basic Hardware

Ropes

Nearly all ropes and lines are either made of wire or synthetic fibres. Wire rope is ideal where low stretch or low windage is required, but is too hard on the hands to be handled by the crew. Splicing on a rope tail overcomes this problem, and in this form wire is used for halyards and long control lines. Whilst stainless steel is best for standing rigging, galvanised wire is better for running rigging due to its greater durability when run round blocks.

There are several types of synthetic fibre used in ropes, their different properties suiting them to different tasks. Nylon is very strong and also very elastic; these properties are used to good effect in anchor warps and mooring lines, as the stretch acts as a shock absorber. Polypropylene is a lightweight, buoyant fibre used for heaving lines, and lightweight spinnaker sheets on smaller boats; however, it is not very strong or durable.

Polyester, or Terylene, has become the standard fibre for all running rigging as, although slightly weaker than nylon, it has much lower stretch characteristics. Finally, there is Kevlar for use on racing boats (a slightly different fibre than that used for hull reinforcement, but closely related). Its characteristics are extremely high strength, and about half the stretch of polyester ropes. As such it is used as an alternative to wire, offering reduced weight and easier handling, though slightly greater windage. Early problems due to fatigue failure and ultra-violet degradation have now been largely overcome, but the rope is weakened by knots and kinks; also the rope requires extra large sheaves.

In addition to the fibre used, the construction of the rope may also vary considerably. In order of increasing flexibility and stretchiness, 1×19, 7×7 and 7×19 construction is used for wire.

Rope may be three strand or braided; the former is most resistant to chafe, but also stretches more and is harder on the hands than braided rope. The smallest sizes of braided rope are of solid construction, but in the larger sizes extra strength is obtained by a braided sheath enclosing either a braided core or continuous longitudinal filaments.

The strands of rope may be made up of continuous or short fibres. Continuous fibres, characterised by a shiny appearance, have less stretch and a longer life than those using short fibres, which have a matt, fluffy appearance, but the latter are gentler on the hands.

Shackles

The basic choice here is between screw and snap shackles; a variety of other shackles have been developed, either for specialist applications or for retaining lines under little or no load.

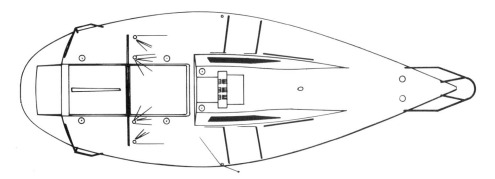

Fig. 4.14.   Deck plan of a half tonner. (*Courtesy Rob Humphreys.*)

The screw shackle is ideal for use on lines where speed of attachment is not of prime importance. They are often used for near-permanent fittings, in which case the pin should be wired up or secured with a thread locking fluid. The loss of shackles and shackle pins need no longer occur, as shackles with captive pins and with a retaining pin across the body of the shackle are widely available.

Snap shackles are intended for use where ease or speed of attachment is important, such as on genoa and spinnaker halyards, spinnaker sheets, and removable baby stays. Side opening shackles, with the hinge set off to one side, have the greatest strength but do not always open easily under high load. Thus top opening shackles, with the pin at the centre, should be used for spinnaker sheets and guys, and in any other situation where they will be released under load.

Blocks

Blocks are used either to alter the lead of a rope, or to increase the mechanical advantage in a system. Apart from the need for adequate strength, the block should be designed for low friction and for minimum wear on the rope.

The strength aspect is easily dealt with by calculating the loads on the rope and referring to the manufacturer's literature for breaking loads or safe working loads

129

– remembering to apply a safety factor of at least 4 where breaking loads are quoted.

Friction is generally an undesirable trait, as it means that the rope is both more difficult to haul in and more reluctant to pay out; however, it is put to good use in a ratchet block, often used in the mainsheet system on smaller boats. When under load the sheave is pulled against a ratchet that permits it to rotate when the rope is hauled in, but locks it in the other direction. Thus the friction of the rope on the specially grooved block makes it easier to hold high loads in the mainsheet.

In most cases a plastic sheave running on a metal axle is sufficiently free running, but racing boats may make extensive use of blocks running on roller or ball bearings. These are used to best effect on lines requiring rapid adjustment under load, such as the mainsheet, traveller, and headsail halyards; their use on items such as the main halyard and spinnaker pole uphaul/downhaul is hard to justify.

Whenever a rope passes over a sheave, the inner part is placed in compression and the outer part in tension; the smaller the sheave diameter, the greater these internal loads. In time they will destroy the rope, unless adequately sized blocks are used.

Where the rope is turned back on itself through 180°, polyester and nylon ropes require a sheave diameter of four-and-a-half to six times the diameter of the rope (the larger the rope, the larger the relative size of the block required); due to its poorer resistance to bending, Kevlar needs sheaves with a diameter at least twelve times greater than the ropes.

With wire ropes, the sheave size depends upon the flexibility of the wire, and therefore upon the construction used. Ropes of 1×19 construction require sheave sizes at least fifty times the wire diameter; for the more flexible 7×7 construction the multiplication factor is reduced to twenty-six; whilst for 7×19 rope this is reduced to sixteen. For both synthetic and wire ropes, where the rope is turned through a smaller angle than 180° the block size can be reduced, as the internal stresses are lower. The sheave sizes need only be three-quarters of the values given above where the change in angle does not exceed 90°.

The other source of wear is chafe, usually caused by a poorly aligned block, or one with insufficient freedom of movement. Before fastening any block in place, ensure that it lies in the same plane as that of the rope entering and leaving the block. In most cases this means that a packing piece will be required.

Where the lead of the rope is likely to vary in use, such as with the spinnaker sheets and halyards, a free-swinging or hinged block will be required so that it can align itself to the rope. If the block is hinged it is only free to move in one plane, and so it still needs careful alignment.

Cleats and stoppers

Although many different devices are now available to make fast a rope, the traditional cleat is still the best choice for many purposes. Its advantages are that it has a very high holding power yet does not damage the rope; also, the rope is unlikely to work loose accidentally, and when released it can be eased out against the cleat. Its disadvantages are that it does take a little while to make up or free off the rope, and the cleat cannot be used to make fast a rope before a winch, thereby freeing the winch for other uses.

The cleat needs to be large enough to take the rope, both in its length and the clearance above the deck. Although it looks neater if the fastenings pass through the body of the cleat, this type is not as strong as those which have feet projecting out from the cleat to take the fastenings. The latter type should always be used where the cleat is subjected to high loads, for example on mooring and anchor cleats. Nylon cleats are suitable for flag halyards and other light lines, but are not as strong or long lasting as metal ones.

When positioning a cleat it needs to be at least 18 inches from any winch or block used by the line, so that any twists in the rope can work themselves out. It should also be angled at 10° or 15° to the pull of the rope, both so that the rope cannot jam on the cleat, and so that it can be eased out under control by checking it on the cleat.

Cam cleats are ideal for quick and easy cleating of lightly loaded lines, such as those controlled by rope purchases; however, under high loads it is often difficult to release the rope. Plastic jaws are quickly worn out by the rope, and so alloy or stainless steel is used for either the teeth or for the complete cams, though this results in some additional wear on the rope. When positioning the cleat it must be absolutely square to the rope in both the horizontal and vertical planes, otherwise it will be difficult to cleat and release, and the holding power of the cleat may be reduced.

Clam cleats share many of the advantages and disadvantages of cam cleats. It is easier to cleat the rope, as it is simply dropped into the groove rather than pulled through the jaws, and this means that it can be used to cleat off lines leading from or into winches. Against this, the fact that the cleat is open means that a rope may easily drop into the cleat after being released and jam itself; also, the rope is not held very securely under conditions of no load. To overcome the difficulty of releasing the rope under high load conditions, and also to prevent the rope re-cleating itself, quick release clam cleats have been developed. These are hinged at the forward end, so that the pull on the rope is trying to trip the cleat; this is opposed by a spring-loaded catch to the rear of the cleat, until the release line is pulled and releases the catch.

Rope stoppers and clutches enable ropes to be cleated off before the winch, and so one winch can be used for several lines simultaneously – this is particularly useful with control lines. The rope is held by a cam pressing against a base plate; with a rope stopper the cam is simply released by a lever, which can be difficult under load unless the load is first taken on the winch; a rope clutch has the cam spring mounted, so that it can always be released with very little effort.

As there is no winch to take the load off the rope, the cam presses down heavily on the rope. This inevitably results in damage to the rope, which may not always be visible from the outside. Thus on boats large enough for the rope sizes to be calculated purely on the grounds of strength, clutches and stoppers should only be used to secure ropes temporarily; even on smaller boats, where the size of rope is often larger than strictly necessary, one has to beware of localised wear on halyards and other ropes which are always cleated in the same place.

Banks of several stoppers leading to a single winch are often used for control lines, but not all of these can give a fair lead to the winch. Thus it is essential that the sides of the stopper are well rounded to avoid chafe. Another common use of stoppers is to secure a headsail sheet, for example when changing sails and the new sheet leads to the same winch as the old one. For this application the stopper can be built into the turning block, or a sheet stopper can be placed on the deck between the turning block and the winch so long as the sheet runs very close to the deck. In this way it is possible to have just one pair of sheet winches on quite large boats, without losing anything when it comes to sail changes.

Winches

Winches enable much higher loads to be dealt with than is possible with a rope purchase, with a mechanical advantage (called 'power ratio' by the winch manufacturers) of anything from 6:1 to 100:1. The power ratio is obtained by multiplying the gear ratio by the ratio of the handle length to the radius of the drum – when quoting power ratios, manufacturers assume a standard 10 inch handle is used, which is much more efficient than the alternative 8 inch size.

The optimum winching efficiency is obtained when the crewman applies a force of 40–60 lb to the handle, and this, together with the load on the rope, should determine the power ratio required. However, this assumes a well positioned, easy to work winch; a more powerful winch may be required if it is badly positioned. The most efficient position for a winch is one where the centre of the top of the winch is about 28 inches off the deck, and 16 inches away from the crewman. If he has to kneel when winching, his efficiency drops by as much as 20%, and so a larger winch may be required.

It is also interesting to note that the force one can apply to the winch handle is reduced by some 60% at the points where the handle is closest to and furthest away from the operator. Thus a ratchet action enables the crew to avoid these 'hard spots' when the rope is under load, allowing more efficient winching. Almost all single speed winches have a ratchet action, and some two speed winches have a limited action over an arc of about 150°; however, the majority of two speed, and all three speed winches, lack this facility. Ratchet winch handles are available, but they are not popular due to their bulk and expense, together with the need to re-set the direction of rotation whenever one changes gear.

Fig. 4.15.   Here stoppers and clam cleats enable nine lines to share one winch –
very neat until two lines need adjusting simultaneously. The lines from the mast
run under a cover to keep the coachroof clear, and are then led through special
rollers from the stopper to the winch.

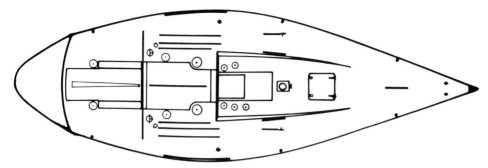

Fig. 4.16. Deck plan of '*Jade*', a masthead rigged Admiral's Cup contender, LOA 39 ft 6 in. (*Courtesy Rob Humphreys.*)

The smallest winches cope with relatively small loads, and so only a single speed action is required for efficient winching over the entire load range. As the loads increase, though, efficiency falls off at the high winching speeds unless a second, and eventually a third gear, is introduced. Sheet winches are often given one more gear than is strictly necessary for the loads so that once the sheet has been brought home it can easily be trimmed by small amounts to give the optimum sail setting.

Boats over about 50 feet in length are not able to extract sufficient power for rapid trimming of the genoa and spinnaker sheets from one man operating a winch. Thus the winches may be cross-linked with each other or a separate winching position, thus enabling a greater amount of effort to be applied. At first this was achieved by cross-linking two conventional winches, so that by engaging a clutch two crew members could wind in the one sheet; a logical development of this was the molehill, a cross-linked winch handle socket without the winch beneath it. Greater efficiency is obtained by a pedestal linked to one or two winches, though, as the crew are able to work more efficiently with the handles rotating about a horizontal axis.

Self-tailing winches have proved to be the most significant recent development in winch design, enabling one person to do what previously required two pairs of hands. On racing boats they are generally used where the speed of winching is not too critical, for example on control lines, the main halyard, and runners. However, they are not used on sheets, for example, as two people can bring the sail home much faster than one with a self-tailing winch. On cruising and short-handed boats, though, speed of operation is not very important, and there is no reason why all the winches cannot be self-tailing. Self-tailing winches do not need a cleat for the rope, as it is held sufficiently securely in the jaws; however, the jaws do cause some wear on the rope. Also, all the speeds in a self-tailing winch must be geared, and so if the top gear has a ratio of 1:1, this is often omitted from the winch.

Whilst bronze and stainless steel are the only really suitable materials for the internal workings of a winch, a variety of materials may be used for the drums.

Aluminium alloy is the cheapest and lightest option, but is quickly scored by wire halyards; plastic may be used on the smallest winches, but is even less resistant to wire than aluminium. Bronze and stainless steel are both very durable, but also heavy; stainless steel has the slight advantage over bronze in that the chrome plating on bronze winch barrels eventually wears through.

When installing a winch, it should be angled so that the rope approaches the drum at an angle of 5° to 15° below the horizontal; if the angle is any less than this, the winch will develop riding turns. On self-tailing winches, the stripper arm should be at the 5 o'clock position, pointing towards the operator's right shoulder, so that the rope falls away clear of the crewman.

Hydraulics

Hydraulic rams are best suited for moving large loads over short distances. Thus their main use is in adjusting the standing rigging and the kicking strap; they may also be used for raising ballasted lifting keels, or on large boats for the clew outhaul, flattener reef, or fine mainsheet control.

To prevent the ram applying too great a load to the rigging, a pressure relief valve is fitted; the maximum permitted load should not exceed one third the breaking load of the rigging. The load applied is shown by a pressure gauge or, on some self-contained units, by a graduated slide on the ram.

If only one or two rams are required, self-contained units with the pump built into the ram present the simplest solution. On more extensive systems a central pump and valve chest will be fitted, connected to all the rams by hydraulic hose. Secondary control panels can also be incorporated, for example in the side deck for controlling the kicker or fine mainsheet control.

So that none of the stroke of the ram is wasted due to slack rigging, the ram needs to be connected to a turnbuckle, so that the ram is at maximum extension in the no-load condition.

Long distance boats should consider using rams with mechanical locks, so that the rigging can be tensioned manually should there be a hydraulics failure. The lock must not be used to override the hydraulic system, though, as this renders the pressure relief valve inoperative, and so may cause a rigging failure.

Self-steering Systems

On long offshore passages a self-steering system is of great benefit to the crew, especially if short-handed. However, a proper lookout for shipping must always be maintained. The system may either be a mechanical wind vane or an electronic autopilot, each type having its own advantages and disadvantages.

Wind vanes have the great advantage of being independent of any power supply, and they are also relatively easy to repair. On the other hand they are

Fig. 4.17. A yacht sailing under 'Aries' vane steering gear. The vane pivots about a horizontal axis and is connected to a servo rudder to magnify the force, before being used to move the tiller or wheel. (*Courtesy Marine Vane Gears.*)

unable to steer to a compass course, and are prone to damage by breaking seas. In winds under about 5 knots they are unable to generate a large enough corrective force to perform well, and on fast multihulls they are totally unsuitable as the rapid acceleration of these craft means that the apparent wind direction varies considerably according to the true wind speed.

Autopilots are generally designed to follow a compass course, and so they are unaffected by wind shifts; thus unless a wind vane can be fitted they must steer about 5° off the close-hauled course to allow for wind shifts. In addition they are totally dependent on having an electrical supply, and many of the popular cockpit-mounted designs fail due to inadequate waterproofing. However, their performance is generally superior to wind vanes, and is unaffected by light airs or fluky winds. They are discussed in greater detail in Chapter 9.

Wind vanes

In essence, a wind vane self-steering system consists of a wind vane which can be rotated so that it is feathered to the wind when on course, linked to the rudder in such a way that a change in the apparent wind direction results in corrective action being taken by the rudder. However, considerable ingenuity has gone into creating a sensitive system, and into amplifying the corrective force.

The simplest type of vane pivots about a vertical axis, but with this arrangement the force developed is proportional to the amount by which the boat is off course. Thus most systems now use a counterbalanced vane mounted on an almost horizontal axis, providing a much greater corrective force for small deviations in the wind direction, and therefore more accurate course-keeping.

If it is to be a reasonable size, the wind vane alone is unable to generate sufficient force to steer any but the smallest of craft, and so some form of amplification is required. In many ways the simplest arrangement is to use a trim tab on the trailing edge of the rudder, but the need for a linkage means that this arrangement is only feasible if the rudder is transom-hung or incorporated into the wind vane.

The other approach that has been used is to incorporate a servo-pendulum into the vane gear. This is a small, high aspect ratio foil mounted on a vertical stock that can rotate and pivot laterally. The wind vane rotates the servo blade, thus setting it at an angle to the water flow. It then swings up sideways, creating a much larger force due to the greater density of water compared to air. This force is transmitted to the wheel or tiller by a rope linkage, and thus to the rudder; alternatively it may be coupled directly to a rudder incorporated in the vane gear. If the vane gear incorporates its own rudder it is likely to be comparatively expensive. However, it does mean that there is a back-up steering system, and the cockpit is not cluttered up with control lines.

Chapter 5

Interior Design

The yacht's interior layout is constrained by several factors. Firstly there is the shape of the hull; deep, beamy, heavy designs will be much more spacious than narrow, low freeboard, light displacement hull forms. The deck layout, especially the cockpit and coachroof design, will also have a major influence on the interior. The long cockpit of racing yachts, for example, inevitably means that they will have a small saloon, and quarter berths placed right aft will not be easily accessible. The need for structural members, such as bulkheads, frames and tie bars, will also place limitations on the layout. Finally, the weight and position of the centre of gravity of the interior joinery must be considered with respect to the boat's displacement, centre of gravity position, and pitching performance.

In addition to the above constraints, it must always be remembered that the boat must be habitable at sea, when it will be well heeled and moving violently at times. It is comparatively easy to design a comfortable, spacious interior for use when the boat is in a marina, but the same layout may well prove totally uninhabitable in bad weather at sea.

Materials

The need for lightweight materials is almost as important on a cruising boat as it is on a racing yacht. For the racing yachtsman it means a lighter displacement, lower centre of gravity, and less weight in the ends of the boat. On a cruiser it means that a much more extensive interior can be fitted, without the need for excessively heavy displacement.

Plywood has now replaced tongue and groove panelling to reduce the weight and cost. Many racing yachts are now reducing the weight even further by using a foam, balsa or paper honeycomb core faced with Formica or thin plywood. However, as with the hull, a well designed structure is just as important in keeping the weight down as is the use of the the latest exotic materials.

Fig. 5.1. Interior layout of a racing yacht. The small saloon is determined by the large cockpit. The whole interior is strictly functional, and very habitable at sea despite the stark appearance. (*Photo courtesy of William Payne.*)

Although most yacht owners seem to have a predilection for the relatively sombre veneers of mahogany, sapele and teak, lighter veneers such as sycamore or oak can be used to give the boat a much lighter, more spacious effect. Plastic laminates such as Warerite, Formica and GRP tend to produce a cold appearance, and are best used in strong, bright colours. Textured laminates are attractive, but not that easy to clean. The great advantage of plastics is their durability, ease of cleaning, and impermeability to water; this makes them ideal for areas such as the heads and galley.

Just as on deck, the cabin sole needs to have a good non-slip finish. Plywood with thin strips of a contrasting veneer laminated into the face, imitating a laid deck, is a commonly used material, and offers a good non-slip finish if oiled or painted with a non-slip varnish. Other materials that can be used are cork tiles and non-slip linoleum or rubber-based materials.

Fabrics used on board must be both hard-wearing and resistant to rot and mildew. From the safety angle they should also be fire resistant, at least around the galley. Many of the man-made materials are ideal, but natural fibres may also

Fig. 5.2. The saloon. In a boat of this size there is no need to incorporate berths. Note that the floor level is raised outboard, thus giving more floor space without sacrificing headroom along the passageway. (*Photo courtesy of William Payne.*)

be used if suitably treated. Some boat builders use a vinyl fabric to cover berth cushions; although water resistant, it is clammy to sleep on, as when sleeping one's body gives out over half a pint of moisture, and this cannot escape into the mattress.

The Saloon

Much of the social life on board centres round the saloon, and a large spacious area is often a major selling point. However, the saloon must never be allowed to impinge upon equally important areas such as the galley, chart table and berths.

In smaller boats the saloon may well have to double as chart table, or the seats may need to convert into berths. This is not an ideal situation, though, as it means that the off-watch crew will interfere with the navigator, or the saloon will not be usable because of sleeping bodies.

Some dimensions for saloon joinery are given in Fig. 5.3. Seat cushions may be anything from 3 to 6 inches thick, but the seat back cushions can be an inch thinner. All cushions need to be held in place by a low fiddle, press studs, velcro, or some other similar means. If the cushions have removable covers so much the better, as it makes cleaning a lot easier.

Fibreglass interior mouldings can be used to contour the seats, which makes

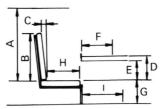

Fig. 5.3. Saloon dimensions. A Sitting headroom 3 ft 0 in (minimum); B Backrest height 20 to 24 in; C Seat back rake 3 in; D Table top height above seat 11 to 12 in; E Table base height above seat 9 in (minimum); F Table width (for eating) 1 ft 3 in (minimum);
G Seat cushion height   10 in, 12 in, 18 in;
H Seat width   20 in, 16 in, 15 in;
 I Legroom   26 in, 24 in, 19 in.
Each person requires a seat width of at least 20 in, and preferably 24 in.

them more comfortable and can also improve the styling. Comfort is also improved, and headroom increased, if the seat base is dropped down slightly at the back.

On monohulls, only seats running fore and aft are comfortable when heeled, as everybody slides down to one end if the seats run athwartships. For this reason, a dinette arrangement is not suitable for use at sea.

The saloon table may be removable so that it can be taken up on deck in good weather, or to give more space for laying out sails and packing spinnakers on a racing yacht. If fixed in place, the central spine can provide useful stowage for bottles; the table may also be able to be lowered so that it can convert a single berth into a double for harbour use.

To keep things on the table, fiddles at least 2 inches high are required all round; these may drop down or be removable for harbour use. The leaves of the table also need to be able to be securely locked into place in both the raised and the lowered positions.

Full headroom is only required where people stand, and not above the seats. Considering the fact that people spend most of their time sitting down in the saloon, full headroom is not strictly necessary, though at least 4 feet 10 inches is required to make it comfortable to walk along the vessel.

Reducing the width and height of the coachroof makes the deck easier to work, and the boat's lines more attractive. The height can be minimised by having the cabin sole as low as possible, perhaps curving or stepping it to match the rocker of the hull. A large amount of deck camber is another useful ploy, as is increasing the freeboard. However, if the coachroof is too low, the crew will not be able to see anything out of the windows unless they are placed in the topsides.

Berths

Berths can be classified into two groups. Firstly there are sea berths, which are designed for use at sea and don't interfere with the rest of the accommodation

Fig. 5.4. This motor sailer has a comfortable interior steering position and chart table. Note the large number of windows, giving the helmsman good all round vision. (*Photo courtesy of William Payne.*)

space. Secondly there are harbour berths, which may be positioned too far forwards to be habitable in a seaway, or may require the saloon to be completely rearranged for the berth to be made up. Obviously, the total number of berths must match the number of crew, but there also need to be sufficient sea berths to cater for all the off watch crew.

Sea berths are best placed amidships or in the stern, where the motion is least. They must run parallel to the centreline to avoid the crew being head down on one tack, and feet down on the other, as the boat heels. The outboard side of quarter berths is a common culprit in this respect, as it all too often follows the curve of the hull; this can be overcome by having a stowage space outboard of the berth, although it does move the berth further inboard.

To keep the crew in the berth, a leecloth or leeboard is required. Leeboards are best designed as an integral part of the bunk, and must be padded for comfort; leecloths easily stow away under the cushions, and are more comfortable than an unpadded leeboard. The only instance where leecloths or leeboards are not essential is on pipe berths fitted with a block and tackle, so that they can be adjusted for heel; even in this case they provide a useful safeguard against a surprise tack or a severe roll.

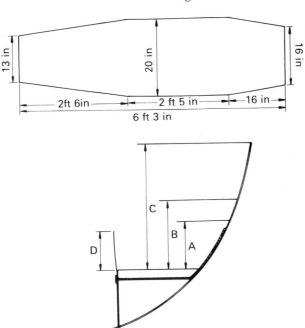

Fig. 5.5. Minimum bunk dimensions. A Minimum headroom for sitting up 35 in; B Minimum headroom over head and shoulders 18 in; C Minimum headroom over legs 13 in; D Height of leecloths, and cushioning up hull side, 10 in.

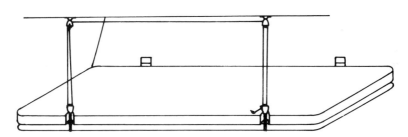

Fig. 5.6. A pipe berth. The tackle enables the occupant to adjust the angle of the berth to suit the conditions. On racing boats only the windward berths will be used at sea, so the berth can be fitted with stops to prevent it dropping below the horizontal.

Pipe cots and root berths can be extremely comfortable, as they can be adjusted to allow for the amount of heel. Root berths achieve this by having several sockets to take the inboard pole, whilst pipe cots have a block and tackle system that permits the occupant to adjust the berth from the warmth of his sleeping bag. The only drawback to these configurations, except for their somewhat stark appearance, is that the berth must be adjusted to the new heel angle whenever the boat alters course.

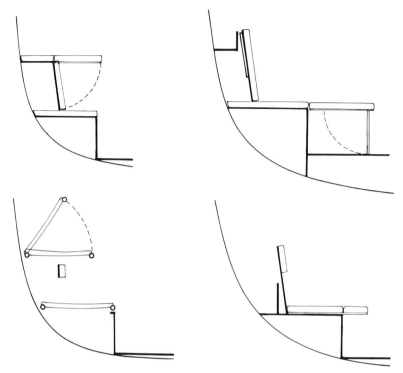

Fig. 5.7. Some methods of converting settees into berths.

Most boats are designed so that the saloon settees can be converted into harbour berths. For example, a dinette table may drop down to form a double berth, or an extension may slide out from under the settee base. Alternatively, the settee back may hinge up to form one or two single berths. However, a settee is too narrow to form a comfortable berth without an extension, and a berth is too large to make a comfortable settee.

The Galley

Cooking at sea is not easy at the best of times, and in bad weather is often well nigh impossible. Thus it is well worth taking care over the galley layout to make this task as simple as possible.

The workspace is best designed in an L- or U-shaped configuration, so that the cook has only to turn round to reach anything. A straight layout is less satisfactory as the cook has to walk up and down all the time, and it is often placed in a gangway, so the crew will be squeezing past as well.

The prime requirement is for adequate worktop space, protected by fiddles at least 2 inches high. Large worktops can be divided up with extra fiddles to keep everything in place. Fiddles are often fitted with gaps at the corners to wipe crumbs through; these are often oversized, – they should not be large enough to let cutlery escape.

To give a smarter appearance, and extra workspace, the galley may be fitted with removable worktops over the sink or cooker. Those that simply drop in place are a nuisance, as stowage always needs to be found for them; the variety that hinge up against a bulkhead are to be preferred. Lockers in the galley should never be accessed from above, as this means that part of the worktop has to be cleared before the locker can be opened. The one exception to this is the fridge or icebox, as a lid in the top helps prevent the cold air escaping when it is opened. Any break in the worktop, whether for sink, cooker, or icebox, should be protected by fiddles.

The other important requirement is for plenty of stowage space. This means stowage specially designed for cutlery, crockery and saucepans, as well as lockers for staple foods, herbs etc, and a gash locker.

There are basically three types of cooker fuel available. Bottled gas is the most convenient to use, but there is the risk of an explosion, and in the United States its use is hidebound with regulations. Paraffin (or kerosene) burns with an equally hot flame, and has the advantages of being available almost anywhere, and of being free from the risk of an explosion. However, the fuel does need pre-heating, or priming, before lighting, and the cooker cannot have a grill. Also, if improperly lit, or if the fuel jets clog, the paraffin may flare up and cause a fire risk. Methylated spirits (or alcohol) cookers are cheap, but have little else to

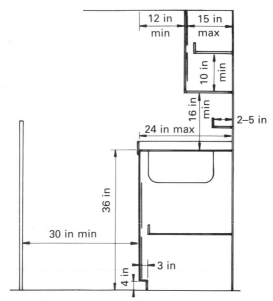

Fig. 5.8. Galley dimensions. The clearance behind the cook should be increased if the galley is in a passageway. Note the deep fiddles on all worktops and shelves.

145

recommend them. They burn with half the heat of a gas flame, or even less if the fuel is not pressurised, and the fuel is expensive and not always easily obtainable.

On monohulls and trimarans the cooker needs to be gimballed so that it can swing to 50° each side of the vertical; anything less and the pans may fly off when the cooker comes against its stops in bad weather. Catamarans do not need gimballed cookers if deep pans are used with strong pan clamps, but if gimballed the cooker should be free to swing to 25° off the vertical. All cookers, whether gimballed or not, need to be fitted with a fiddle rail and pan clamps to keep the pans in place.

Due to its extra height, a cooker with an oven swings out quite considerably when heeled, and so occupies considerably more space than a simple cooker with grill. The gimbals need to be designed so that the cooker cannot jump out in the event of a knockdown, and also so that the cooker can be locked upright when in harbour.

The cooker needs to have an air gap of at least ¾ inch down the sides, but a larger gap will make cleaning much easier. The area surrounding the cooker needs to be made of a heat resistant, easily cleaned material. Formica is most commonly used, but ceramic tiles or copper or brass sheet can be used as attractive alternatives.

The sink must be deep if it is not to spill its contents when the boat heels; if space permits, the sink can be combined with the cooker and the whole unit gimballed. Where the sink drains directly into the sea, it is best positioned as close to the centreline as possible to ensure that it remains above the waterline when the boat is heeled. For some reason, many sinks are fitted with a ½ inch drain pipe; this is far too small as it clogs up very easily, a 1 inch drain being much better. Round sinks should never be fitted in the galley unless at least 12 inches in diameter, as plates inevitably wedge themselves in the bottom and are very difficult to extricate.

When at sea, sinks are used just as much for stowing opened tins and cartons as they are for washing up. Thus it is well worth fitting two sinks where space permits; if fitted with hingeing covers, no workspace need be lost, only some locker space below the units.

As most of the waste on board is produced in the galley, it is the obvious location for the gash locker. Many poorly designed boats make no provision for rubbish, and so the crew have to resort to a bucket or cardboard box jammed under the companionway ladder. Perhaps the best solution is to use domestic bin bags, the holder being located in a locker of its own hinged at the side or base. When full these can easily be sealed and taken ashore.

Ideally every boat should have a locker designed as a larder, specifically for keeping fresh food. This needs to be in a cool place, sited away from hotspots such as the engine, and provided with plenty of ventilation. The locker door can be louvred, or have ventilation holes top and bottom, with a fly screen to keep insects out. Inside, the shelves need to be of wooden slats or netting to ensure a good flow of air, and are best divided into several compartments to segregate the contents.

Nowadays most boats are fitted with an icebox, which is ideal for keeping things cool over a weekend but not much use on longer passages. To keep the cold in, a minimum of 4 inches of foam insulation is required all round, though 6 inches is a better figure to aim for. The locker obviously needs to be watertight to cope with the melting ice, and this makes a fibreglass moulding ideal for the job. A small drain is also required to cope with the melt water; this can be T-ed into the sink drain rather than letting it drain into the bilge. Wire racks are very useful for keeping items off the ice, and for holding opened tins and cartons upright.

It is not worth having an icebox unless it can be filled with ice every few days, and so many larger boats carry a fridge or freezer. It is not necessary to buy a complete fridge, though, as manufacturers also produce separate cooling systems, enabling an icebox to be converted or a compartment to be specially built to the shape of the yacht.

Fridges operate on one of two principles: absorption or compression. The chief advantages of the absorption type are that it can run off several types of fuel, such as gas, electricity or paraffin, and that it is totally silent in operation. However, its efficiency falls off dramatically when heeled, and so it is best suited to catamarans unless it is gimballed.

The compressor variety is more efficient than an absorption fridge, and is also unaffected by heel. It may be run off the boat's batteries, cutting in and out as required by the thermostat, but this places a heavy load on the electrical system. Alternatively, the compressor may be directly driven by a belt off the engine, and the cold stored by fitting dole plates inside the fridge. This means that no strain is put on the batteries, and the dole plates only need recharging once a day when the engine is run to charge the batteries.

In the galley area there must either be full standing headroom, or a seat for the cook. There is nothing worse than trying to cook with one's head banging against the deckhead. Assuming the cook is standing, a galley strap is needed at hip level to give him something firm to lean against. Another important safety feature is a crash bar in front of the cooker, to prevent the cook being thrown against the cooker and spilling the pans all over himself.

The Heads

In order to have sufficient height to struggle in and out of oilskins, at least 4 feet 10 inches of headroom is required; the lower the headroom, the greater the floor area needed. The dimensions shown in Fig. 5.11 should be regarded as the absolute minimum requirements; if there is less space than this, the boat would

Fig. 5.9. This well planned galley has plenty of stowage space, with portholes for ventilation and a vent hood over the cooker to eliminate odours. Although the cooker is not gimballed, it is fitted with good pan clamps. (*Photo courtesy of William Payne.*)

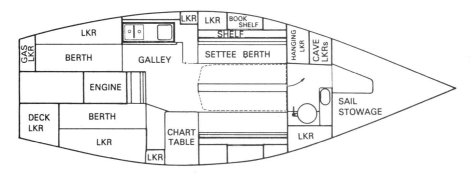

Fig. 5.10. The interior of a 30-foot cruising yacht.

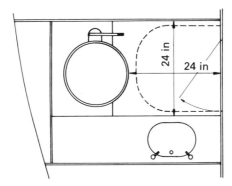

Fig. 5.11. Minimum dimensions in the heads. Where possible, more floor space should be available, especially if a shower is fitted. Note the shower curtain (dotted), which slides behind the doorway when not in use.

be better off without a separate heads compartment. Covering one bulkhead with a large plastic mirror makes the compartment seem lighter and more spacious, even though it doesn't make it any larger in reality.

When the boat is heeled it is easier to use a heads facing athwartships than one lying fore and aft; it is also easier to stay on if the seat is not too high, 12 inches being about right. To give greater security in rough weather a couple of handholds, and perhaps a footrest, are a great asset, as is a catch to hold the toilet seat in the raised position.

As in the galley, the handbasin needs to be nice and deep. Ideally the basin should be let into a worktop, with lockers beneath; however, where there is insufficient space the basin may hinge up against a bulkhead, or be built into a drawer that slides out over the toilet. The heads compartment should also contain a number of small lockers for the crew's washing tackle, a towel rail, a razor socket, and a mirror over the basin.

If the boat has a pressurised water system, and if there is standing headroom in the heads, a shower may be fitted. This does require a considerably larger compartment, though, at least 3 feet square at shoulder level and 16 inches square on the cabin sole. A step at least 4 inches high is required at the door to contain the shower water, and a grating or drain hole leading to a sump tank; a shower curtain will also be needed to keep the rest of the compartment dry.

The Chart Table

The amount of space devoted to the chart table varies considerably, according to the size of boat and its intended uses. However, on any offshore boat it is well worth making sacrifices elsewhere to ensure a reasonably sized chart table.

On boats up to about 30 feet there is often no other option than to use the saloon table; sometimes it is possible to have two table tops, the top one carrying the chart and hingeing out of the way when not in use. Another possibility is to have a chart table that slides away over a quarter berth.

Unfortunately, there is no such thing as a standard chart size. All British Admiralty charts fold down to Double Elephant size, 20½ inches by 28 inches, whilst most American charts measure 20 inches by 40 inches. Thus the minimum size for the chart table should be 22 inches by 30 inches, but any increase on this up to about 30 inches by 48 inches is worth having.

If the navigator can be given a deep bucket seat it will hold him securely against the motion of the yacht, and so make his job much easier; sloping the chart table down towards him slightly will also help. On some boats there may be insufficient space for a decent seat, and rather than fit an uncomfortable one which will seldom be used, it is better to omit the seat and have the navigator stand. This means raising the chart table to a height of 42 inches, with full standing headroom, and a strap for the navigator to lean against in bad weather.

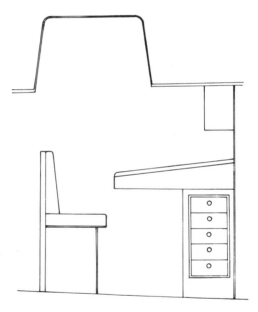

Fig. 5.12. Here the chart table has been placed under a bridge deck in the middle of the cockpit. The navigator has a hatch in the bridge deck. Note the gap left under the bookshelf to give the maximum possible working space, the generous legroom, and the stowage drawers under the chart table.

The navigation area is best sited close to the cockpit, so that there is good communication with the helm, and the navigator can easily come up on deck to take sights or bearings. If the chart table is right by the hatch, though, it may be necessary to fit a perspex panel to protect the charts and instruments from spray. On some racing boats with a shallow cockpit and a wide bridge deck the navigator

150

may sit under the bridge deck, often on the engine cover, and talk to the helm through an opening porthole.

The charts are best stowed flat under the chart table, with access either from the side or by the table top hingeing up; if the top hinges, a flush fitting piano hinge must be used, otherwise it will not be possible to use a parallel ruler. To cope with a reasonable number of charts, the stowage space is best made 4 – 6 inches deep. At the side of the chart table there should also be secure stowage for pencils and rubbers, parallel ruler, hand bearing compass and RDF equipment.

Fig. 5.13. All that is missing from this chart table is somewhere to stow reference books. Note the deck lights above the chart table to give extra illumination. (*Photo courtesy of William Payne.*)

Sailing and navigation instruments need to be mounted where clearly visible by the navigator, preferably on a bulkhead immediately in front of him; any instruments requiring tuning or data entry must be close enough to come within easy reach. Radio equipment, and often the electrical control panel, are usually also sited by the chart table; as these need to be within easy reach but are not always required they can be placed to one side of the chart table. Finally, a bookshelf is essential to keep the necessary reference books; it must be of adequate size to hold these often bulky items.

Lockers and Stowage

It is all too easy to design a boat with plenty of living space yet with insufficient locker space, or with badly designed lockers that cannot be utilised to the full. Apart from a few bulky items such as the sails and the inflatable dinghy, most items carried on board are fairly small; thus the lockers themselves need to be small and numerous, so that things do not end up buried in the depths of some locker.

The insides of lockers are best painted a light colour; this makes it easier to examine the contents, and also encourages regular cleaning by showing up the dirt. If condensation is a problem, a foam-backed vinyl lining or one of the anti-condensation paints can be used. All lockers require limber and ventilation holes, so that moisture is free to escape and there is no build-up of stale, musty air.

One problem with all modern flat-floored designs is that the bilge water rides up the sides of the boat as soon as she heels, unless a deep sump has been designed into the top of the keel. One way to prevent the water getting into stowage spaces under the berths is to have a watertight join along the settee front, though this means that any water that does get into the locker, for example through a deck leak, remains there until mopped up. An alternative solution is to fit PVC locker liners, but this is more expensive and they may become holed or torn.

Under-berth lockers may be accessed from above or from the front. Although access from above is a nuisance when the berth or settee is occupied, it enables the locker to be filled completely, and also eliminates any risk of the contents spilling out when the locker is opened.

A simple trough can often be useful outboard of a berth for stowing bedding and personal effects; it also aligns the berth fore and aft, thus making it more comfortable at sea. A shelf with a deep fiddle, at least 3 inches, is similar in concept, and is useful by the galley or chart table for stowing odds and ends. If the fiddle is made of clear plastic it is easy to see what is on the shelf.

Front opening lockers with shelves are most useful for keeping frequently used items. To prevent the contents flying out when the locker is opened, the shelves must be fitted with deep fiddles. The door needs to be fitted with a positive catch, either fitted into the handle, or as a finger hole and elbow catch. A magnetic or ball catch is not secure enough, and the locker door will fly open as soon as bad weather is encountered.

On lockers with long fronts, or where space is restricted, a sliding door may be fitted; if this is made of perspex the contents of the locker will be visible from outside. On monohulls, sliding doors fitted athwartships must be secured with a catch, otherwise they will slide open when the boat heels.

The cheapest form of locker to construct is the simple cave locker, with a deep fiddle along the front. However, unless fitted with a zip-up fabric front, the contents are not secure in bad weather, especially if the opening faces inboard.

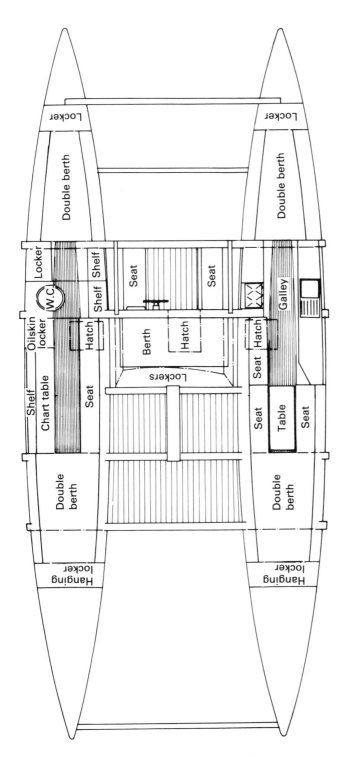

Fig. 5.14. 42-foot 'Captain Cook' catamaran, designed by James Wharram. To give a pleasing appearance and plenty of deck space, the coachroof on the bridge deck is small for a cruising cat. Thus the starboard hull has been used for the chart table, and the port hull for the galley. The bows are used for stowing sailing gear. (*Courtesy of J. Wharram.*)

153

Drawers are best avoided where possible, as they are expensive to construct and, generally, wasteful of space. However, they are essential in some cases, such as for stowing cutlery in the galley. Flush fitting drawers must be fitted with a positive catch, but where the drawer front lies proud of the joinery the 'lift and pull' variety may be fitted. Every drawer needs to be fitted with a stop to prevent it coming off its runners when fully open.

Bookshelves are best fitted with vertical dividers every few inches, so that the books remain in place even if the shelf is not full. A fiddle is required along the base to keep the volumes in place, as well as a drop-in fiddle rail at half height for rough weather.

Hanging lockers are extremely useful for stowing wet oilskins and, in a separate locker, shore gear. A minimum height of 36 inches is required for shirts and jackets, and 56 inches for dresses and oilskin trousers. Coat hangers require a width of 18 inches, and each item occupies about 1½ inches of the hanger rail. If the locker is for wet gear it is best placed right by the hatchway, and hooks are better than coathangers; a rack for boots is also useful. The locker needs to be well ventilated, and should drain into the bilges.

Doorways

In many ways doors present a problem on boats. They may require large holes to be cut in structural bulkheads, they require plenty of space to open and close, and they may sometimes be jammed shut by the flexing of the hull. However, they do divide up the interior and give some privacy, and with careful design the drawbacks can largely be overcome.

A door does not need to be particularly large for the human frame to pass through it; the minimum dimensions are 5 feet high and 20 inches wide for the body, tapering to 12 inches wide below knee height. However, where possible these dimensions should be increased, particularly if sailbags or other bulky items are likely to be carried through the doorway.

If the aperture for the door is made with square corners, or carried right up to the deckhead, the sharp corners will result in a very high localised stress point; this will eventually result in the formation of cracks, and the door may well jam due to movement in the bulkhead. Instead, the door should be designed with the maximum possible corner radius, and with an adequate depth of bulkhead left intact top and bottom. On a lightly built boat the door may still tend to jam, but this can be avoided by mounting the door proud against one of the faces of the bulkhead, instead of setting it in flush.

Ventilation and Heating

The interior of the yacht needs to be well ventilated to keep the air fresh, to

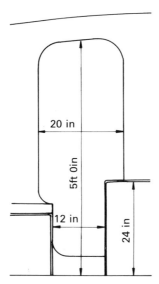

Fig. 5.15. Minimum doorway dimensions. Here the doorway has to be tapered to allow for the seats on one side, and the engine box on the other. Note the generous amount of timber left at the top and bottom of the bulkhead.

disperse smells, and to minimise condensation. The amount of ventilation required depends upon the climate in which the boat is sailed; in temperate climates the saloon requires one 6 inch diameter vent per two crew members, but in the tropics the requirements are trebled.

The saloon is not the only area requiring ventilation, though. Cabins and quarter berths need ventilating to prevent the air going stale, whilst the galley and heads need ventilating to disperse odours.

On all but the largest of yachts, powered ventilation imposes an excessive drain on the batteries, and so natural ventilation must be used. The simplest form of ventilator is the opening hatch or porthole, but as these also let water in they can only be regarded as auxiliary vents, for use in fine weather or in harbour.

Perhaps the commonest type of vent, and one of the most efficient, is the Dorade vent, so named after its use by Olin Stephens on the yacht of that name. A cowl, usually of flexible PVC, catches the air and leads it down below; a baffle box acts as a water trap, and water escapes through drain holes on each side onto the deck. If the water rises above the level of the baffle plate, though, water will find its way down below. The only real drawback of the Dorade vent is that the cowl is prone to catching ropes, particularly if placed forward of the mast. This can be avoided by fitting guards over the cowls, which can also double as handholds for the crew.

Many boats use Tannoy vents; their low profile makes them unobtrusive, and they cannot snag ropes. The centre of the vent may be made of clear plastic, so that it doubles as a decklight. Unfortunately, the low profile also means low baffle

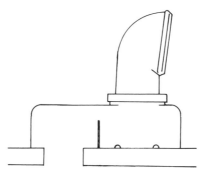

Fig. 5.16. The Dorade or cowl vent. The cowl can be turned to avoid spray or catch the breeze. The higher the baffle plate, the more water resistant the vent.

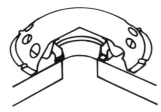

Fig. 5.17. The Tannoy vent. Instead of having a single deep baffle, a series of shallow baffle plates are used to keep the profile low.

plates, and so the vent is best placed on the coachroof top, where it is unlikely to be covered by green water.

Mushroom vents simply consist of a cap with a central spindle that can be screwed up or down from below decks. Once again they have a low profile, but they can be screwed right down to make them watertight in bad weather. However, the spindle protrudes below the deckhead by several inches when the vent is shut, and plastic spindles are easily broken off by passing heads.

When positioning the vents, both the deck plan and the interior layout must be considered. Below decks the vent must not be placed directly over a bunk, the chart table, or anything else that may be affected by water coming down the vent. On deck they should be kept clear of the crew's working areas, and as high up and as far inboard as possible to avoid getting swamped by a wave.

A cabin heater can do much to make the crew more comfortable, particularly on those chilly nights at the beginning and end of the season. There are basically two types of cabin heater in use: those that are mounted in the cabin, from which they draw their air supply and into which they radiate their heat; and those which are sited remotely, having a ducted air supply and exhaust, and a separate duct to blow hot air to one or more cabins. Both types may use gas, paraffin or diesel as a fuel.

The first type is the cheapest and the simplest, and the most suitable on small boats where one heater may serve the whole vessel. Although this type of heater does not need a ducted air supply, it must have an exhaust leading up on deck.

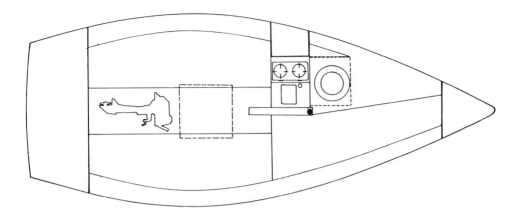

Fig. 5.18. Interior layout of a 'Gem' 18 ft Micro Cup design. On a boat of this size there is no room for a separate galley or heads, everything must be fitted into the one area. The central box is for the keel, which can be raised when towing but otherwise remains locked down. (*Courtesy Rob Humphreys.*)

Those without an exhaust, usually catalytic gas heaters, will release carbon dioxide and moisture, the products of combustion, into the air. The extra ventilation required to dispel these products will result in much of the heat being lost, and in all probability heavy condensation will build up inside the boat.

A remotely sited heater need not take up any space in the cabin, and can be ducted to supply each cabin; it can also be fitted with a thermostat for automatic operation. The fuel is pumped into a combustion chamber where it is ignited by an electric element, and the heat is transferred to air drawn from the cabin or the outside, which is then blown into the various cabins. As the systems for combustion and heating are kept totally separate, the air is dry and odour free. Apart from the extra expense of this system, though, a constant electric supply of 1 – 3 amps is required, depending upon the size of the unit.

Lighting

The obvious sources of natural lighting include windows in the coachroof sides, and glass or perspex hatches; other possibilities include windows below the sheer line or, if there is an aft cabin, in the transom, and lights set into the deck.

Windows may be of acrylic or polycarbonate plastic, or toughened or laminated glass. Plastic is easily worked in the boatyard, and can be bent to take up curvature in the window, but scratches easily. Thus glass is best used for hatches, decklights, and windows from which a watch is kept. Because of the very brittle nature of glass it cannot be bolted directly into place, but must be mounted in a frame which is bolted to the coachroof. On the other hand, the flexibility of plastic means that it may pop out of a frame if not thick enough, and it is best bolted directly to the boat; this also means one less joint which may leak in time.

For privacy, all windows should be fitted with a curtain. To prevent it swinging around at sea, the curtain should be attached to rails at both the top and bottom. Deck hatches can also be fitted with curtains, and this is particularly useful when the hatch lies over a cabin or berth.

Electric lights may use a light bulb or a fluorescent tube. The latter consumes about one third the current for the same intensity of light, and has a much longer life; however, some models can cause interference with radio equipment. Light bulbs have the advantage of being more compact, and can give a more intense, focussed light; replacement bulbs are also more widely available.

There are two requirements for lighting: firstly, all living areas need a good all-round level of illumination; secondly, areas such as the galley and chart table, the engine compartment and the head of bunks need a more intense, concentrated light to read or work by. These lights must be carefully positioned to give the maximum light and yet not shine into the user's eyes or cast a shadow over the work area.

To preserve night vision when sailing after sunset, no lights should be placed so that they shine through the hatch into the helmsman's eyes. A second set of lights with red shades can be fitted over the chart table and galley, so that these areas can be worked with no loss of night vision. These lights should be positioned so that they do not shine into the faces of any sleeping crew members. A red decklight may also be fitted to help with sail changes at night, and racing boats may have lights set into the foredeck to illuminate the headsails.

Chapter 6

The Engine and Propeller

Power Requirements

If an engine is to be worth its while, it must be capable of driving the boat at a speed of at least $1.1\sqrt{LWL}$ knots; small boats in particular should be capable of higher speeds, and a minimum speed of about 5 knots is necessary to make any sort of headway against tides.

The nomograph given in Fig. 6.1 can be used to estimate the power required at the propeller (i.e. after allowing for transmission losses); the speeds given are those attainable in smooth water. It is only a guide, though, as the exact figure will depend upon the propeller efficiency as well as the boat's resistance.

The engine's output may be quoted for the bare engine, the engine and gearbox, or the power delivered to the propeller (generally assuming a normal directly driven propeller). If the figure quoted excludes the gearbox, a 5% reduction must be applied for a mechanical gearbox, or 12% for a hydraulic gearbox (fitted to larger engines). An allowance may also have to be made for the alternator, which absorbs about 1 horsepower per 250 watt output.

Propeller Selection

Performance under power is just as dependent upon having the correct propeller as it is upon having a powerful enough engine. Choosing a propeller is a complex task, as many factors have to be taken into account. These include the engine's power, the boat's speed, the propeller speed, and the effect that the hull's lines have on the water flow over the propeller. Expert advice should be obtained from the engine manufacturers or a yacht designer.

It is only possible to optimise the propeller for one boat speed, and the intended cruising speed should be used. Knowing the engine's power (P_1) and the propeller speed at which this is produced (R_1), and reading the power required at cruising

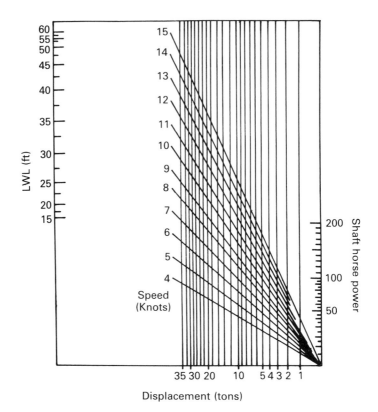

Fig. 6.1. Nomograph giving power requirements. Note that the shaft horse-power and the load displacement (including the crew) must be used. To find the speed attainable by a given engine, join the waterline length and the engine horse-power by a straight line, and then read off the speed where this line crosses the displacement. To find the power requirements for a vessel, draw a line joining the waterline length and the intersection of the required speed and the displacement, then continue the line to the power requirements. (From *Power Requirements and Speed of Vessels up to 50 t Displacement*, 1979. Courtesy of KHD.)

speed (P_2) off Fig. 6.1, the approximate propeller speed can be calculated from the formula:

$$R_2 = R_1\left(\frac{P_2}{P_1}\right)^{0.357}$$

The propeller is defined by three main dimensions. Most fundamental of these is the diameter, which determines the amount of water that is accelerated by the propeller. The blade area, governed by the number of blades and their dimensions, controls the amount of grip that the propeller has on the water, and also has a major effect on drag when sailing. Finally, the pitch controls how much the water is accelerated by the propeller; it is defined as the amount by which the

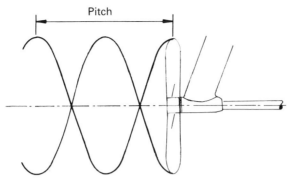

Fig. 6.2. Propeller pitch. This is the distance that the propeller would move through the water in one revolution, assuming that there is no slip.

propeller would advance through the water, assuming no slippage. For design purposes the pitch is converted into a non-dimensional form, the pitch ratio, given as pitch:diameter.

For the relatively slow speeds of sailing boats under power, the most efficient propeller is slow-turning with a large diameter, low pitch and plenty of blade area. However, the optimum propeller is seldom fitted because of the high drag when under sail, and the large installation that would be required. In particular, almost all yachts carry a two-bladed propeller with narrow blades to minimise the drag under sail, despite the diameter needing to be about 7% greater than for an equivalent three-bladed propeller.

Figure 6.3 indicates the optimum propeller diameter for a given engine power and propeller speed, and also shows the efficiency at which it is operating. In most yachts the propeller speed lies somewhere between 900 and 1200 rpm, and so the greatest efficiency that can be hoped for is about 55%.

Once the propeller diameter has been selected, the pitch ratio is dependent upon the boat's speed. The greater the boat speed, the more the water must be accelerated, and so the greater the pitch ratio required. Sailing boats have an average pitch ratio of about 0.75, though values ranging from 0.65 to 0.9 have been fitted. If the propeller has the correct pitch the engine will just reach full revs with the throttle wide open; if the engine cannot attain full speed the pitch is too large, whilst if it reaches full speed before the throttle is fully open the pitch is too small. To a limited extent the pitch can also compensate for too large or too small a propeller diameter; too large a propeller requires a reduction in pitch, and vice versa.

Propeller drag

The most efficient propeller under power is also the least desirable under sail, as its high drag causes a marked reduction in performance. This is why few boats carry a three-bladed propeller, despite its greater efficiency and lower vibration.

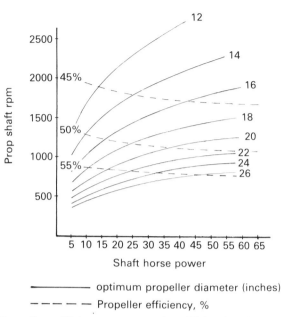

optimum propeller diameter (inches)

Propeller efficiency, %

Fig. 6.3. Propeller efficiency curves. At efficiencies below about 43%, cavitation may be a problem. (*Courtesy Volvo Penta.*)

Some boats eliminate prop drag entirely by using an outboard motor or, in the case of multihulls, a retractable strut drive mounted between the hulls. Others minimise drag by fitting a small, high revving prop, accepting the loss in efficiency; many also fit a folding or feathering propeller.

Folding propellers simply have the blades hinged at the root, so that they close under water pressure when sailing, and open under centrifugal force when the engine is running. Their main drawback is that they are not very efficient in reverse, as the forces developed by the blades oppose the centrifugal force, and so partially close the propeller. Also, on propellers where the blades are not linked together by gears, one of the blades may swing open when sailing, or fail to close.

Feathering propellers have a more complex mechanism that uses the rotation of the shaft to angle the blades under power, and the water pressure to feather them under sail. The shaft should be marked so that it can be locked with the propeller blades aligned with the P-bracket when sailing. Feathering propellers are considerably more expensive than the folding variety, the mechanism is more prone to seizing up, and the blades are more likely to catch weed when sailing. They were chiefly developed to exploit a loophole in the IOR, which rates them on a par with the considerably bulkier variable pitch propeller.

The effect that the various propeller types have on performance is shown in Fig. 6.5. This also shows that a freely rotating propeller has considerably less drag than a fixed one. The only disadvantage to a free spinning prop is the increased wear on the bearings; also, some hydraulic gearboxes are not designed for continuous

Fig. 6.4. A feathering propeller. The blades are rotated by the prop shaft, which is locked when sailing so that the blades are aligned with the P-bracket.

operation without the engine running, and this should be checked with the manufacturer.

Engine Selection

A large number of engines are available on the market, and it is worth taking some care when choosing a suitable model. As with any piece of machinery, one of the most important factors is the availability of service and spares in the cruising area. Here the larger firms, and those marinising car or truck engines, are at an advantage.

For a given output, engines may be designed to have a large capacity and be slow revving, or to have a small capacity and a high speed; the trend is currently towards high revving engines. The faster turning engines are undoubtedly lighter and cheaper, but they also tend to be thirstier on fuel, and their higher speed results in greater wear, and therefore more maintenance.

There are many good arguments for buying an engine that is slightly oversize, in addition to that of having some power in reserve. Running at reduced power means that the stresses on the components will be less; this is also the case when engine manufacturers offer one standard cylinder block in different engines with different power outputs, controlling the power produced by means of the engine speed. Running below full speed also generally means that more torque will be

163

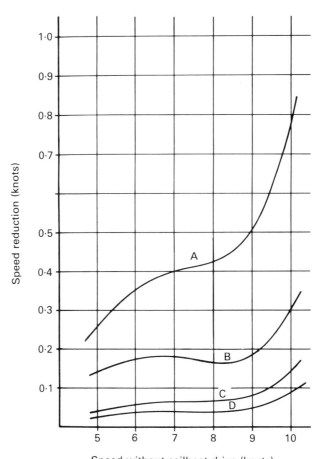

Fig. 6.5. Propeller drag characteristics. These tests were carried out on a 25-foot waterline boat, fitted with a saildrive unit. The peaks and troughs correspond to the wavemaking resistance 'humps', and not to the propeller characteristics. A Fixed two-bladed propeller, 16 × 11.
        B Freely rotating two-bladed propeller, 16 × 11.
        C Feathering propeller, 18 × 9.
        D Folding propeller, 15 × 12.
(*Courtesy of Volvo Penta.*)

available, and the specific fuel consumption (fuel consumption per horsepower) will also be reduced.

Engines may use diesel oil or petrol as a fuel; the choice of fuel used to be a matter of some debate, but nowadays in sailing boats outboards are petrol driven, whilst almost all inboards use diesel. Petrol engines are cheaper, lighter, quieter and smoother running than diesels; against this there is the risk of an explosion if there is a fuel leak, and the damp atmosphere makes their ignition system unreliable. However, this problem can largely be overcome by electronic ignition and fuel injection. Also, their fuel consumption is about 40% higher than a diesel, requiring larger tanks to be fitted, and eventually offsetting the initial cost advantage.

Diesel engines are extremely reliable, as they do not need any electrical systems once started; also the flashpoint of diesel is sufficiently high for there to be no risk of an explosion. The modern high revving diesels are also not much heavier than petrol engines. However, diesel engines do tend to be smelly, and have a smokey exhaust.

Even if two banks of batteries are fitted, there is always the possibility of not having sufficient power to start the engine. Thus it is always worth having some form of manual starting. On engines up to about 35 horsepower, a decompression lever and a crank are adequate, but on larger engines the energy must be stored in a spring or other device before being released to start the engine. Starting in cold weather can also be a problem, particularly with high revving engines. Thus some heating device may be fitted, either pre-heating the fuel, or heating the combustion chamber.

In addition to propelling the yacht, the engine may also be called upon to drive one or more ancillary items. These may include an additional alternator, a compressor for a fridge, a hydraulic pump for the anchor windlass, or a bilge pump. Many engines make provision for this either by connecting the device directly to the drive shaft, or by carrying a power take-off pulley for a belt drive. The first system is preferable as it imposes no extra strain on the engine bearings, though it does increase the length of the installation. Any intended auxiliary drive system should be referred to the engine manufacturers for approval before installation.

The Cooling and Exhaust Systems

There are three methods of engine cooling: air, raw water (sea water) and fresh water. Air-cooled engines, although not currently popular, are inherently reliable due to the simplicity of their design. A fan mounted on the engine draws air over the surface of the engine, and then expels it through an exhaust duct; this air may be used to heat the cabin. The air intake and exhaust ducting is obviously fairly bulky due to the large quantities of air required, and the fan tends to be noisy unless well silenced. Also, the engine is not cooled as efficiently as a water-cooled unit, and so its power output is slightly lower.

Air-cooled engines must be fitted with a dry exhaust, unless a sea water inlet and pump are specially fitted. The main disadvantage of a dry exhaust is the fact that it is relatively expensive. It needs to be made of steel, type 316 stainless steel providing the best resistance to the hot, corrosive gases. It must also be covered in lagging at least ¾ inch thick to prevent any risk of a fire, or burns to the crew. A short length of flexible metal hose is needed by the engine to allow for its movement, and also for thermal expansion in the system. A silencer is also required to bring the noise down to an acceptable level.

Raw water-cooled engines draw up water through a skin fitting, circulate it round the engine, and then discharge it over the side. Although a simple system, the salt water will inevitably cause some corrosion in the engine block; most manufacturers fit sacrificial zinc anodes to guard against this. However, if the engine block is of aluminium, copper pipe should not be used for the coolant intake pipe.

There is a lot to be said for fresh water cooling. Here the engine is cooled by recirculating fresh water, and the heat is transferred by a heat exchanger to a flow of sea water. This is the most efficient cooling system, allowing the maximum power to be extracted from the engine. Also, the fresh water largely eliminates corrosion problems, as well as being available to heat up hot water, or to drive a desalination plant.

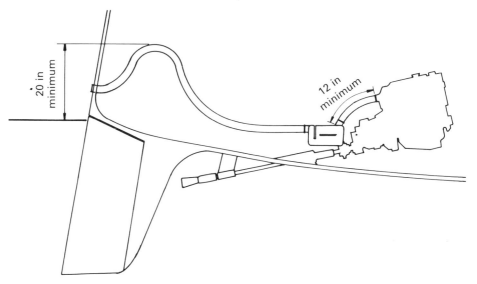

Fig. 6.6. A water cooled exhaust system, fitted with a water trap at the lowest point of the system. If the engine exhaust outlet is less than 6 inches above the waterline, an air bleed must be fitted between the engine and the water trap, to prevent coolant siphoning back into the engine when it is switched off.

To prevent debris from clogging the cooling system, the sea water intake needs to be fitted with a strainer; this should be fitted facing aft to prevent water being forced in when sailing. A cleanable filter can also be fitted, either incorporated into the seacock or mounted on the engine. To minimise the risk of leaks or fire damage the pipe is best made of metal, with a short length of fire resistant hose to take up engine movement.

Water-cooled engines are normally fitted with a water-cooled exhaust, whereby the exhaust gases are cooled by injecting the sea water coolant where the exhaust leaves the engine. This enables a flexible heat and oil resistant rubber exhaust hose to be used. The exhaust should leave the hull above the waterline to minimise back pressure in the system, and to enable the flow of coolant to be checked.

Two precautions need to be taken to prevent water working its way up the exhaust and into the engine. First of all, a water trap needs to be fitted at the low point of the exhaust to hold the coolant in the system when the engine is switched off. Secondly, the exhaust should be looped up, or a gooseneck fitted, where the exhaust leaves the hull; this is to prevent sea water entering the system from the skin fitting. The water injection silences the exhaust, and a separate silencer is seldom required.

Engine Controls and Monitors

Engine controls need to be positioned where they can be reached by the helm, yet in a sheltered position to prevent ropes snagging on them or water seeping in. A common solution is to recess the controls into the cockpit side, where they can be operated by hand or foot. A single lever controlling the throttle and forward/reverse gears is generally fitted, being easier to operate than a twin lever system.

The engine may be monitored by instrument dials, or audible or visual alarms. Instruments give more information and can give advance warning of a problem, but audible alarms will attract the crew's attention even if they are involved with something else on board; for this reason, warning lights are best fitted in conjunction with an alarm buzzer.

Every engine ought to be fitted with sensors for low lubricating oil pressure, and for too high an engine temperature. The engine temperature is monitored by measuring the temperature of the coolant circulating round the engine. In the case of a fresh water-cooled engine, if a leak or pump failure occurs in the sea water system the alarm will not be triggered off until the whole fresh water system has been heated up; by this time the uncooled exhaust gases may have melted or set fire to the exhaust hose. To guard against this possibility, a flow meter can be fitted into the sea water system immediately before the injection elbow.

Other instruments that can be useful are a tachometer to indicate engine speed, and an engine hour meter to ensure that services are carried out at the correct intervals.

Engine Mounts

The engine bearers not only have to support the weight of the engine, but also have to transmit the thrust of the propeller to the hull (except in the case of a hydraulic system). To ensure that the load is spread sufficiently, they should run fore and aft for at least twice the length of the engine and gearbox before being tied in to the rest of the hull's framing system; cross-bearers may also be required to provide adequate lateral rigidity.

The incessant vibration of the engine means that screws or coach screws will work loose in time, and only bolts should be used to fasten the engine down. Timber or fibreglass bearers need to be protected against local crushing, both beneath the engine feet, and underneath the nuts, by metal strips or plate washers.

Nowadays almost all engines are flexibly mounted, as this reduces the amount of vibration transmitted to the hull by at least 30%, and so reduces the noise and vibration levels. The mounts need to be suited to the engine, but in general the more flexible the mounts, the quieter the installation will be.

All piping and cables connected to the engine need to have a short flexible length to accommodate the movement of the engine. Also, any belt driven ancillary devices must be mounted onto the engine itself, to ensure a constant belt tension.

The engine must be accurately aligned with the propeller shaft; as all hulls are slightly flexible, the final adjustment is best left until the boat is afloat. Alignment may be achieved by using adjustable mounts, or by fitting shims under the feet. Even if flexibly mounted, an incorrectly aligned engine will result in increased vibration and wear in the bearings.

The Engine Compartment

One of the most important requirements of the engine compartment is good access; this makes it easier to maintain the engine, and so makes it more likely that it will be given the attention it deserves. In particular, there must be ready access to items that are regularly serviced, such as filters, oil and water dipsticks, fillers and drain plugs, belt tension adjusters, and the fuel injectors or carburetter and distributor. Also, there must be plenty of space to swing the starter handle if fitted.

In a well designed compartment it will be possible to carry out almost all of the work with the engine *in situ*, but at some stage in its life the engine will probably have to be removed, and the designer must plan for this from the start. On some boats a considerable amount of joinery has had to be dismantled before the engine could be removed.

The engine compartment must be ventilated, both to satisfy the needs of the engine, and to disperse any fumes that build up. Separate inlets and outlets are required on larger craft; as the inlet must also supply the engine with air, it needs to be bigger than the outlet. For combustion, the engine requires about 2½ cubic feet/min per horsepower; this means an inlet area of about 1 square inch per horsepower. On top of this, allowance must be made to ventilate the compartment.

In many yachts the air inlet draws air from the bilge, and if there is an outlet it either goes back into the cabin or into a cockpit locker. This draws fresh air through the interior, preventing pockets of stale air building up, and keeping condensation down. However, it also allows noise to escape into the accommodation space. The alternative is to have the inlet and outlet ducted directly to the open air, but with this system precautions need to be taken to prevent water entering the compartment.

A metal or fibreglass drip tray ought to be fitted below the engine to catch any oil or fuel spillages. This helps to keep the bilges clean, and also protects the hull in wooden or ferro-cement craft. In metal or fibreglass hulls the drip tray may be built into the engine bearers. The tray needs to be deep enough to contain any oil even when the boat is heeled.

Engine noise can largely be contained within the compartment by minimising the number of air gaps leading to the cockpit and the cabin, and by lining the sides and top of the compartment with sound absorbent materials. A foam/lead/ foam sandwich is the best sound absorber, although some manufacturers substitute mineral wool for the foam to improve fire resistance. The outer foam layer absorbs the high frequencies, the lead the low frequencies, and the inner layer of foam insulates the lead from the walls of the compartment. A heavily built engine box will further help to contain the noise.

The Propeller and Drive Train

The water flow round the propeller must be as undisturbed as possible, both to increase propeller efficiency and to reduce vibration. This means that the clearance between the propeller blades and the hull should be at least 15% of the propeller's diameter; increasing this up to 35% will reduce vibration still further, but on no account should the clearance drop below 10%.

A skeg or P-bracket immediately in front of the propeller will obviously disturb the flow; for this reason P-brackets are raked forwards on cruising boats. However, on racing boats the P-bracket may be vertical or raked aft to minimise drag under sail.

The steeper the angle of the propeller shaft, the more energy is wasted in trying to push the boat's stern up out of the water. An angle of 15° is often quoted as the maximum desirable angle, but obviously the more horizontal the shaft can be, the better. Mounting the propeller too close to the rudder will reduce the rudder's efficiency under sail, due to the eddies shed off the propeller blades.

The propeller is secured to the shaft by locating it onto a taper cut into the shaft with a keyway, followed by a lock nut. Thus the key takes the shear loads, and the lock nut prevents the propeller dropping off the end of the shaft. However, the taper is not standardised, and so the propeller must be fitted to both the shaft diameter and the taper. If the flexible coupling has the same taper as the propeller, the shaft life can be prolonged by turning it end for end when there are signs of wear at the bearings.

Fig. 6.7. Volvo Penta MD17D/MS2 diesel engine. Note that the gearbox is angled down to make installation easier. (*Courtesy Volvo Penta.*)

Direct drive

The simplest and commonest drive system has the propeller shaft fitted directly to the gearbox. To give a better installation, some gearboxes have the prop shaft emerging at a lower height than the crankshaft, thus improving the shaft angle; others have the prop shaft angled at up to 10° below the horizontal, helping keep the engine level and so reducing its height at the forward end.

If the prop shaft is rigidly supported at two bearings, a flexible coupling is required to absorb the engine's movement; in most cases the coupling is bolted directly onto the engine, although it is sometimes sited close to the gearbox. Alternatively, if the prop shaft is only rigidly held at one point, the flexible coupling must be omitted. In this case the bearing must be rubber, and the stern gland must be mounted on a short length of flexible hose, so that the movement of the prop shaft can be accommodated.

The flexibility of the engine mounts and the flexible coupling is limited by the thrust of the propeller. However, the engine can be mounted much more flexibly if a thrust bearing takes the propeller's load, and a flexible coupling incorporating a thrust bearing is now available. The coupling is also designed to be able to be angled at up to 8°, thereby reducing the height of the engine.

Shaft bearings are normally made from synthetic rubber or white metal, and water lubricated; other hard wearing substances such as Tufnol may also be used on occasion. To avoid excessive bearing pressures, the length of the bearing needs to be about four times the diameter of the shaft. Rubber bearings are particularly suited to inshore waters, as the softness of the rubber prevents the shaft being scored by grit. However, they must have a good supply of water, and they wear more quickly than metal bearings.

The stern tube may have a rubber or a metal outer bearing, but where an inner bearing is fitted it needs to be metal, due to the inadequate flow of water. Lubrication is achieved by small scoops forcing water into the tube, though no scoops may be fitted if the tube is short and only has one bearing.

A stern gland is required to prevent water working its way into the boat via the prop shaft. It usually consists of a stuffing box, containing a fibrous packing material that is compressed by tightening up a flange plate, and lubricated by grease. A remote greaser can be sited in a locker to make greasing the stern gland easier. The flange should be tightened to a point where almost no water comes in, yet not so tightly that the gland overheats. Solid rubber stern glands which require no maintenance are also available, but must be replaced when they wear out or are damaged. This could present a problem if a leak started when at sea. Every stern gland or bearing will absorb 1–1½% of the engine's power.

The P-bracket is subjected to surprisingly high lateral loads, and so it must be securely bolted or bonded into place. Ideally the bracket should bend before becoming detached from the hull – this means that most P-brackets need to be of solid stainless steel or aluminium bronze.

The shaft diameter depends upon the material used, and the power output divided by the shaft speed, a slower turning engine requiring a larger shaft diameter. Another factor on some boats is the distance between the bearings. Manganese bronze, as we have seen, is not a good material for use underwater from the aspect of corrosion; neither is it very strong, and so a large diameter shaft is required. Type 316 stainless steel is better on both counts, though still subject to some corrosion problems. The best materials are aluminium bronze, titanium and the cupro-nickel alloys Monel 400 and Monel K500; all are corrosion free and strong, especially Monel K500 and titanium.

V-drives

A V-drive is an extra gear train used to turn the shaft angle through an angle of or close to 180°. Its main use is on high speed power boats, where the engines are frequently mounted right aft. However, it is also used on sailing boats where the propeller is positioned just behind the keel and the engine is well aft. The V-drive gearbox will absorb about 10% of the engine's power.

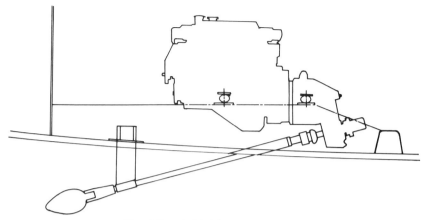

Fig. 6.8. A V-drive installation.

On sailing boats the V-drive is usually built into the gearbox, or it may alternatively be mounted at the end of an intermediate shaft. Long intermediate shafts, or prop shafts for that matter, may require additional bearings to prevent the shaft whipping at speed. The maximum unsupported length varies with the diameter and material of the shaft, but generally lies between 4 feet and 7 feet.

Hydraulic drive

A hydraulic drive permits totally independent positioning of the engine and propeller. The price to pay for this is a comparatively large power loss: 13% for the pump and motor, plus a further 1% for every 3 feet of hydraulic hose.

The system consists of a hydraulic pump mounted on the engine, which is connected by a pair of oil hoses to a hydraulic motor positioned at the inboard end of the propeller shaft. As this arrangement is most frequently used where the propeller is on a short shaft unsupported by a P-bracket, the shaft may be incorporated as part of the hydraulic motor.

Sail drives

Sail drives were developed to make the installation of the engine easier on fibreglass hulls. The engine has a drive leg bolted to it, leading through a rubber seal and a hole in the hull to the propeller; the drive leg also incorporates the sea water intake. The whole unit comes mounted on a fibreglass plinth, ready to be cut to shape and bonded to the hull. This means that the builder only has to install the fuel supply, the exhaust, and the engine controls. Two side benefits are that softer mounts can be used to give a quieter installation, and the drag of the drive leg is about half that of an exposed shaft and P-bracket.

VOLVO PENTA
MD 11/120 S

Fig. 6.9. A saildrive unit. Installation is simple, as all the builder has to do is cut and bond in the glassfibre plinth, and connect up the engine. (*Courtesy Volvo Penta.*)

A variation on this theme has been developed for multihulls. Here a conventional engine is fitted, connected to a drive leg mounted between the hulls. The leg can be raised and lowered by a block and tackle or a hydraulic ram to avoid any drag penalty when sailing; it can also be steered, making the boat more manoeuvrable under power.

Outboard Engines

Outboard motors are widely used for powering tenders and small yachts. The main restriction upon the size of the engine is its weight, as it needs to be manhandled on and off its mounting pad.

The engine may be mounted on the transom, or in a well at the aft end of the cockpit. Although having the engine in the cockpit means that it takes up more room, it also means that it is more accessible, and the propeller comes out of the water less when the boat is heeled. The only problem with this arrangement is that, unless properly ventilated, the petrol fumes may build up in the well and cause a fire risk; particular care must be taken if the well is fitted with a hatch cover.

Unfortunately, many outboard engines are designed with high speed craft in mind, with high revving propellers and with the exhaust emerging through the propeller hub, which has a disastrous effect on the stopping power and reversing capability of the engine, as it inevitably ventilates the propeller. Also, not many engines can be started by pulling the starter cord vertically, as is often necessary when the engine is sited well down the transom, or in a deep well. Another major drawback with outboard motors is that relatively few are fitted with an alternator that is large enough to be of any real value. However, one of the main advantages of an outboard motor is that it can easily be brought ashore for servicing.

Two stroke engines are used almost exclusively, as they are both cheap and simple. However, they are very thirsty on fuel, and the lubricating oil mixed with the petrol makes the plugs oil up fairly frequently.

Clearly, negligible installation costs are involved, but the exposed situation of the engine makes damp a problem. The engine should be protected with a water repellent spray, and always kept in a locker; the cylinder block must be kept uppermost, to prevent any cooling water left in the system working its way up into the cylinders.

Chapter 7

Water, Fuel and Gas Installations

Water Systems

Fresh water

The first requirement in any yacht's fresh water system is that the tanks should have a sufficiently high capacity. As a rule of thumb, 4 pints are required per man per day, but clearly requirements will vary widely according to the lifestyle of the crew.

A variety of materials may be used for the tanks: steel, in mild, galvanised or stainless form, aluminium, fibreglass, rigid plastic or flexible rubber. Fibreglass will taint the water, mild steel will corrode, and aluminium will form a hard scale, unless coated with an epoxy-based paint. Flexible tanks, although cheap, tend to burst or become punctured, and so cannot be recommended for offshore use.

To enable repairs and cleaning to be carried out, the tank should be fitted in such a way that it is readily removable; alternatively, it can be built into the hull, and a large access hatch fitted on top.

As fresh water weights 10 lb a gallon, the tanks will be pretty heavy when full. Thus they should be sited low down to lower the centre of gravity, amidships to minimise changes in trim between the full and empty states, and with the weights balanced athwartships to maintain lateral trim. When in a seaway the water will also surge around the tank; baffle plates are fitted in tanks larger than about 11 gallons (13.2 US gallons), spaced between 20 and 30 inches apart. These also serve to strengthen the tank.

To provide some safeguard against leaks, at least two tanks should be fitted, each with their own shut-off valves. They may have separate filler plates, or be cross-connected to the one filler plate. To prevent sea water seeping into the system, the filler plates should be sited in a sheltered area, not in the cockpit sole, nor right by the gunwhale.

In addition to the filler pipe, supply pipes and an air vent will also be needed. All pipes should enter through the top of the tank if possible, as this prevents a leak if the tank fitting fractures. The vent pipe needs to be taken as high as possible, higher than the filler pipe, to prevent water being lost when heeled, or spillages occurring when filling the tank.

A means of discerning the amount of water present in the tank is clearly useful. If the filler pipe goes straight down to the tank a dipstick, graduated in gallons, provides the simplest solution, though a strengthening plate should be fitted where the dipstick strikes the tank bottom. Another simple solution, suitable when one of the tank sides is visible, is a sight glass. However, in many cases a mechanical or electro-mechanical gauge is required, usually a pivoting float with a sender that is wired to a tank contents gauge. Obviously, none of these systems will give an accurate reading when the boat is heeled, nor can they be fitted to flexible tanks.

The use of PVC hose is now almost universal, being cheaper and easier to install than copper, though it must be of food grade if it is not to affect the taste. As it softens and expands on heating, hot water pipes must be reinforced by having a nylon braid embedded in the hose. The hose also tends to squash down on itself it subjected to a pressure drop, as may happen on the suction side of a blocked pump. Thus all hoses on the suction side of powered pumps or high-capacity manual pumps should be reinforced with a plastic spiral.

The simplest and most reliable supply system simply has a hand or foot operated pump at each faucet. Foot pumps leave the hands free, but unless carefully sited they can be difficult to use when the boat is heeled. The pumps can be kept permanently primed if a non-return valve is fitted at the low point of every supply line.

Most larger boats have a pressurised water system, though at least one hand pump must be fitted as a back-up. A pressurised system means that water is available at the turn of a tap, and a shower and hot water system can be fitted if desired; however, water consumption will be increased because of its ready availability. Two types of installation are available, both using an electric pump.

The first system is kept permanently pressurised at about 15 lb per square inch,

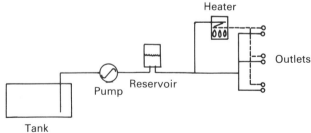

Fig. 7.1. A pressurised water system. The reservoir damps out any surges in the supply, resulting in a smoother system.

with a pressure-sensitive switch activating the pump whenever there is a drop in pressure due to a tap being turned on. Unfortunately, the pump will also be switched on if a leak develops, causing a rapid loss of water; also, after a few years the pressure difference across the pump may cause its seals to fail, and so it will operate continuously to maintain the required pressure.

The other system is not permanently pressurised, but instead has a micro-switch incorporated into each tap. The switch turns the pump on and off whenever a tap is used. This arrangement is clearly more reliable, but the choice of taps is limited.

Hot water

The most efficient way of obtaining hot water is to use the waste heat of the engine coolant water by fitting a calorifier (or heat exchanger). However, the engine must be fresh water cooled, as raw water does not get hot enough; also, water can only be heated when the engine is run. The calorifier is simply a well-insulated water tank with a network of pipes inside it to carry the engine coolant; it is connected in parallel with the raw water heat exchanger, so that it can be switched in or out as desired.

The size of the calorifier is limited by the power and amount of use of the engine, as too large a tank will not become hot unless the engine is run for a considerable length of time. Once heated, the water will remain hot for many hours due to the insulation – this could be further improved by lagging the hot water pipes.

To provide 'instant' hot water, an on-demand gas heater may be fitted. When the tap is turned on, the pilot light ignites the burners, which heat the water as it passes through the unit. The heater must be placed in a well-ventilated area, both because it gives out a lot of heat, and because it rapidly consumes the air's oxygen. If the oxygen level falls, first of all poisonous carbon monoxide will be emitted, and eventually the flame will go out. If it is to be used for more than about 5 minutes at a time, a chimney leading through the deck is required to ensure an adequate supply of air. This must be heavily lagged where it passes through the deck, and it needs a cover to keep rain and spray out.

Water purification

On yachts intended for extended cruising the water tanks will occupy a considerable amount of space, as well as increasing displacement, and so methods of obtaining fresh water whilst at sea are well worth looking at.

The traditional approach has been to catch rain water off the sails or coachroof top with a bucket and funnel, but this is clearly dependent on the weather. Another possibility is to use a solar still, but this requires sunny weather, and even then will need about 15 square feet of surface area to produce 1 gallon a day.

Fig. 7.2. An Aquaheat calorifier, capacity 21.3 gallons. The water can be heated by the engine coolant, or by an electric immersion heater. (*Courtesy G & M Power Plant.*)

An approach gaining popularity on large yachts is to purify the sea water by evaporation, getting most of the energy required from the engine coolant. The sea water is pumped through a low pressure chamber, which has the effect of reducing its boiling point to about 45°C. Whilst in this chamber it is heated by a network of

Fig. 7.3. This desalination unit (left) measures only 31 × 19 × 7 inches, yet is capable of producing 50 gallons per day. (*Courtesy Bravac Ltd.*)

tubes containing the engine coolant. Some pure water evaporates off, is condensed, and pumped to the tanks, whilst the remaining brine is discharged. A 40 horsepower engine will be able to produce about 3 gallons of fresh water per

179

hour (3.7 US gph). However, the electrical requirement is high; also, the low boiling point means that the water is not sterilised, so that all distillate obtained in coastal waters will need sterilising. River or harbour water must not be used.

Waste water

Waste water from the sinks and shower may be discharged in several ways. The simplest is to take it directly to a seacock, close to the centreline to maximise the fall of the pipe at all heel angles. However, the motion of the yacht will cause fluctuations in the air pressure, which will force the plug out of its hole. To avoid this a non-return valve should be incorporated in the pipe.

Another arrangement is to have a small discharge pump, and to pump the water out of the sink. This ensures that the sink can be drained at all times, but it is a nuisance to operate, and is not suitable for showers unless an electric pump is fitted. Occasionally the shower water is simply allowed to drain into the bilge, where it is dealt with by the bilge pump. However, as some water will inevitably be left in the bilges this practice is to be condemned, as it makes the bilges smelly and unhygienic.

Perhaps the best approach for larger craft is to fit a sump tank in the bilges that collects all the waste water. It can then be pumped out periodically, either manually or by an electric pump.

Sea water

Apart from its use as an engine coolant, dealt with in the previous chapter, sea water is used to flush the heads, and may be piped to the galley.

The heads inlet seacock must be forward of, or to one side of, the waste seacock to ensure that it always sucks up clean water. It also needs to be close to the centreline, so that it is below the waterline at all angles of heel. Screw-down gate valves are cheap, but ball valves are easier to use as the handle only needs to be turned through 90°. Flush closing valves are available, primarily designed for racing boats, that present no disturbance to the water flow when shut. Nylon skin fittings are also on the market, but are only acceptable if used above the waterline due to their low fire resistance.

If the piping is looped up to the deckhead before being taken to the heads, it will prevent water flowing in when the seacocks are left open; a small release valve is required at the high point of the loop to enable air locks to be removed. If the pipes are led directly to the heads the seacocks must be shut when not in use, as water may come onboard if the pump seals fail. Opaque plastic piping is generally used, reinforced on the suction side of pumps to prevent it collapsing in the event of a blockage.

The traditional marine toilet has two pumps, a lift pump for the inlet, and a diaphragm pump for the outlet. However, many modern designs have a single twin chamber pump fitted with a changeover switch, enabling the bowl to be emptied, or flushed and emptied simultaneously. This system is more compact and easier to use, but the diaphragm pump of traditional design is less likely to become blocked. The Lavac toilet uses a single diaphragm pump and an airtight seal round the lid, thus creating a vacuum when the bowl is emptied, which sucks in water to flush it.

As the number of pleasure craft increases, more and more harbour, marina and inland waterway authorities are insisting on non-discharging toilets to minimise pollution. If the discharge pipe is simply connected to a holding tank, a capacity of about 1½ gallons per man per day is required. Thus most boats fit a recirculating holding tank and use a chemical flushing fluid. This reduces the tank capacity requirements by one third.

To keep the boat free from odours, the holding tank's air vent is best taken up the outside of the mast to a point well above deck level.

For smaller boats, a portable recirculating chemical toilet will take up less space and be cheaper. However, it cannot be piped in to act as a marine toilet for use offshore, and the holding tank, which has to be emptied by hand, has a maximum capacity of 30 man days.

A sea water supply taken to the galley will help to reduce fresh water consumption, as the crew will not need to put a bucket over the side each time they want some sea water for washing up or cooking. It will also reduce the number of buckets lost overboard.

Bilge pumping systems

A bilge pump is mainly called upon to deal with small quantities of water that have accumulated in the bilges. It may also have to deal with large quantities of water in an emergency, though, and this must always be regarded as its prime function.

A graph giving the recommended bilge pipe diameter and total bilge pump capacity is given in Fig. 7.4. A minimum of two pumps should be fitted, so that a back-up system is provided; each pump should ideally have its own suction and discharge lines. Where two or more suction lines are taken to the one pump, a valve chest or other switching system should be sited close to hand. The discharge skin fitting needs to be taken to a point above the waterline so that the flow rate can be checked, yet low down to minimise the pressure head. It must be taken straight overboard, and not emptied into the cockpit.

Plastic hose is generally used, though copper pipe is equally satisfactory so long as the flow rate is below 3 feet/min (corrosion will take place at higher velocities). The suction end of the line must have a strum box fitted to prevent debris blocking the pump; to minimise its resistance to the water flow, the total area of its holes should be at least twice the cross-sectional area of the pipe. A

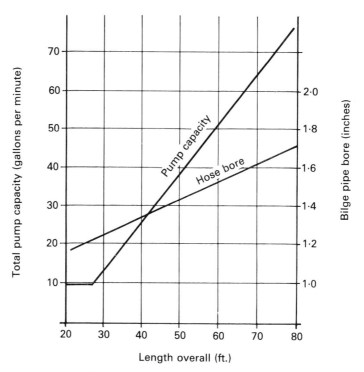

Fig. 7.4. Recommended bilge pump and hose sizes.

non-return valve should also be fitted close to the strum box, to keep the system primed.

Manual pumps are most reliable, being independent of any power supply. Thus at least one, and preferably two, must be fitted; two are required when racing under the IOR. One should be sited on deck and the other down below, both in easily worked positions. The handle must either be kept in a holder by the pump, or permanently fastened in its socket.

Diaphragm pumps should always be used, as they are very resistant to blockages. Those with a metal casing have proved more durable than plastic ones. Capacities range from 7 – 25 gallons per minute (8.4 – 30 US gpm), and through bulkhead mountings are available to give a neat installation.

A mechanical pump, driven by a belt drive off the engine, is the only type capable of dealing with large quantities of water. It will continue to operate until the engine air intake, or the ignition system on petrol engines, is submerged, though of course the engine must be able to be started in the first place. It can also be connected to suck up sea water and operate a deck wash or fire hose. For some reason, though, it has not become popular amongst yachtsmen.

Electrical pumps, on the other hand, are extremely popular, perhaps more so than they deserve. Their main drawback is a pretty hefty electrical consumption,

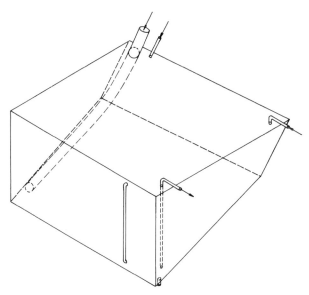

Fig. 7.5. A diesel fuel tank. Note the filler pipe has been taken to the bottom of the tank, so that a liquid seal is formed in the pipe.

about 0.35 A per gallon per minute output (0.3 A per US gpm). Thus in the event of prolonged usage a flat battery may result.

The pump may be a submersible unit located in the bilge, or a remotely sited self-priming pump. The submersible pumps tend to break down after a couple of years due to inadequate waterproofing, but they are quick and simple to install. A remote pump is much more durable, has a lower power consumption, and can be connected to several suction lines. Neither type of pump should be permitted to run dry, as the bilge water is used to lubricate the seals.

Fuel Systems

Most of the comments made about fresh water tanks apply equally to fuel tanks, though there are some important differences. Because of the risk of fuel spillage in the event of a fire, plastic or flexible rubber tanks must not be used, and fibreglass is only acceptable if laminated from woven rovings and a fire-retardant resin.

The water and the sulphur compounds present in diesel fuel sediment out at the bottom of the tank and cause corrosion, so copper, brass, or galvanised steel tanks should not be used. Mild steel, stainless steel, one of the cupro-nickel alloys, or 3103 grade aluminium alloy are to be recommended.

A sediment trap with a drain tap ought to be fitted at the lowest point of the tank, so that the sediment can be drained off periodically. The supply line should not extend right to the bottom of the tank, where it could pick up contaminated fuel.

Petrol (gasoline) is virtually free of water, and has far fewer corrosive compounds; thus tinned brass and tinned copper are suitable in addition to the materials recommended for diesel. Galvanised mild steel, copper and brass are also used for petrol tanks, but in the long term a gummy deposit is formed. Fibreglass cannot be recommended either, because of the increased fire risk. Because of the high purity of petrol and the greater dangers of a leak, no sediment trap should be fitted, neither should an access hatch be fitted.

Fuel lines are usually annealed copper, though one of the cupro-nickel alloys or stainless steel are also acceptable. However, to prevent metal fatigue a short length of fire-resistant neoprene hose must always be fitted where the supply line is connected to the engine or any other item, and also where the filler pipe is connected to the filler plate.

Joints should be brazed, or use flange, cone or compression connectors. Soldering is not acceptable, as both its fatigue strength and its melting point are unacceptably low.

If static electric charges are allowed to build up, a spark may be discharged, which could result in a fire. To prevent this, all tanks, piping and other major metal components must be electrically connected and taken to a common earth point.

The air vent must be taken to a sheltered spot on deck to prevent a build-up of fuel vapour in the cabin. In the case of petrol tanks, the vent must have a flame arrester gauze on the end to prevent a fire flashing back to the tank. A further precaution to prevent the contents of the tank from catching fire is to take the filler pipe down to the bottom of the tank. This means that if a fire travels down the filler pipe the fuel forms a liquid seal to prevent it spreading further.

The supply line must have a shut-off valve right by the tank, in an easily accessible position. This should be followed by a water separator, coupled with a filter. In conjunction with the engine's fuel filter, these will remove 99% of all impurities. A clear plastic or glass filter bowl permits easy inspection of the water level, but a metal bowl will not melt or shatter in the event of a fire.

Diesel engines will have an excess fuel return line from the injectors. As this fuel is warm it will reduce the engine's efficiency if T-ed back into the supply line; instead, it must be taken back to the fuel tank to cool off.

Gas Installations

Liquefied Petroleum Gas (LPG), like petrol, forms a potentially explosive mixture with air, and so the installation must be to a high standard. Butane gas is generally used, but propane may be preferred if sailing in very cold weather. This is because it has a lower boiling point than butane (which liquefies at between $-1°C$ and $-10°C$) and so it will maintain full pressure at lower temperatures.

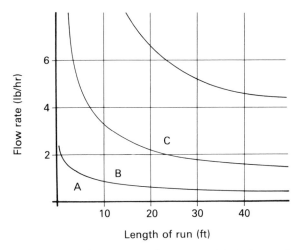

Fig. 7.6. Gas pipe sizes. A ¼ in bore; B ⅜ in bore; C ½ in bore. The pipe sizes should be chosen using the maximum possible gas flow. The following is a guide to the maximum consumption of various appliances: Two burner cooker 0.6 lb/h; Three burner cooker 0.9 lb/h; Two burner cooker with grill 1.1 lb/h; Four burner cooker with grill and oven up to 3.0 lb/h; Air heater 1.0 lb/h; Water heater 2.4 lb/h; Fridge 0.03 lb/h.

Every supplier of LPG has his own gas bottle design, and it may prove difficult to find an agent in remote areas; however, some suppliers are able to fill their competitor's bottles with special adaptors.

The simplest type of installation has the gas bottle screwing directly into the bottom of the cooker, and the absence of piping makes leaks very unlikely. However, it makes it impossible to have an oven, or any other gas appliance. It also takes up a considerable amount of space in the galley, where space is usually at a premium.

On most boats the gas bottle is kept in a deck locker, and the gas is piped to the various appliances. A special gas locker should be used, air tight except for ventilation to the deck, and with a ½ inch diameter gas drain pipe at the bottom of the locker going overboard to a point above the waterline.

Piping may be annealed copper or stainless steel, with the number of joints kept to a minimum; all joints should be of the capillary or compression type, sealed with PTFE tape or a gas-tight compound. To minimise the risk of a fire or explosion if a leak should occur, the piping must be run well up the sides of the boat, clear of any electrical wiring or heat sources. A length of flexible hose will be required at the gas bottle and the cooker to permit movement; this should be flameproof, but not natural rubber, as it is attacked by the gas.

In theory, the gas ought to be switched off at the bottle when not in use; in practice, though, this is not always done, and so a shut-off valve should be fitted where the piping enters the cabin. It is also recommended that each burner has a flame failure device to cut off the gas supply if the flame is blown out; this is essential on items such as fridges and water heaters, which operate unattended and use a pilot light. Where several appliances are fitted, each one should have its own shut-off valve.

Chapter 8

The Electrical System

Electricity Afloat

Water and electricity do not mix. This fact must always be borne in mind when dealing with any electrical equipment on board a yacht. There are three routes by which water can come into contact with electrical equipment. Firstly, there is direct immersion. This is only likely to occur in the bilge, and can be avoided by siting all wiring and equipment well up the sides of the hull, unless specifically designed to withstand immersion.

Secondly, there is the problem of spray and rain. Obviously, any equipment sited on deck will get wet from time to time; equipment sited close to hatches may also be vulnerable. Therefore all sockets and equipment used on deck must be waterproof, and preferably sited in a sheltered position.

Finally, the inevitable fluctuations in temperature and humidity result in the formation of condensation. This results in corrosion, and may create short circuits; ultimately it is bound to cause the failure of the equipment. To prevent condensation, all electrical equipment should be contained in a waterproof housing; also, dissimilar metals should be avoided whenever possible, to prevent bimetallic corrosion.

Water is not the only source of electrical problems. If the electrical fabric is not properly installed and maintained, small currents may leak out and run to earth via metal hull fittings. This can cause electrolysis at quite an alarming rate.

Sparks from switches and motors present a hazard if there has been a build-up of petrol fumes, hydrogen, or butane gas. Thus spark-proof equipment must be used in areas such as the petrol tank, engine compartment, battery and gas bottle stowage areas. Also, a gas detector should be fitted, so that the presence of any inflammable gas can be detected long before it has reached a dangerous concentration.

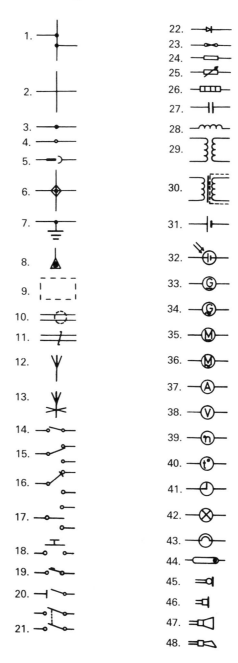

Fig. 8.1. Electrical symbols. 1, Wiring connection. 2, Wires crossing. 3, Permanent connection. 4, Readily separable connection. 5, Plug and socket. 6, Junction box. 7, Earth. 8, Sacrificial anode. 9, Screening. 10, Screened cables. 11, Wires twisted together. 12, Aerial. 13, Direction finding aerial. 14, Single pole on/off switch. 15, Break before make changeover switch. 16, Make before

The Circuit Diagram

Figure 8.1 shows some of the commonest electrical wiring symbols, and Fig. 8.2 shows a typical circuit diagram for a yacht. Note that a two wire system is used; an earth return will cause extensive corrosion below the waterline if a short circuit occurs. A separate supply circuit is used for each main system, such as interior lights, navigation lights, sailing instruments, radio equipment, and refrigerator; where necessary, the supply circuit is subdivided to supply each piece of equipment.

Unless fitted with a voltage regulator, electronic equipment should not be connected in parallel with equipment that is intermittently switched on and off. This will cause fluctuations in the voltage, and so may interfere with the performance of electronic circuits.

In most cases a 12-volt system is perfectly adequate; in larger vessels, though, a 24-volt system may be used (or 32-volt in the USA). This extends the useful life of the batteries, and allows lighter cables and switches to be used. Against this the weight of the batteries is considerably increased, along with the stowage space required. There is a much wider range of 12-volt appliances on the market, though many of the more powerful radio and radar sets require the higher voltage system.

Unless the engine can be hand started, separate engine start and supply batteries ought to be installed. This ensures that the engine can be started even if the supply battery is flat. Yachts carrying a large amount of electrical equipment may carry three banks of batteries, separating the navigation and lighting circuits.

Each bank of batteries needs to be fitted with an isolation switch, so that the batteries can be disconnected when the boat is left unattended, or when work is being carried out on the electrical system. Unless the isolation switch incorporates advanced field switching for the alternator, the batteries must not be isolated whilst the engine is running, as this will result in damage to the alternator rectifier diodes.

If more than one bank of batteries is fitted, a battery changeover switch is required. This enables either battery, or both batteries in parallel, to be used for starting the engine. It can also be used to determine which batteries are charged, unless this is being done automatically by blocking diodes.

Each supply circuit, and each item of equipment, needs to have its own switch. Clearly, if a circuit contains only one piece of equipment, and that equipment carries its own switch, no separate switch is required; the only exception to this is if

---

break changeover switch. 17, Two way contact with off position. 18, Push-button non locking switch. 19, Circuit breaker. 20, Isolation switch. 21, Double pole on/off switch. 22, Rectifier (permits flow from left to right). 23, Fuse. 24, Resistor. 25, Variable resistor (or rheostat). 26, Heater. 27, Capacitor. 28, Inductor. 29, Transformer. 30, Screened transformer. 31, Battery (left side +ve). 32, Solar cell. 33, d.c. generator. 34, a.c. generator. 35, d.c. motor. 36, a.c. motor. 37, Ammeter. 38, Voltmeter. 39, Tachometer. 40, Thermometer. 41, Clock. 42, Indicator lamp. 43, Filament lamp. 44, Fluorescent lamp. 45, Microphone. 46, Earphone. 47, Loudspeaker. 48, Horn.

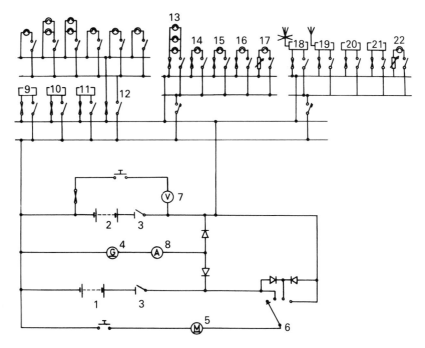

Fig. 8.2. A typical circuit diagram. Key: 1, Engine start battery. 2, Service battery. 3, Battery isolation switch. 4, 25 A alternator. 5, Engine starter motor. 6, Battery changeover switch. 7, Battery state meter. 8, Ammeter (30-0-30 A). 9, Refrigerator. 10, Water pressure pump. 11, Gas detector. 12, Interior lights. 13, Sidelights and sternlight. 14, Masthead light. 15, Anchor light. 16, Deck light. 17, Compass light. 18, Radio direction finder. 19, VHF radio. 20, Echo sounder. 21, Sailing instruments. 22, Instruments light.

the switch is automatic, in which case an additional manual switch should be fitted. Each switch must be rated to take the maximum possible current in the circuit that it controls.

In most cases, single pole switches (i.e. switches fitted in only one of the supply wires) are perfectly adequate. In metal hulls, though, double pole switches (i.e. switches that make or break contact in both the positive and the negative supply wires simultaneously) are to be preferred for the battery isolation switches and for each of the primary supply circuits, as the conductivity of the hull increases the risk of a short circuit.

Each distribution circuit needs to be protected by a fuse, though once again metal hulls need the additional protection of a fuse in both the negative and the positive wires. The fuse should be rated to blow at a current no more than 50% higher than the maximum current of the circuit it protects.

A circuit breaker is a switch that is designed to turn itself off automatically whenever the rated current is exceeded. They prevent anybody from 'curing' the fault in the circuit by fitting a larger fuse, and cannot be reset until the fault is corrected. They also make it immediately obvious which circuit is at fault, and there is no need to carry a set of spare fuses on board.

Wiring

The size of cable is determined by the maximum current that it will carry, and by the voltage drop that occurs along its length.

If the current flowing in a wire is too great, the wire will heat up, melt the insulation, and eventually blow like a fuse. Thus the higher the melting point of the insulation, the greater the current that the wire can carry. Figure 8.3 shows the cross-sectional area required to carry a given current for some of the insulation materials available. Obviously any fuse in the circuit must be rated to blow at a current below the capacity of the wiring in the circuit it protects.

The voltage drop between the battery and the equipment should not exceed 0.9 volts for a 12-volt system, 1.8 volts for a 24-volt system, or 2.4 volts for a 32-volt system. It is calculated by:

$$\text{Voltage drop } (mV) = VDF \times \text{cable length (ft)} \times \text{current (amps)} \ (1000 \, mV = 1V)$$

The current should be taken as the maximum that can flow in the circuit. *VDF* is the voltage drop factor; Fig. 8.4 gives a graph of the voltage drop factor against the cross-sectional area of the wire.

The wires may be run inside conduit, or may be supported at regular intervals by clamps. Conduit is essential to protect wires inside the mast from chafe, and should also be used in inaccessible areas, such as behind fuel tanks. It allows easy addition or replacement of wires, and provides a high degree of protection. Metal conduits must be earthed to protect against earth faults, and to prevent radiation of interference.

If the wire is supported by clamps, these should not be spaced at intervals greater than 15 inches. Additional clamps will be needed where the cable run changes direction, or where it passes through a bulkhead. A rubber bush will also be required where the wire passes through a bulkhead, to prevent chafing.

All wiring should be run out and back along the same side of the vessel, otherwise a magnetic field will be set up which may affect the compass and radio direction finder. It is for this reason that a ring main is not used.

Batteries

The capacity of a battery can be expressed in several ways but the most usual form is in amp hours. This is the product of the current that is drawn from the battery, and the time for which that current can be sustained. For lead/acid batteries, the amp hour rate is quoted on the basis that the battery will take 10 hours to discharge; for alkaline batteries a period of 5 hours is used, except for the high

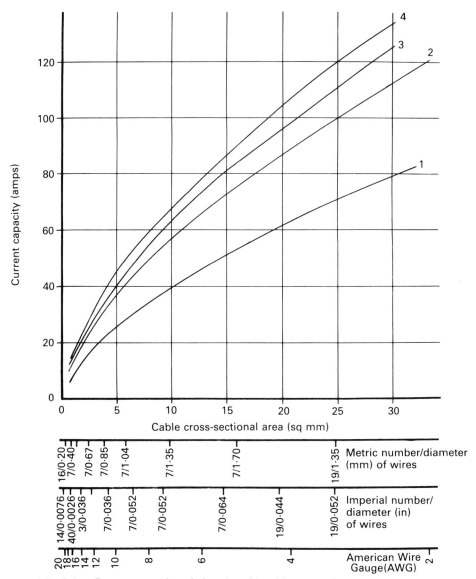

Fig. 8.3. Current capacity of electric cables (single core). For two core cables reduce the capacity by 15%. Key: 1, General purpose rubber and PVC insulation. 2, Heat-resistant PVC insulation. 3, Butyl rubber insulation. 4, Ethylene propylene rubber and cross-linked polyethylene insulation.

performance type which work on a 2 hour rate. If a higher current is drawn, the capacity will be less than that quoted, and vice versa.

To determine the capacity required for the service battery, the interval between charging periods must first be decided upon. Then the period of operation between charging periods must be estimated for each piece of equipment, and multiplied by the current drawn by the equipment. This gives the number of amp

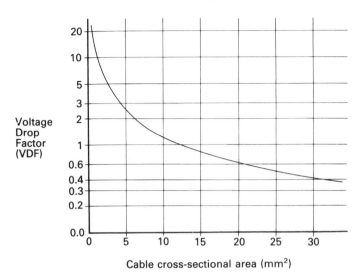

Fig. 8.4. Voltage drop factor of electric cables.

Petrol Engine	Battery capacity (AH)
Up to 1500 cc	40
1500–2000 cc	50
2000–4000 cc	60
Diesel Engine	
Up to 2000 cc	70
2000–3500 cc	100
3500–5000 cc	125

Fig. 8.5. Engine start battery capacity requirements.

hours drawn by each piece of equipment; the battery capacity is found by summing up the power consumption of each item and adding on 20% to allow for variations in the load. If wind, water or solar powered generators are carried, the battery capacity can be reduced by their estimated output between charging periods.

For the start battery, the capacity can be found by reference to Fig. 8.5. However, most owners have both start and service batteries of the same capacity, as regular rotation of the batteries will prolong their life span.

Virtually all yachts use lead/acid batteries, as these are both cheap and compact. The conventional unsealed type needs periodic topping up with distilled water, and loses its charge at a rate of about 1% a day. The sealed type of battery, although more expensive, is totally maintenance-free, has a negligible rate of charge loss, and is considerably smaller and lighter.

The voltage of the battery will vary from about 13.5 volts at full charge, down to 10.8 volts at full discharge. The battery should never be used if the voltage drops below this point, as permanent damage to the plates will occur, reducing the efficiency of the battery.

A few yachts are fitted with alkaline nickel-cadmium batteries, though many of their advantages are offered by sealed lead/acid batteries at considerably lower cost. They offer a very long life span, some four times greater than a conventional lead/acid battery, a negligible rate of charge loss, and a more rapid rate of charging. On the other hand they are about twice as bulky as lead/acid batteries, and considerably more expensive. The standard type should be used for supply circuits, but the high performance variety is necessary for engine starting.

An ammeter and a voltmeter should be used to monitor the battery. The ammeter measures the current drawn by the supply circuit, and the voltmeter measures the voltage of the battery. One of the types using an expanded scale of 8–16 volts is to be preferred, often called a battery state indicator. An on/off switch should be fitted, to avoid the small but unnecessary power drain, and the meter should be protected by a fuse.

Batteries are heavy, and so should be positioned where access for removal and maintenance is good; they should also be positioned centrally in the yacht, as low down as possible, whilst remaining clear of the bilge water. The start battery must be sited close to the engine, to minimise power losses in the leads to the starter motor (a starter motor for a 2 litre diesel engine may draw up to 75 amps); however, hot spots should be avoided, as these will reduce the life of the battery.

The battery box must be designed to hold the batteries securely, even in the event of a knockdown. It should be lined with fibreglass, to prevent damage from any spilled electrolyte. If the battery box is situated inside another compartment, a lid should be fitted to prevent the terminals from being shorted out by loose equipment.

When the battery is being charged, hydrogen gas is emitted. As hydrogen forms an explosive mixture with the air, good ventilation is essential. Hydrogen is lighter than air, and so the inlet should be low down, and the outlet at the highest point in the compartment. Obviously, any electrical equipment in the battery compartment must be vapour tight, to prevent sparks igniting the hydrogen.

Battery Charging

With the ever-increasing amount of electrical and electronic equipment fitted to yachts, it is essential that an efficient means of battery charging is provided. Every engine, with the exception of most small outboard motors, carries an alternator for this purpose; there are also a variety of alternative charging systems that may be carried.

The current required to charge the batteries can be determined from the following formula:

$$\text{Charging current} = \frac{\text{battery capacity } (AH) \times 1.4}{\text{charging time}} + \text{mean current load}$$

The mean current load is found by dividing the capacity of the service battery by the time interval between charging periods. A charging time of 10 hours is recommended for lead/acid batteries. Although shorter times can be used, they may damage the battery by overheating.

In installations using two or more banks of batteries or charging devices, it is necessary to prevent current flowing from a fully charged to a discharged battery, or from an operational charging device to one which is switched off. In most cases the best way of achieving this is to use blocking diodes. These permit current to flow in the arrowed direction of their symbol, but not in the opposite direction, and so can provide automatic protection.

The only disadvantage of blocking diodes is that each diode causes a voltage drop of about 0.7 volts. Some alternator regulators allow for this by providing low, medium or high voltage outputs. The energy released by the drop in voltage is dissipated as heat, and so the blocking diode must be sited where it has a reasonable air supply. Alternators and battery chargers incorporate blocking diodes in their voltage regulators, and so only solar cells and dynamos need to be protected with separate diodes.

The use of blocking diodes ensures that each battery is charged in accordance with its needs; if it is desired to charge only one bank of batteries, the other banks must be isolated, unless the charging is controlled by a changeover switch.

The Engine's Alternator

Most yachts rely on the engine's alternator for battery charging, and this suggests that an alternator with a large output should be fitted to provide rapid battery charging.

As can be seen in Fig. 8.6, the output of an alternator increases with its speed up to about 5000 r.p.m. and then is virtually constant right up to the maximum operating speed, usually between 10 000 and 15 000 r.p.m. Thus the sizes of the drive pulleys should be chosen so that the alternator is giving maximum power at the engine's tickover speed, yet does not exceed the maximum operating speed when the engine is operating at full speed.

Propeller-driven Alternators

Boats over about 30 feet in length travel sufficiently fast to drive an alternator off the freely-spinning propeller. Lucas have developed an alternator specially for this arrangement that starts charging at about 3 knots, and provides a maximum output of 12 amps.

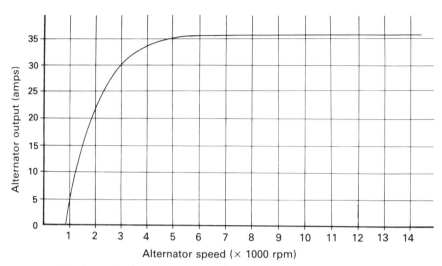

Fig. 8.6. Performance curve of Lucas 17ACR"M" alternator.

As far as performance is concerned, the drawback to this arrangement is that the drag of the propeller is increased, reducing the speed of the boat by between 1% and 5%. A large propeller, with large blade area, will produce more power and a lower cut-in speed for the alternator, but will also increase the drag penalty, even when the batteries are not being charged.

The alternator is driven by a belt drive off the propeller shaft, with the larger pulley on the propeller shaft, giving a step-up ratio of between 4:1 and 6:1. It is important to ensure that the maximum permitted alternator speed is not exceeded; if it is driven too fast, a variable pitch propeller, a smaller propeller, or a clutch must be fitted.

The advantage of a variable pitch propeller is that a large pitch can be used at low speeds to give an earlier cut-in of the alternator, whilst at high speeds the pitch can be reduced to prevent the alternator speed from becoming excessive. When the alternator is not being used, the blades can be feathered to minimise the drag.

The alternator is usually mounted close to the gearbox; however, the gearbox manufacturer should be consulted to ensure that this will not damage the gearbox. Some units, especially the hydraulic types, are not able to free-wheel without damage; in this case, a sailing clutch should be fitted. Others may not be able to withstand the additional loads transmitted by the propeller shaft; in this case, the alternator will have to be sited away from the gearbox, and an intermediate bearing will need to be fitted to prevent the propeller shaft from bending.

Water-driven Generators

As can be gathered from the previous section, the installation of a propeller-driven alternator can be quite a complex operation; in existing boats it may be

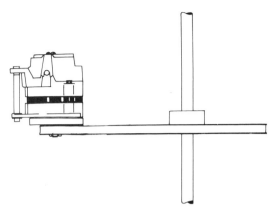

Fig. 8.7 An alternator driven off the propeller shaft. Note the large drive wheel required on the shaft to give the correct drive ratio. (*Courtesy Lucas Marine.*)

impossible, due to insufficient clearance for the drive pulley, which will be between 10 and 15 inches in diameter. Thus several self-contained water-driven generators have appeared on the market, designed to fit onto the stern of the yacht.

Although the output of these units is generally less than could be achieved with a propeller-driven unit, they can be taken out of the water when not in use, thus minimising the drag penalty. All of the units have integral voltage regulators, and so are very easy to install.

The most powerful type of unit resembles a small outboard motor, with the engine being replaced by the alternator. This cuts in at about 1.5 knots, producing ¼ amp; at speeds in excess of 5.5 knots the output is about 10 amps. The drag results in a speed reduction of about 3% in a 35-foot boat.

The other variety consists of an impeller towed on a length of braided line, connected to an alternator mounted on the toe-rail or pushpit. Although very compact, the output of this type is generally limited to about 4 amps. It may be combined with a wind generator, enabling the batteries to be charged whilst in harbour as well as when sailing.

Wind-driven Generators

The great advantage of a wind-driven generator is that the batteries will be charged day and night, in harbour and at sea, except in calm weather or on a run, when there may be insufficient wind to turn the windmill. Also, the drag penalty upwind is considerably less than a water-driven generator, and downwind it will help to propel the yacht.

There are several units on the market, with a wide range in performance; for example, one 17-inch diameter unit produces an average charge rate of 0.25

Fig. 8.8. A wind-driven generator. The large boss can be connected to a trailing impeller for use in light airs.

amps, whilst a 26-inch unit produces 2.5 amps. In general, larger units should give a higher output, but some designs are very inefficient due to poor aerodynamic design; in a 10 knot wind, a well-designed unit should have an output close to that given by:

$$\text{Current (amps)} = 0.0038d^2 \text{ (at twelve volts)}$$

where d is the diameter of the windmill in inches. Most of the commercially available units have an output of less than 5 amps.

Solar Cells

Solar cells are ideal for racing yachts, as they create no extra drag; however, they are relatively expensive for their power output, and are dependent on a good supply of light (though not necessarily sunlight) to generate electricity.

Once the intensity of the light falling upon the cell exceeds a certain relatively low level, electricity is generated. The voltage is virtually independent of the lighting conditions, but the current rises in direct proportion to the light intensity. As each cell produces about 0.6 volts, a number of cells (at least twenty) need to

Fig. 8.9. Solar panels. These should be mounted flat on the deck, so that they catch the sun at all times. (*Courtesy Mars Marine Systems.*)

be connected into a panel to provide a 12-volt supply.

At night, or in low light conditions, the voltage will drop below the battery voltage, and the battery will slowly discharge through the solar cells. This can be prevented by fitting a blocking diode, or a manual on/off switch; a blocking diode provides automatic control, but the voltage drop may absorb a considerable amount of the power in smaller installations.

The output of a panel is generally given in watts (watts = volts × amps), and values may range from 2 to 36 watts. To give some idea of what this means in practice, a 10 watt panel will produce about 15.7 amp hours per week in southern England, 23 Ah/week in the Mediterranean, and 29 Ah/week in the Caribbean.

Mains Electricity

Mains electricity presents few problems on board a yacht, and it enables a full range of domestic appliances and power tools to be used. The power supply can come from a d.c./a.c. inverter, a shore line, or an on-board generator.

If mains electricity is only required for an electric razor and other low power devices, it is best supplied by an inverter. This converts the d.c. battery supply to a 110 volt or 240 volt a.c. supply. Modern solid-state inverters have a conversion efficiency of about 85%, so relatively little power is lost.

On yachts making extensive use of mains appliances a generator may be used at sea, and a shore line in marinas. A battery charger enables the batteries to be charged without running the main engine.

Both the frequency and the voltage of mains electricity varies from one part of the world to another. Europe, Africa and Oceania use 220/240 volts at 50 Hz, whilst the Americas, the Middle and Near East use 115 volts at 60 Hz, and South East Asia uses 115 volts at 50 Hz. The frequency will affect the running speed of motors, but will not affect resistive loads such as heaters. However, all equipment must be run at the correct voltage.

All mains equipment must be either double insulated or properly earthed. If a generator is being used, the earth should be connected to a sacrificial anode below the waterline.

Generators

A 10 horsepower main engine would typically be fitted with a 30 W alternator; a 2 horsepower generator would give the same electrical output, whilst a 10 horsepower generator would supply a hefty 4 kW (1 kW = 1000 W). This means that vessels requiring a large amount of power can drastically cut their fuel consumption and engine running times by fitting a generator, as well as having the advantages of a mains supply on board.

A generator is usually rated in volt-amperes (VA). This is simply the product of the maximum current and the maximum voltage produced by the machine. However, the voltage and current do not necessarily reach their maximum values at the same time, and this reduces the available power. The extent to which the voltage and current are in phase is measured by the power factor. The actual usable power (in watts) is found by multiplying the output in volt-amperes by the power factor.

The cheapest form of generator is the portable petrol unit. This is both compact and cheap, and incurs no installation costs. Depending on size, up to 4 kW may be produced. Many of these sets incorporate a voltage regulator, providing 6 volts, 12 volts, or 24 volts d.c. in addition to a mains supply.

One of the drawbacks of this type of generator is that it must be used on deck, to avoid a build-up of exhaust fumes. As it is not waterproof, it must be protected from rain and spray, and this may severely limit its usefulness. Also, fuel costs can be up to twice as high as a comparable diesel unit, and the small fuel tank means that there is a fire risk whenever it is refilled at sea.

For larger yachts, a permanently installed diesel generator is a better option, though it is not available with outputs below about 3 kW. The generator is installed in much the same way as any other engine, and is often installed in the same compartment as the propulsive machinery. However, as the engine and alternator form a self-contained unit, they can be very flexibly mounted, minimising noise and vibration levels.

The generator can be connected to appliances in such a way that it will start up automatically as soon as the appliance is switched on, and shut down when it is switched off. This is particularly useful for high power devices that are only run intermittently, such as deep freezes and MF/HF radio transmitters. However, it should be possible to power all essential equipment, and all equipment likely to be used at night, by the d.c. supply. This provides a safeguard against failure of the generator, and prevents the crew from being disturbed by the generator starting up in the middle of the night.

Battery Chargers

A battery charger is necessary if a generator is fitted (except in the case of a portable generator with an integral voltage regulator), and is also very useful if the boat is going to spend a fair amount of time in marinas.

In its most basic form, a battery charger consists of a transformer to produce a 12 V supply, and a rectifier to convert the current from a.c. to d.c. This is perfectly satisfactory if the batteries are disconnected from the yacht's electrical system before charging, and are watched to prevent over-charging. However, for marine use two additional facilities are desirable.

Fig. 8.10. A 4AC1W generator, producing 3.2 kW, and based on a 6.5 bhp engine. (*Courtesy G & M Power Plant.*)

The main requirement is that the set should have automatic voltage regulation. This does two things: firstly, it monitors the state of charge of the batteries, and when about 80% charged it reduces the charge rate to a trickle charge, thus minimising gassing and preventing over-charging; secondly, it adjusts the charging current so that the charger is supplying enough current both to charge the batteries, and to meet the needs of any equipment in use.

An automatic overload cut-out is also desirable, as this will prevent the charger from being damaged by trying to supply too high a current, as may be the case when trying to start the engine with the battery charger in operation, or if there is a short circuit somewhere.

Interference Suppression

Interference consists of electro-magnetic waves, generated from equipment on board the vessel, that are picked up by, and interfere with the operation of, other items of electronic equipment. There are many possible sources of interference; some of the more common ones are alternators and their voltage regulators, fluorescent lights, electric motors and pumps, switches, and the ignition system of petrol engines.

If an item is inadequately suppressed, there are three routes by which the interference may be transmitted to other equipment. Firstly, the electrical wiring, and in some cases the metal components of the boat, will conduct the interference directly from the source to the equipment. Secondly, the wiring will act as an aerial, and radiate the interference. It may be absorbed and re-radiated several times by the rigging, but will eventually be picked up by the equipment. Finally, if two wires are placed close together, the magnetic field created by the current flowing in one wire may be large enough to induce interference in the other. This is only likely to occur in high-powered equipment.

Although it is not always possible to eliminate interference entirely, the aim should be to reduce it to a level at which it does not affect the operation of any piece of equipment. Radio equipment, especially the radio direction finder, is clearly prone to interference; however, radio navigation equipment, radar, echo sounders and electronic logs may also be affected.

There are four main methods used to minimise interference. Firstly, all equipment should be carefully sited away from sources of interference; for example, aerials are best sited at the masthead or the transom, and all equipment should be kept well clear of petrol engines. This will reduce the chances of picking up radiated interference.

Secondly, all major metal items on board should be bonded together and earthed; this establishes a common potential throughout the vessel, and prevents the re-radiation of interference. The bonding wires should have a cross-sectional area of at least 0.02 square inches (12.5 mm^2); they may be incorporated with the corrosion protection system.

Thirdly, filtering, by the use of capacitors and inductors, prevents interference from travelling along the wiring. Thus the filters should be placed as close to the source of interference as possible, and any wiring between the interference source and the filter should be screened.

Finally, screening consists of placing equipment or wiring inside an earthed metal container, preventing the radiation of interference. It is sometimes necessary for equipment to be screened where wires pass close to sensitive items. Obviously, all wires will need to be fitted with filters at the point where they leave the case, to prevent their transmitting the interference. At times it may be necessary to screen a length of wire; this can be achieved by using special screened cable, or by running the wire inside a length of copper pipe. In both cases, the screening must be earthed at approximately 18 inch intervals.

Chapter 9

Instrumentation

Sailing and Navigation Instruments

Many instruments may be powered either from the boat's electrical system, or from internal batteries. Use of the boat's supply is to be preferred, as batteries are an expensive power source, and there may be problems in obtaining replacements in remote areas. Some indication of the current consumption is given for each instrument discussed here (at 12 volts unless indicated otherwise); this excludes any current required for illumination.

The data may be displayed in either digital or analogue (dial or meter) format. Unfortunately, there is an increasing trend towards digital display, regardless of whether or not it is the most appropriate form. With the possible exception of chart table displays, an analogue display is always to be preferred for directional information. The case is not so clear cut when displaying speed or depth; digital displays are capable of displaying data with greater accuracy, but in some cases the accuracy displayed may exceed that of the measuring equipment. Also, digital displays are often difficult to read in strong sunlight. Analogue displays are easier to read at a glance or from a distance, and a change in the reading is more likely to catch the eye than with a digital display.

Illumination is essential for night sailing; it may be in the form of a small light bulb, or a luminous display. Luminous displays require no power supply, but after about ten years will become too dim for use. A light bulb will draw about 150 mA per display; a diffuse red light will have the least harmful effect on night vision, and a dimmer is useful to adjust the brightness.

As most deck instruments are set into a bulkhead with one face on deck and the other inside the yacht, conditions are ideal for condensation forming on the inside. Thus it is imperative for the unit to be fully waterproof if a long working life is to be expected.

The compass

The compass needs to be gimballed to allow for the pitching and heeling of the vessel. Traditionally this was achieved by means of external gimbals, but nowadays most compasses are gimballed internally, by mounting the card inside a spherical compass bowl. With this arrangement the compass is much more compact, and may be set into a bulkhead or the deck. If mounted on a vertical surface, a card that can be read from both the edge and above is to be preferred for ease of reading.

External gimballing is necessary for grid compasses, which are very easy to steer by. The face of the compass has a rotating bezel mounted over it, with the perimeter graduated in degrees and a pointer over the face. The inscribed bezel is rotated to the compass course, and when on course the pointer will be aligned with the north-south axis of the compass card, which is marked boldly. Thus parallax is eliminated, and all the helm has to do is keep the card aligned to the bezel. The drawback is that the compass can only be read from above, which can make siting the compass a problem.

All magnetic compasses work by having a magnet mounted underneath the compass card, which is attracted towards the earth's magnetic poles. However, electronic compasses are also available, offering some advantages.

The Magnesyn system is based on a magnetic compass, but the magnetic field of the compass's magnet is sensed by a flux gate (a net of coils) which may be designed into the compass, or may be fitted to an existing magnetic compass. All magnetic compasses suffer from swirl and eddy currents in the damping fluid when subjected to rapid motion, and so this type of compass is best sited amidships, where the vessel's motion is least.

A flux gate can be used to measure the earth's magnetic field directly, and this system offers the greatest accuracy. As there are no moving parts apart from the gimballing, and no damping fluid, the compass is almost totally unaffected by motion. This is particularly useful on steel or ferro-cement boats, as it enables the compass to be mounted well up the mast, where deviation will be minimal.

In addition to enabling the compass to be sited where deviation is low, most electronic compasses are capable of driving several repeaters, so compass displays may be mounted in several places with only the sensor unit needing correction. An increasingly common reason for fitting an electronic compass is to interface it with other electronic navigation equipment. In all cases, though, a properly corrected magnetic compass should always be fitted to guard against power failure. The power consumption is about 150 mA for a modern electronic compass, though older models may consume considerably more power.

The log

The simplest types of log operate on purely mechanical principles, a rotator in the water turning the register. The best known type consists of a rotator trailed on a thin line which is connected to a register clamped on the transom. As the length of the log line (in feet) needs to be about ten times the maximum speed of the boat it is pretty long, and must be handed whenever entering harbour or going astern; it also tends to pick up seaweed, or occasionally be eaten by fish. When running in big seas the log over-reads, as it follows the contours of the waves, whilst at speeds below about 2 knots the force produced by the rotator is insufficient to overcome the friction in the system.

The VDO Sumlog works on similar lines, but uses an impeller mounted through the hull, connected to the recording head by a flexible transmission cable. This overcomes the drawbacks of a trailed rotator, and gives greater freedom in siting the recording head, but otherwise is identical to a trailed log.

Most yachts are now fitted with an electronic log, in which a paddle wheel, impeller or electro-magnetic sensor sends an electronic signal to one or more display units. The log will draw only about 0.1 or 0.2 mA.

The paddle wheel type is unlikely to be fouled by weed, but some accuracy is lost as it operates within the boundary layer. The impeller is intended to operate clear of the boundary layer, but is more prone to being damaged or picking up weed, though most models incorporate a weed deflector to provide some degree of protection.

The sensor used by electro-magentic logs contains an electric coil which generates a magnetic field, and two electrodes mounted in line fore and aft. As the water flows past the electrodes a voltage is induced between them, directly proportional to the speed of the water. Because the sensor is virtually flush with the hull it is unlikely to pick up weed or be damaged, and offers minimal drag; however, it is operating within the boundary layer, and accuracy is highly dependent upon the electrodes being clean and properly aligned with the water flow.

Obviously, the hull unit must be positioned so that it is permanently immersed, with an undisturbed flow of water over it. This is best achieved by placing it on the centreline, about one third of the waterline length aft of the stem; if this is not possible, two transducers should be fitted, positioned slightly further aft and about 12 or 15 inches off the centreline. A gravity switch is then used to select the leeward unit automatically. It is essential that the hull unit can be withdrawn, and the skin fitting sealed by a blanking cap, for cleaning and servicing.

The distance is of necessity displayed in digital form, but the speed may be in either digital or analogue form. To detect small changes in boat speed with an analogue display, an amplified water speed (or trim) display is also required, and this has to be zeroed to suit the boat's speed.

As the water flow conditions vary from one boat to another, the chances are that the log will need to be calibrated, and most manufacturers provide some

Fig. 9.1. A log transducer unit. This protrudes from the hull just far enough to get out of the worst of the boundary layer, and so offers more accurate results than flush-mounted paddle wheel transducers. (*Courtesy Brookes & Gatehouse.*)

means of adjustment. When properly set up in calm conditions errors will be less than 1½% for distance, and 3% for speed. However, in bad weather the errors may well be doubled.

The echo sounder

An echo sounder operates by sending an ultrasonic signal towards the sea bed, and recording the time lapse between the emission of the pulse and the reception of its echo. As the speed of sound in water is known, the time taken by the signal can easily be converted into a depth.

The most important factor in choosing an echo sounder is the power of the transducer, with the maximum attainable depth varying with the square root of the power available, and powers ranging from 50 – 150 watts. Obviously, no prediction can be made as to the actual attainable depth, as it depends so much on the nature of the bottom, a hard sea bed reflecting a much stronger signal than a soft one.

To ensure good performance, attention must be paid to the siting of the transducer. It must not be close to the log transducer, to avoid interference; it must be far enough aft to prevent air bubbles passing over it and causing spurious signals, and it must be well clear of the keel, which will mask part of the beam and cause false readings. In practice, this means siting it about 35–45% of the waterline length aft of the stem, and also in a position such that a cone making an angle of 30° with the axis of the transducer clears the keel.

One vertical transducer is perfectly satisfactory on multihulls, but monohulls need to allow for heel by having two transducers with a gravity changeover switch. They should be positioned about 15 inches off the centreline, and angled outwards by about 12°. Where the transducer emerges from the hull a fairing block is required, both for protection and to prevent air bubbles being formed. As with the log unit, the transducer should be retractable, and a blanking cap should be attached to the skin fitting.

As fibreglass is virtually transparent to the echo sounder's signal, many boats have the transducer mounted internally. This is satisfactory on hulls up to about 1 inch thick, and means one less hole below the waterline. However, some power will inevitably be lost, and the return signal will be woollier. The transducer is mounted inside a tube bonded to the hull, which is filled with castor oil to ensure a good acoustical connection.

The depth may be displayed by a rotating flasher, a meter, or a digital display; recording paper and cathode ray tube displays are also available, but these are considerably more expensive, and offer no significant advantage to the yachtsman.

The rotating flasher display consists of a rotating arm with a light emitting diode mounted on the end. The diode lights up at the zero point when the signal is

Fig. 9.2. A rotating flasher echo sounder, with a digital repeater for the cockpit. (*Courtesy Seafarer Navigation International Ltd.*)

transmitted, and again when the echo is received, the depth being read off a scale on the perimeter. The great advantage of this system is that some indication of the nature of the bottom can be had by turning up the gain control. A hard bottom will give a single, sharp echo, whilst a soft bottom will give a broad band of weak echoes. Unfortunately it is difficult to read in bright light, and so is best used by the chart table in conjunction with a meter display on deck.

Meter and digital displays both suffer from the same problem: they are only capable of displaying the depth given by the strongest echo. This means that if a rock bottom is covered by a sandbank, the depth displayed will be that of the rock, until the sand is thick enough to return a stronger signal; this could be detected on a rotating flasher display by increasing the gain.

Wind instruments

Wind speed and direction instruments consist of a combined wind vane and anemometer at the masthead, connected via a control box to three displays. The wind speed display shows speeds up to about 60 knots, with analogue displays often having an expanded scale at the lower end where changes in windspeed are more critical. The wind direction is displayed on a 360° meter for general use, with

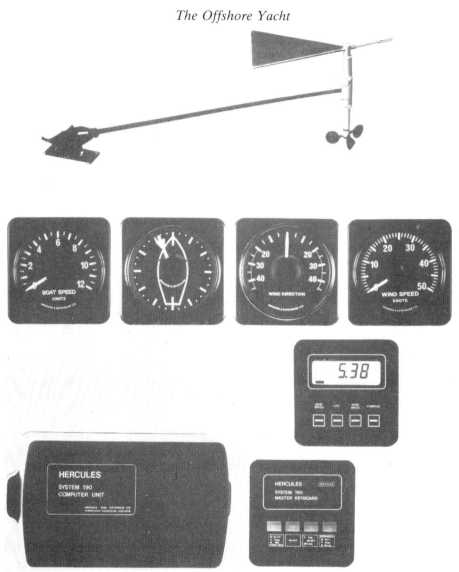

Fig. 9.3. A masthead wind speed and direction unit, and a selection of digital and analogue displays. The Hercules computer unit provides simple functions such as speed made good to windward, and a comparison of actual boat speed against that of a hypothetical boat with a similar rating. (*Courtesy Brooks & Gatehouse Ltd.*)

an optional amplified wind direction, or trim, display for use when close hauled and running; this uses an amplified scale to show the wind direction up to about 50° each side of the centreline. Power consumption is low, at about 100 mA.

The masthead unit must be well damped against the violet motions of the masthead, yet sensitive enough to detect small changes in the wind. There must be a method of adjusting the mounting arm so that it is aligned exactly along the centreline if accurate wind direction readings are to be obtained.

Fig. 9.4. On board computers are becoming increasingly powerful. Those that are interfaced with the instruments are restricted to the chart table, but others, like Tacticalc shown here, are designed for use on the weather rail. Although pocket sized, this computer contains a program just as powerful as that carried within many desk top computers.

Microcomputers

Computers were first used on a one-off basis for analysing the performance of 12-metres, but some systems are now appearing on the open market. These vary from compact pocket computers able to be used on deck, such as Tacticalc, right through to large microcomputers with disc drives and a printer. The most important feature is the program, though, not the computer. Fairly simple programs can analyse the current sailing situation, but much more important is the ability to predict what will happen on future legs, and a means of logging the boat's performance to provide tuning data.

Radio Navigation

The development of microchip technology has resulted in a marked reduction in the price, power consumption, and bulk of radio navigation systems; thus Decca, Loran, Omega and Satnav are now becoming increasingly common on yachts.

Reliability is paramount, and so most sets incorporate a self-test facility to detect, and sometimes diagnose, faults that may occur. Some incorporate a rechargeable battery to protect against short-term power failures, and it may also power the system's memory bank when the equipment is switched off, allowing data to be stored for periods of up to about one month; this is most useful if the equipment is used on an intermittent basis, or if the same data is entered each time the set is switched on.

In addition to providing a fix, Satnav, Decca and Loran systems may offer waypoint navigation facilities. A waypoint is simply a point lying on the boat's course; it may or may not be a turning point. Once the intended course has been plotted on the chart, a series of waypoints are selected and entered into the navigation system; it will now act as a navigational computer, and will be able to supply the rhumb line course and distance to the next waypoint, and the course and speed made good.

Other data available may include the great circle course and distance to the next waypoint, the estimated time of arrival, and the distance and ETA to the final waypoint; it may also sound an alarm when a waypoint is reached. Satnav can also compare the DR course with the last two fixes, enabling the set and rate of any tide, current or leeway to be obtained.

Radio direction finders

Radio direction finders utilise a series of shore-based radio beacons; these broadcast a morse identification signal, followed by a continuous tone, in the 283.5–415 kHz band. In areas where there are a large number of beacons, up to six may use the same fréquency, transmitting in sequence. The RDF set consists of a directional aerial coupled to a sensitive receiver, and it finds the bearing of the beacon either by rotating the aerial to find the null point at which the signal strength is a minimum, or by comparing the signal strengths detected in a pair of mutually perpendicular aerials, known as a Bellini-Tosi loop.

RDF equipment is of great assistance when sailing inshore, having errors of less than 3° by day, assuming that the set is properly installed and set up. When sailing offshore, though, the equipment is of less use, as even the most powerful beacons are restricted to a range of about 200 miles.

Errors are considerably greater at night, as part of the signal is received as a sky wave (reflected off the ionosphere) with constantly varying polarisation, resulting in an indistinct and unstable null. This night effect is particularly severe at dawn and dusk, but all bearings taken during the night must be regarded as suspect. The increase in error is usually less than 4°, but may be considerably greater.

The simplest type of RDF equipment is the hand-held self-contained unit with an internal ferrite rod aerial and a compass mounted on top. When tuned in, the set is rotated to obtain a null, and the compass bearing read off. Although simple and cheap, there are drawbacks. The set should always be used in the same place, so that quadrantal errors and compass deviation are constant and can be calibrated. Also, the set must be held upright, otherwise the compass card may jam; some designs are better than others in this respect. Power consumption is minimal, long life batteries giving about 100 hours of use; however, a means of checking the battery is clearly useful.

Many general purpose marine radio receivers can take a hand-held combined compass and RDF aerial. As there are no limitations on the size and weight of

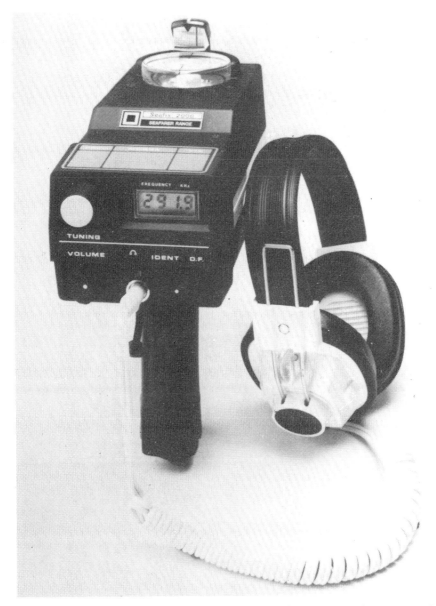

Fig. 9.5. Seafix 2000 hand-held RDF unit. (*Courtesy Seafarer Navigation International Ltd.*)

the receiver, it is generally of better quality than a hand-held unit, and the aerial/ compass unit is lighter and easier to use.

Automatic direction finding equipment offers the best performance, though it is more costly. Signal reception can be enhanced by mounting the aerial high up, and accuracy is improved, especially in rough weather or when there is a

213

considerable amount of magnetic deviation present. The only drawback is that the bearing is given relative to the vessel's head, and so the helmsman must maintain a steady course when a reading is taken; however, some sets can now be interfaced with an electronic compass to give the reading as a compass bearing.

The aerial may be a Bellini-Tosi loop, or a rotating ferrite rod aerial inside a protective housing, and the bearing is displayed digitally or on a 360° meter. Power consumption is about 1.5 amps, though it varies considerably between one design and another.

Consol and Consolan

Consol, or Consolan in the United States, provides a simple, cheap navigation system. All that is required is a radio receiver covering 250–320 kHz in Europe, or 190–195 kHz in USA, and a set of tables or Consol charts.

The system consists of a number of land-based radio transmitters. Each transmits a Morse identification signal and then a series of dots followed by dashes, or dashes followed by dots, numbering sixty in all. The point at which the dots and dashes change over, the equisignal, varies according to where the vessel lies within a 20-degree arc, the signal being repeated every 20°. To determine the vessel's position within a given arc, the number of signals before the equisignal is counted, and their type noted; then the bearing is obtained by reference to the tables in the Admiralty List of Radio Signals, or by use of special Consol charts. To decide which arc the vessel is lying in one must use the DR position, or take an RDF bearing on the transmitter.

The system's range is good, about 1000 miles by day and 1500 miles by night, though there is a minimum range of about 25 miles. However, accuracy is poor at long range, with errors of up to 1.2° by day and 2.7° by night.

Unfortunately, the system is now almost totally redundant as far as commercial shipping is concerned, and so is being phased out. At present, coverage in Europe is limited to the area between 40°N and 60°N, and to the east of 20°W; in the USA there is only one Consolan station operational, at San Francisco.

Radio lighthouses

In Britain and France a radio lighthouse system is being evaluated, working on a principle similar to Consol. The radio lighthouse broadcasts a signal on VHF Channel 88 over a 120-degree sector, consisting of a Morse identification signal followed by a series of up to 67 pulses with a silent null amongst them.

The number of pulses to the null are counted, and converted to a true bearing by reference to a simple conversion table, each pulse representing a two-degree arc. Accuracy is high, with errors being limited to 2° or 3°.

The advantages of this system are that the only equipment required is a VHF radio, and its accuracy is unaffected by night effect, quadrantal errors and so on. Against this, the use of VHF means that its range is restricted to about 30 miles. At present there are no immediate plans to introduce the system on a wider scale, but the possibility of replacing foghorns with radio lighthouses has been discussed.

Decca

A Decca chain consists of a master and three (or sometimes two) slave radio stations, designated red, green and purple. Each slave transmits on its own frequency in a fixed phase relationship with the master station, which transmits on all three frequencies. The yacht's receiver measures the phase difference between the master and slave signals, which varies according to the difference in the distance travelled by the two signals. The phase difference is converted to a hyperbolic position line, and by using the best two master/slave pairs a fix is obtained.

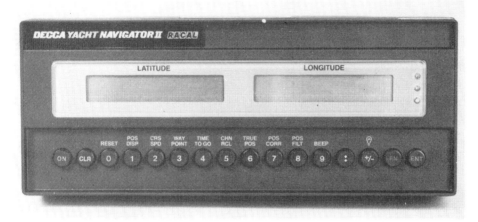

Fig. 9.6. A Decca navigator. This type, giving latitude and longitude directly, is for sale; commercial units giving the decometer readings are only for hire. (*Courtesy Racal-Decca Ltd.*)

The receiver is set up by entering the approximate position, whereupon it automatically selects the best chain. The position is displayed directly as latitude and longitude, to the nearest 0.01 minutes. Accuracy is to about 0.1 miles by day, and 1 mile by night at maximum range.

At present there are fifty-one chains in existence. The present coverage is given in Fig. 9.7. The system's range is about 350 miles from the master station by day, and 250 miles by night.

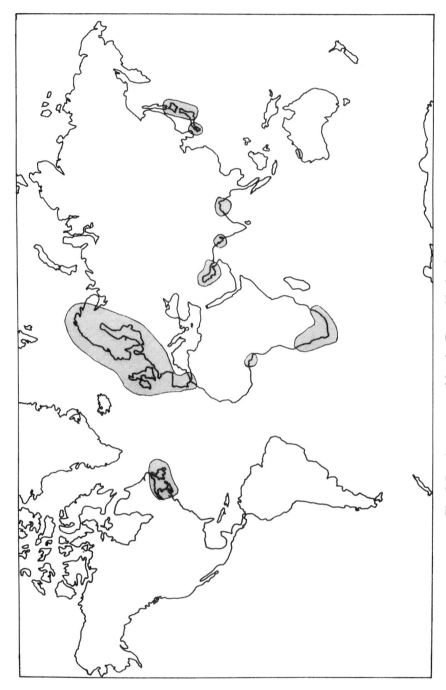

Fig. 9.7. Areas covered by the Decca Navigation system.

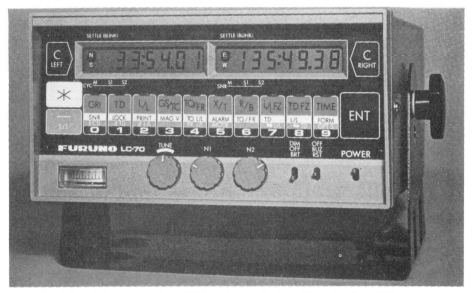

Fig. 9.8. A Loran receiver. This unit can display either the time differences or the latitude and longitude, and is also capable of being interfaced with an autopilot. (*Courtesy Furuno Ltd.*)

Loran

Loran operates in a way similar to Decca, but offers greater range at the expense of some accuracy. During the day, using groundwaves which follow the earth's surface, the range is about 1000 miles, with errors generally being less than 200 yards; at night, sky waves bounced off the ionosphere increase the range to about 2300 miles, though errors increase to about 400 yards using groundwaves, and up to 10 miles using skywaves.

Each chain consists of one master and between two and four slave stations, designated W, X, Y, and Z, spaced several hundred miles apart. The chain is identified by the time taken for one complete set of master/slave transmissions (in seconds $\times 10^{-5}$), known as the Group Repetition Interval (GRI).

The master station transmits a signal, which triggers off a transmitter in each slave after a fixed time delay. The time difference between the arrival of the master and the slave signal at the receiver is measured in micro-seconds, and this is plotted as a line of position (LOP) either directly onto a chart with a Loran lattice, or by the use of Loran tables; as with Decca, the LOPs have a hyperbolic shape. A fix is obtained by plotting two or more LOPs. Many of the more modern sets are capable of converting the time differences directly into latitude and longitude; this is easier to use, but some accuracy is lost.

As Loran operates on a frequency close to that used by Decca, it tends to pick up interference if used in areas with Decca coverage; in these areas a high quality receiver is essential, with tunable notch filters to minimise interference. Power

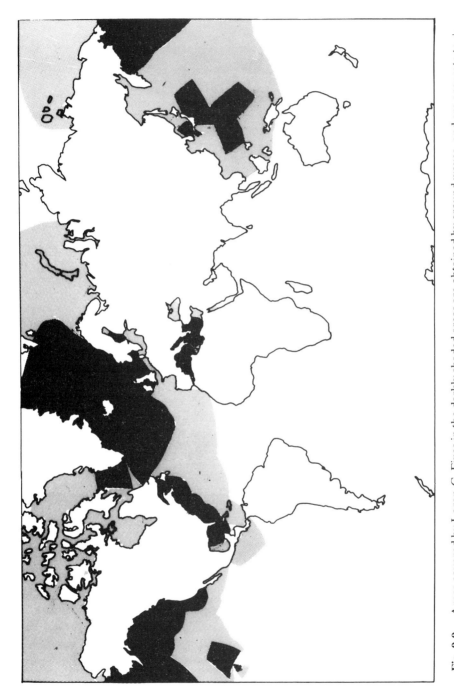

Fig. 9.9. Areas covered by Loran-C. Fixes in the darkly shaded areas are obtained by ground waves, and are accurate to ± 500 m. The lighter shading signifies that only sky waves can be received, with a worst possible error of 8 miles.

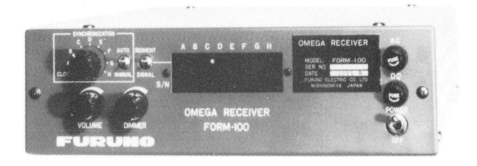

Fig. 9.10. An Omega receiver. This model is designed to be connected to a Satnav set. As the errors in the Omega system are almost constant over short periods of time, this gives the maximum possible accuracy, with Satnav giving good fixes and Omega providing a position between satellite passes. (*Courtesy Furuno Ltd.*)

consumption is around 1.75 amps at 12 volts, and the equipment is slightly cheaper than Satnav.

As can be seen in Fig. 9.9, coverage is very good over North America and the Mediterranean, but is very poor over Britain. However, the system is still being extended, and a station might be set up in France to cover northern Europe.

Omega

Omega uses very low frequency radio signals to provide worldwide groundwave coverage from only eight transmitting stations. The transmitters send out signals in a fixed phase relationship on four frequencies, and the receiver measures the phase difference between any two transmitters to give a hyperbolic position line.

The more basic sets just monitor the 10.2 kHz transmissions, displaying the stations in use and the lines of position; the fix is then plotted on US Hydrographic Office charts after various tabulated corrections have been applied. Although up to five position lines can be obtained at any one time, many sets cannot display more than two.

More advanced sets monitor three frequencies, 10.2, 11.33 and 13.6 kHz, and all eight transmitters; they then convert the position lines into latitude and longitude. This is more reliable and more accurate, especially at dawn and dusk when reception is poor, or in the event of a fault developing on one frequency.

The receiver uses an 8 to 12-foot whip aerial, as used by Loran, and has a power consumption of between 1 and 1.5 amps. Accuracy is to within one or two miles, and the position is updated at intervals of about one minute. Although more expensive than Satnav, it does offer an up-to-date fix at all times, though it is best suited to continuous operation. At dawn and dusk, however, radio interference may mask out the Omega signals, requiring the whole system to be set up from scratch.

Satellite navigation

Satellite navigation, or Satnav, is a highly accurate worldwide navigation system; its only drawback is the system's inability to give a fix on demand. However, it has become very popular with yachtsmen, the appeal of its high accuracy tending to mask its limitations.

The system is based upon six US Navy Transit satellites in trans-polar orbits, each transmitting a signal every 2 minutes, containing details of its orbit. When a satellite rises above the yacht's horizon, the receiver picks up its signal, records the orbit data, and measures the change in signal frequency due to the relative motion of the satellite and the receiver (the Doppler shift). Then, using the course and speed of the yacht and data giving the shape of the earth, the computer calculates the position of the vessel in latitude and longitude.

The equipment is set up by entering the height of the antenna above sea level, the approximate time and the position of the yacht. The course and speed may be entered manually through the keyboard, or automatically by interfacing a suitable log and compass with the receiver.

Accuracy is very high, to within 0.05 miles for a stationary vessel, with additional errors of up to 0.2 miles per knot error in the speed data. The average time interval between fixes is 1½ hours; however, the satellites are not equally spaced and not all passes are capable of giving an accurate fix, so intervals of 4 hours are not uncommon, with considerably longer intervals occasionally being reported.

Although the time between fixes is relatively unimportant when sailing well offshore, it is generally too great for coastal navigation. With most sets this shortcoming can be overcome to some extent by using the compass and log interfaces to provide a DR position, based on the last fix. It is also possible to obtain the DR position from log and compass data entered manually, but this is not nearly as accurate, being dependent upon the helm's ability to estimate the vessel's course and speed accurately.

The small antenna is usually contained within a sealed plastic housing for protection; unlike aerials receiving land-based transmissions, there is no advantage to be had from mounting it at the masthead, though it should be kept clear of large metal objects which may impair reception.

Power consumption varies tremendously; commercial equipment may consume as much as 6 amps, but yachting sets usually require from 0.5 to 1.75 amps. If it is intended to use the set continuously, some sets incorporate a standby mode for when the DR position is being updated but no fix is being calculated. When on standby power consumption drops to about 100 mA.

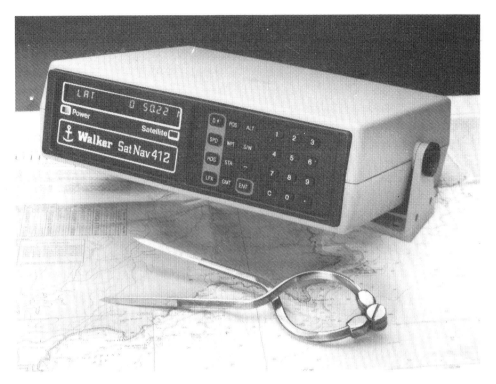

Fig. 9.11. A satellite navigation display and computer unit. (*Courtesy Thomas Walker & Sons Ltd.*)

Radar

Radar operates in a similar way to an echo sounder: the rotating aerial transmits a very high frequency radio pulse. The range is found by recording the time taken from the transmission of the pulse to the reception of an echo reflected off the target, and the bearing is found from the position of the aerial. The information is then displayed on a cathode ray tube, with the boat in the centre of the screen, the bows pointing towards the top.

The power transmitted by the aerial may vary from 3 kW upwards; the higher the output the greater the maximum range of the unit, and the better the discrimination between targets. However, as radar operates on a line of sight basis, an aerial mounted 25 feet above the waterline is only able to see about 7 miles to the horizon, and at 36 miles, maximum range for most 3 kW units, an object would have to be about 550 feet above sea level to be visible.

Most aerials are mounted inside a fibreglass radome; this enables a lighter aerial to be used, and reduces the power consumption of the aerial's motor. It also minimises windage and prevents damage due to halyards snagging on the aerial.

Fig. 9.12. This radar aerial has had to be given considerable protection as it is not mounted inside a radome. To minimise the loadings on the mast it has been positioned at the spreaders.

As the aerial is relatively heavy, between 30 and 60 lb, it can exert considerable loads on the mast when the boat is pitching and rolling. Thus it is usually mounted close to the spreaders, where the mast is amply supported.

The display unit is centred round the cathode ray tube; obviously a larger display will be easier to read, and make it easier to differentiate between targets. As the display is not very easy to read in bright light a detachable viewing hood is supplied; this normally incorporates a magnifying glass to increase the size of the display effectively.

As anyone who has used radar will know, it is an invaluable aid to collision avoidance and coastal navigation, especially at night or in poor visibility. Unfortunately, it draws a fairly hefty current, between 4 and 8 amps for a 3 kW set, and this has limited its use in sailing boats.

Radio Communications

VHF radiotelephones

VHF radiotelephones are quite deservedly very popular. They enable yachtsmen to call up the race committee, clubhouse or marina, as well as the coastguard, and also offer telephone link call facilities, all for a relatively small financial outlay.

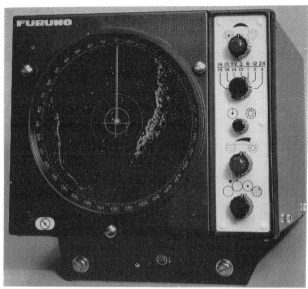

Fig. 9.13. A small boat radar display unit, the Furuno FR-240 Mk III. (*Courtesy Furuno Ltd.*)

Designated use	Channels
Distress and calling	16
Inter ship	6, 8, 10, 13, 9, 70, 72, 73, 69, 67, 77, 15, 17
Port operations (simplex)	12, 14, 11, 13, 9, 68, 71, 74, 10, 67, 69, 73, 17, 15
Port operations (duplex)	20, 22, 18, 19, 5, 7, 2, 3, 1, 4, 78, 82, 79, 81, 80, 60, 63, 66, 62, 65, 64, 61, 84
Public correspondence	26, 27, 25, 24, 28, 4, 1, 3, 2, 7, 5, 84, 87, 86, 85, 88, 61, 64, 65, 62, 66, 63, 60, 82
Racing yacht intership	72
Radio lighthouses	88
HM Coastguard small vessel safety channel	67

Fig. 9.14. Allocation of VHF frequencies. (Note that the most frequently used channels are placed first in each list.)

VHF operates between 156 and 174 MHz, with a 25 kHz channel spacing. Each channel has one or more specific uses allocated to it, as indicated in Fig. 9.14. Of particular interest to the yachtsman are channel 67, used by the British coastguard for safety traffic; channel 72, which is the preferred yacht to yacht channel when racing; and channel 88, for radio lighthouses. A number of private channels are also available. Of these, channel M has been designated for use by marinas and yacht clubs, and in the USA channels WX1 and WX2 are used for weather reports.

Some of the channels are designated simplex, whilst others are duplex. A simplex channel only uses one frequency, and so it is not possible to transmit and receive simultaneously; a duplex channel overcomes this by using two channels and a duplex filter, or sometimes separate transmit and receive aerials. Sets aimed at the yachting market offer simplex and semi-duplex operation; the latter enables duplex channels to be used, but functioning in a simplex manner.

The maximum permitted transmitted power of a VHF set is 25 watts, but at ranges up to about 3 miles power should be reduced to 1 watt to avoid interfering with nearby operators using the same channel. There is a slight tendency for the radio waves to follow the earth's curvature, and so the maximum range is about 15% greater than the line of sight distance between the aerials. Power consumption is about 0.5 to 1.0 amps on receive and standby, and 4.5 to 6.0 amps when transmitting.

The output of an aerial is given by its gain (in decibels, dB), with longer aerials generally having a higher gain figure. However, the gain takes no account of the direction in which the signal is transmitted; for example, a high gain aerial may

Fig. 9.15. Seavoice 550 VHF set. (*Courtesy Seafarer Navigation International Ltd.*)

transmit most of its power within a narrow horizontal band, resulting in a marked drop in performance when heeled, whilst another aerial with a lower gain may have a more uniform distribution, and so be more suitable for a sailing boat.

Although long aerials, available up to about 8 feet long, tend to have high gain characteristics, this is normally concentrated into a narrow horizontal band. This, coupled with the great range available by siting the aerial at the masthead, means that there is little advantage to be had from fitting a long aerial, and a short stub aerial is normally perfectly satisfactory.

Radio receivers

A radio receiver is another useful item to have on board, enabling weather reports, time signals, and radio broadcasts to be received. Whilst a portable transistor radio is perfectly adequate for inshore yachtsmen, when sailing well offshore a more sensitive radio with good coverage of the marine and short wave frequencies is to be preferred.

The frequency coverage of radio receivers varies widely, from complete coverage of all frequencies in a set aimed at radio hams, down to a set just covering the MF marine band. For the yachtsman, the frequencies shown in Fig. 9.16(a) are likely to prove most useful.

There are a variety of ways of sending a radio signal, denoted either by a description or by a code. Obviously the receiver must be designed to be able to cope with the desired transmission modes, whether AM, SSB, FM broadcast, F1 or F4. The main ones in use are shown in Fig. 9.16(a).

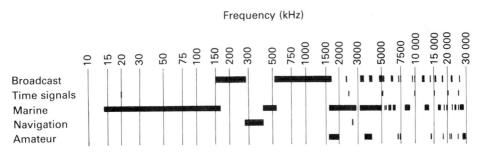

Fig. 9.16(a). Radio frequency allocations in the marine wavebands.

Whilst a small built-in aerial will prove adequate for short-range reception, a properly installed, earthed aerial will greatly improve performance at long range, and is essential when transmitting. It may take the form of a long, low impedance aerial, usually the backstay, or a shorter, high impedance whip aerial; the longer aerial will always give better performance, though it will obviously become inoperative in the event of a dismasting.

The mode of transmission is designated by three characters.

The first is the type of modulation:
A–Amplitude modulation (AM)
F–Frequency modulation (FM)

The second indicates the type of information transmitted:
1 or 2–Telegraphy (eg Morse)
3–Telephony (eg voice communication)
4–Facsimile

The third gives the strength of the carrier wave and sidebands:
None–Double side band (DSB)
A–Single side band (SSB), reduced carrier wave
B–SSB, two independent sidebands
C–SSB, vestigial sideband
H–SSB, full carrier wave
J–SSB, suppressed carrier wave

The following are the main modes of transmission relevant to yachtsmen:
A1, A2–Double side band Morse telegraphy
A1A, A2C–Single side band Morse telegraphy
A3–Double side band telephony, eg SW, MW and LW shore broadcasts
A3A–Single side band telephony, can be received by a DSB set
A3J–Single side band telephony
F1–Telex
F3C–Radio telephony, eg VHF
F4–Weather facsimile transmissions

Fig. 9.16(b). Modes of radio transmission.

It is vital that the aerial is properly earthed, as this effectively doubles its length. It can be achieved by using the external ballast keel as an earth, or a few square feet of copper plate, or a commercial earth such as the Dynaplate, a block of sintered bronze pellets measuring a few inches square. Use of a skin fitting or the engine generally results in a poor electrical connection with inadequate surface area, and may cause electrolytic corrosion.

To minimise losses heavy gauge, low resistance cables must be used to connect the receiver to the earth plate and the aerial. If no transmitter is carried the aerial cable can be screened by using a co-axial cable below decks, thus minimising interference. However, if a transmitter is carried this will severely reduce its power output, due to the high capacitance of the cable. If a length of rigging is used as an aerial it must be electrically isolated by using insulators top and bottom. The upper insulator should be about 4 feet from the masthead to minimise masking by the mast, whilst the lower one should be high enough off the deck to prevent the crew coming into contact with the aerial. The installation of a radio and its aerial is a technical job, and is best left to professional radio engineers.

Although dial tuning is ideal when scanning for a station, keyboard tuning is best when tuning in to a known frequency. Sets displaying the frequency on a digital display generally permit better tuning, due to the greater accuracy of the display. In addition to tuning controls there will be a switch selecting the mode of the signal, and a volume control. Sensitivity and filtering controls are incorporated to optimise reception of poor signals; these may function manually or automatically. Power consumption varies between 0.3 amps and 5 amps, with the more sensitive receivers generally drawing more current.

Weatherfax

The use of radio fascimile equipment to obtain weather maps whilst at sea is becoming increasingly widespread on long-distance races. It enables up-to-date weather, sea state, and ice maps to be obtained, covering most of the world.

The map is encoded into a radio signal in the 2 – 25 MHz band and the F4 transmission mode. It is then received by the receiver incorporated in the facsimile equipment, or, if suitable, the yacht's radio receiver, where it is decoded and a chart printed on specially treated paper. The whole process takes about 20 minutes, and power consumption is around 2 amps. A special signal at the beginning and end of every transmission enables the system to operate automatically when left on standby.

Radio transmitters

It is debatable how useful a radio transmitter is on board a yacht, especially if its high power consumption is considered. Apart from use in emergencies, for which an emergency radio transmitter may prove a better and less expensive option, its chief benefit is that it enables the crew to communicate with people ashore.

The transmitter is generally combined with a receiver to form a transceiver. Just about all transceivers cover the MF band, and part or all of the HF band may also be covered. The power transmitted obviously has a direct bearing on the range of the set, and is described as the peak envelope power (PEP); this may vary from 100 watts to 400 watts for an MF set, and rise to 1200 watts for an HF set.

Because of the large power drain, most radios are designed to operate at 24 volts. A 200 watts PEP set may draw 13 amps at 24 volts, rising to about 35 amps for a 400 watt transmitter; due to the limited capacity of the batteries, it is normal practice to transmit only when the engine or generator is running. An MF transmitter may be expected to have a range of up to 250 miles, rising to 1000 miles for an HF set in the 4 – 8 MHz band, whilst worldwide coverage is possible in the 9 – 30 MHz band. It must be remembered, though, that the signal

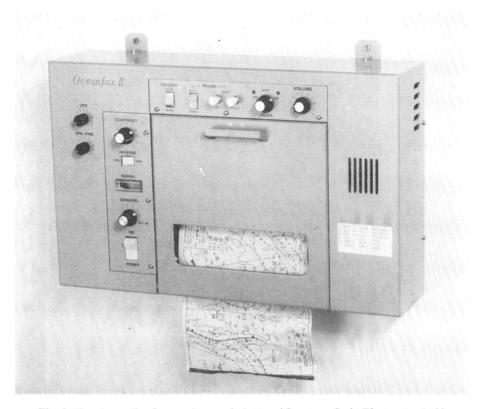

Fig. 9.17. A weatherfax receiver and plotter. (*Courtesy Cody Electronics Ltd.*)

may be drowned by a more powerful ship's transmitter operating on the same frequency.

As with a VHF radio, operation may be simplex, semi-duplex, or duplex. Similarly, there will also be a means of reducing the PEP when operating at short range. However, there will also be a choice of various AM and SSB transmission modes, and a coupler to tune the aerial's characteristics to suit the transmission frequency; in some sets the tuning is carried out automatically.

Autopilots

An electronic autopilot operates by comparing the course set with the course steered, and then activating the drive unit to apply a course correction whenever the boat wanders off course.

The course is usually monitored by an electronic compass, either by entering the magnetic course directly, or by locking in the compass when the boat is on course. The latter system, although less convenient to use, is ideal for steel and

Fig. 9.18. This compact 400 W PEP MF radio transceiver comes in three modules, allowing more versatile installation. (*Courtesy Skanti.*)

ferro boats as it is unaffected by compass deviation. If a wind vane is used, the course may be selected by a dial, or simply by turning the wind vane.

The drive unit may be a linear motor connected to the tiller or rudder quadrant, or a rotary chain drive or hydraulic pump incorporated into the steering system. Clearly the system must be able to apply sufficient torque to steer the yacht, though a high rate of correction is also important, especially downwind, for prompt course correction.

Most autopilots apply a rudder correction whose magnitude is proportional to the angle that the boat is off course; alternatively, the course correction may be proportional to the rate at which the boat is deviating from her course, which generally offers better course keeping. Whichever system is used, there will be a rudder control to vary the amount of rudder applied for a given course error, enabling the autopilot to be tuned to suit the steering characteristics of the boat. As sailing boats have much greater directional stability upwind than down, the setting can be reduced when beating, thereby minimising battery drain.

When a sea is running the boat will tend to yaw to each side of her course. In most cases the boat will go back on course of her own accord, and so no correction is required. Thus there is a weather, sensitivity, or response control which sets the width of the deadband within which no corrections are applied. The rougher the conditions, the more the boat will yaw, and so the wider the deadband needs to be;

Fig. 9.19 A cockpit mounted autopilot. The seals on the course selector and the actuator rod are not always completely watertight on cockpit mounted units, and so the course selector is best sited within the hatchway, and if possible the drive unit should be kept under a cover. (*Courtesy Nautech.*)

too high a setting merely results in excessive power consumption, whilst too low a setting results in poorer course keeping.

A trim system is required to compensate for any weather or lee helm present; this may either be entered manually, or it may be applied automatically. As the amount of helm will vary with the angle of heel and set of the sails an automatic system is to be preferred, as it requires no adjustment by the crew.

Compact, cockpit-mounted autopilots linked directly to the tiller have become very popular in smaller boats. Unfortunately, the seals round the controls and the drive shaft are not always totally waterproof, and so many sets fail due to internal corrosion. Many of these failures could be avoided by fitting a waterproof housing or cover to offer some protection.

The power requirements of an autopilot obviously depend upon the size of the vessel: a cockpit-mounted unit for a 30-foot boat may draw only 0.25 amps, whilst a powerful system on an 80-footer will draw 4 or 5 amps on average. In both cases, the maximum current drawn may be six or seven times greater than the mean value. This must be allowed for when choosing the cable and fuse sizes.

Chapter 10

Safety Equipment

When at sea the yachtsman must be totally self-reliant. If an emergency arises it may not be possible for the rescue services, if available, to render assistance in time. Also, calling out the lifeboat means that one is putting other people's lives at risk, which is inexcusable if the incident arose due to a poorly equipped boat or owner.

Thus the yachtsman's first aim must be to try to prevent incidents by a combination of good seamanship and maintaining a properly equipped, well found yacht. The second line of safety must be to have the means of getting out of an emergency by using safety equipment carried on board. The third and final level is to call out external assistance, but this must always be regarded as a last resort.

Designing for Safety

Clearly the yacht must be strong enough to meet the worst weather that may be expected. However, many racing yachts are lightly built, especially multihulls; the owners of these vessels should know their limitations, and know when conditions are such that the boat may be damaged if driven hard.

In foul weather the boat must be able to be shut down to form a watertight unit. Thus through-hull openings for running rigging are not acceptable, and all hatches and openings must be watertight when closed. If foredeck hatches are hinged at their forward end this will help to keep out any water that comes across the deck when the hatch is open. All monohulls should have their hatches positioned so that they lie above the waterline if the boat suffers a knockdown.

If the cockpit fills with water this may find its way below; even if this is not the case, it will cause the boat to trim down by the stern, and make the boat more prone to being pooped, as well as reducing her stability. Thus the cockpit, including the cockpit lockers and the companionway hatch, must be fully watertight. It must also be self-draining at all angles of heel, with the cockpit floor at least 2% of LWL above the waterline to ensure a sufficient head of water.

For the cockpit to drain quickly the drains must be of adequate size, at least 1 square inch per 30 square foot cockpit area (measured from coaming to coaming), with a minimum of two ¾ inch diameter drains. Drains smaller than ¾ inch should not be used, as they become clogged too easily.

The size of cockpit will also affect how the boat behaves if it is flooded. The ORC Special Regulations lay down a maximum volume for all cockpits of 0.09 × $L \times B \times FA$; here L approximates to the waterline length, B the maximum beam, and FA the freeboard at the stern. For multihulls, MOCRA lays down a maximum cockpit area of 0.2 × LWL × BWL, taking the measurements from the hull in which the cockpit is placed. To put this into perspective, if the cockpit of a 35-foot yacht built to the ORC category 1 limits were completely filled, it would be holding about 3000 lb of seawater.

To prevent water getting down below, the companionway must be able to be blocked off to at least the level of the sheer line; if the cockpit opens aft to the sea the bottom of the companionway should not be below the sheer line, so preventing a wave running along the cockpit and straight down the hatch. The washboards should run down parallel slides to ensure that they cannot fall out in a knockdown if the hatch is shut and the top board has been left out for ventilation. They should also be tied to rope lanyards to prevent their being lost overboard.

Windows may be broken by green water coming on board, and so storm boards should be carried, at least for all windows over 2 square feet in area and preferably for all windows irrespective of size. These may be of stout plywood, bolted to battens passing over the broken window on the inside.

Another possible trouble spot is the skin fittings. All skin fittings below the boat's heeled waterline, and preferably all skin fittings present, must be fitted with seacocks. To guard against the seacocks failing, tapered softwood plugs can be carried on board.

Flooding

A collision or grounding may damage the hull and result in the boat flooding. The first step to combat this is to plug the hole, even if only temporarily; for this reason all of the hull should be readily accessible. Collision mats are commercially available, but in most cases the hole can be plugged with materials on board; if the hole is so large that it cannot be plugged quickly, it is probably too large for a collision mat to deal with.

The only way of preventing the boat from sinking is to have it fitted with watertight bulkheads, so that the damaged compartment can be sealed off. However, these are seldom fitted, for a variety of reasons. For a start, the chances of a severe collision are slim, and the presence of watertight bulkheads would not enhance the peace of mind of the crew. Also, watertight doors and bulkheads would reduce the available space on board, and destroy the open-plan layout used to make yachts appear spacious. A collision bulkhead could easily be placed in the bows, though, saving the yacht from a head-on collision; it could also double as a stowage compartment.

If the boat should begin to flood, a powerful bilge pump is essential to keep the amount of water under control whilst repairs are carried out. If the engine can be started this is where an engine driven pump comes into its own, otherwise the crew will need to do the work with buckets and manual pumps. However, it is surprising how much water can enter the hull before it actually sinks. The problems are much more likely to be due to lack of stability rather than lack of buoyancy, due to water surging to the lee side in monohulls, or one float flooding in multihulls.

Multihull Capsizes

Every multihull sailor should prepare for the worst, namely a capsize. Once again, prevention is better than cure, and the sheets should be fitted with some form of quick release system. In its simplest form this means carrying an axe in the cockpit, but with a nervous crew this can prove expensive. If the sheets are cleated off before passing round a winch, clam cleats with a quick-release line are ideal, or an electronic cam cleat can be fitted that uses a mercury switch to release the sheets at a preset heel angle.

To ensure that the boat floats after a capsize it should either be made from inherently bouyant materials such as wood or foam sandwich, or an adequate amount of foam buoyancy should be fitted under the deck. A hatch must be fitted in the side of the hull to enable the crew to escape from the cabin, and the underside of the vessel fitted with adequate handholds or lines; if painted a bright colour it will be more visible from the air. Although the crew should stay with the boat for as long as possible, should the worst come to the worst the liferaft must be equally accessible from each side of the hull.

Several methods of righting a capsized multihull have been proposed. Although these may work perfectly satisfactorily in calm conditions, they have yet to prove themselves in more realistic conditions. They may use a masthead float to try to prevent total inversion, or flood part of the hull to bring the boat up to the half capsized position. Water bags are then swung out on the end of a derrick and filled, or air bags are inflated, to bring the boat upright, and the hulls are then pumped out.

Fire

After sinking, fire is probably the greatest hazard on a yacht. The obvious fire

Fig. 10.1 Every multihull sailor must be prepared for a capsize. A properly designed multihull will float upside down, enabling the crew to stay with the boat. (*Photo courtesy of Press Association.*)

hazards are the engine and fuel system, the galley, and any gas installations. However, hydrogen gas emitted from the batteries can also build up to an explosive level, and a common cause of fire is a crew member falling asleep whilst having a smoke.

Petrol and gas fumes can build up to form an explosive mixture with air, and so

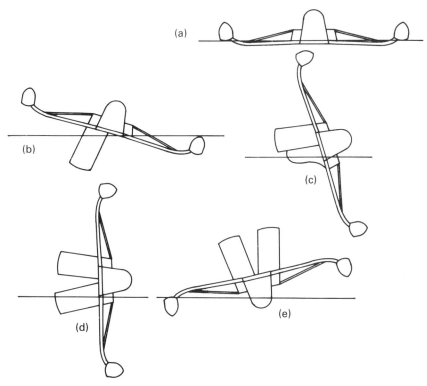

Fig. 10.2. Righting a multihull with air bags. (*Courtesy Derek Kelsall.*)
(a) The central hull has sufficient buoyancy to ensure that it floats high. One outrigger is flooded with sea water.
(b) Once the outrigger is submerged, air bags are inflated on the opposite side.
(c) Next the air bags on the opposite side are inflated.
(d) With both bags fully inflated, the boat quickly passes through 90° of heel, and then rights herself.
(e) Finally the flooded hull is pumped out. This must be done quickly to prevent a capsize over the flooded float.

present a particularly serious hazard. A gas detector should always be fitted in the bilge if either of these fuels are carried, as the vapours are heavier than air and so sink to the lowest point on the vessel. Additional sensors can also be fitted in the engine room or the fuel compartment. In addition to sounding an alarm, some makes can also operate a fuel shut-off valve, or switch on a bilge blower fan.

The speed with which a fire spreads can be reduced by enclosing high risk areas, and using fire retardant or fire proof materials for hull coatings, panelling and fabrics. Where possible, potentially hazardous or essential systems such as gas, electricity or bilge pump runs should not be routed through high risk areas; this is also a good argument for using galvanised steel pipe for the bilge system. Each compartment should have at least two exit routes to prevent crew members becoming trapped by a fire.

Several types of fire extinguisher are available, each with its own particular uses. Whatever types are used, they should be sited close to hatches so that the crew do not have to enter the burning area. At least two 3 lb extinguishers should be carried on board; the Department of Trade requires British vessels over 45 feet in length to carry two fire buckets and two extinguishers, and those over 50 feet must also carry a hand pump and fire hose located outside the engine room, capable of throwing a 20-foot jet of water and reaching any part of the vessel.

Gas extinguishers operate by replacing the oxygen with a non-combustible gas such as carbon dioxide (CO_2), BCF, BTM or Freon. As the gas disperses quickly it is best used in confined spaces such as the engine room or the bilges; a particular advantage is that it can sink into areas not directly accessible by the extinguisher. These extinguishers may be safely used on electrical fires and liquid fires. The drawback is that they replace the oxygen in the atmosphere, which is essential for breathing, and so should not be used if any crew members are in the compartment. BCF and BTM extinguishers also produce a toxic gas on contact with the flames, and so do not comply with Department of Trade regulations.

Dry powder extinguishers cut off the oxygen supply by settling on the burning material, and so are perfectly suitable for use in accommodation spaces, if somewhat messy to clean up afterwards. They are probably the best type of extinguisher for use on small fires. Some extinguishers use a separate gas cartridge to expel the powder, but the powder tends to coagulate and so make the extinguisher useless.

Most larger extinguishers produce a foam, which once again settles on the burning material to cut off the oxygen. This type is at its best on large fires in open spaces, but is not suitable for electrical fires where the voltage exceeds 32 volts. The extinguisher needs annual recharging, but this can be done by the crew.

Water is the oldest known means of fighting fire, both cooling the material and cutting off the air supply. However, it is not suitable for electrical or liquid fires, and the use of large amounts of water may affect the boat's stability.

The best method of fighting a galley fire is to smother the flames with a fire blanket, and one should be carried in addition to fire extinguishers. Although it must be kept close to the galley, it must also be easily reached once a fire has started up and so should not be kept directly over the cooker.

As the engine compartment is not readily visible, it is worth considering a heat sensor and a remote or automatic operating gas fire extinguisher, especially if a petrol engine is fitted. This can either be fully automatic in operation, or the crew can operate the extinguisher once the sensor has triggered off an alarm; the latter system is preferable on large yachts, where a crew member may be in the engine compartment at the time of the fire.

Lightning

A yacht's mast in the middle of an ocean is the highest point for miles, and so makes an ideal lightning conductor. On steel or aluminium hulls any lightning strikes will earth themselves through the hull, but on a non-conducting hull a lightning conductor is required.

This should be a copper wire with a cross-sectional area of at least 0.15 sq inches, led in a straight line from the heel of the mast and the bottom of the standing rigging to the ballast keel, or to a copper plate below the waterline at least 1 foot square. Any sharp bends will result in a corona discharge, and so make the lightning conductor almost useless. On non-metallic masts the body of the mast cannot be used as a lightning conductor, and so the copper wire should be led up the mast to a point just above the masthead.

The entire electrical system will be prone to damage during a lightning strike, and any electronic equipment should be disconnected in a storm. Aerials should be earthed during the storm, or fitted with lightning arresters, as they also act as lightning conductors. The compass will also be thrown completely out by a strike, as will the boat's deviation.

Man Overboard

Good deck design can go a long way to preventing crew members falling overboard. A good non-slip deck finish is the first essential, not only on the deck itself but also on the cockpit coamings and seats, and the coachroof sides. The finish may be one of the non-slip deck paints, an unvarnished wood deck, or sheets of non-slip material glued onto the deck; of these, the rubber/cork compositions provide a better surface than the vinyl variety. Many fibreglass boats have a non-slip finish moulded into the deck; this may be adequate when new, but quickly loses its efficiency after a year or two, and so is best painted over.

Plentiful handholds are also important, running along the coachroof top at least from the cockpit to the mast. Vulnerable areas such as the bridge deck or the foot of the mast can be fitted with guardrails for extra security, and combined handholds/rope guards can be fitted over dorade vents. As grabrails, stanchions and guardrails are subjected to high loads they must have a large baseplate and be bolted through the deck, or welded in place on metal craft.

Around the edge of the working deck lifelines at least 2 foot high should be fitted, together with a second line at half height, of at least 6 mm diameter wire. The stanchions should not be placed more than 7 feet apart to spread the load; the solid aluminium type are more resistant to buckling than the tubular stainless steel variety. In the bows a pulpit is used to give extra space and security to the crew; the lower rail is often omitted above the bow roller to give more space when bringing the anchor aboard. The stern should also have a lifeline led between braced stanchions, unless a solid pushpit is fitted.

A toe-rail, or better still a bulwark on cruising boats, should also be fitted round the deck edge, preferably at least 2 inches high; this is particularly important on the foredeck. It must have sufficient drainage holes or scuppers so that no water is trapped on deck. The slotted aluminium toe-rails are particularly useful as they can be used to bolt together the hull and deck mouldings, and they also provide attachment points for snatch blocks, preventers and so on.

In bad weather safety harnesses should be worn, not to keep the crew attached to the boat if they should fall overboard, but rather to *prevent* the crew from falling overboard. Thus, all attachment points should be sited well inboard if possible.

In the cockpit there should be strong eyes for the crew to clip onto, including one positioned for the helmsman. At least one of these must be close enough to the companionway for the crew to clip onto before coming on deck. Stout wire jacklines should be fitted along the deck, preferably in one length so that the crew don't have to transfer from one line to another at any point. Again, the crew should be able to clip onto the jacklines from the security of the cockpit.

If someone should fall overboard, his chances of survival are much enhanced if a lifebuoy can be thrown to him immediately. At least two should be carried, sited close to the helm and ready for use. The horseshoe type are generally used as they are much easier to get into when in the water; the heavier rigid plastic variety are better than the soft foam ones, as they can be thrown further and are carried less by the wind.

Each lifebuoy should be fitted with a whistle, a drogue to prevent drifting, and a self-igniting light for use at night. A danbuoy will make the lifebuoy more visible from a distance, whilst a dye marker will make the victim visible from the air.

The Department of Trade requires all yachts over 45 feet to carry at least two lifebuoys, one of which must have a self-igniting light and a self-activating smoke signal; 10 fathoms of buoyant line; and one lifejacket per crew member, not totally dependent on oral inflation.

Once the boat has returned to the victim, a buoyant heaving line should be available to throw to the man. A rigid ladder extending below the waterline is invaluable in getting him aboard, and can easily be incorporated into the pushpit or transom.

Pyrotechnics

Flares may be used either to draw the attention of another vessel to one's position, for example where there is a risk of collision, or as a distress signal both to raise the alarm and to pinpoint one's position. The Department of Trade requires all yachts over 45 feet to carry at least six distress flares.

All distress flares are red or orange, whilst white hand-held flares are used to signal one's position; because of their different functions they are best stowed in different compartments, so as to avoid confusion in moments of stress. No flares are waterproof, even when packed in a plastic sachet, and so they must be stowed in dry lockers. Because they are likely to be needed in a hurry they should be kept in or close to the cockpit. All flares have a shelf life of three years, and are stamped

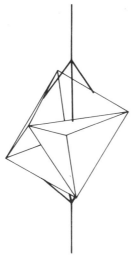

Fig. 10.3. An octahedral radar reflector hoisted in the 'catch water' position.

with the expiry date; out of date flares may work, but have a lower intensity and may be dangerous to use.

Parachute flares are generally the best way of signalling that one is in distress. These shoot the flare up to about 1000 feet, and it then floats down on a parachute whilst burning; some may also release strips of aluminium foil to produce a radar echo. When sailing offshore at least four should be carried, and preferably a dozen when ocean sailing.

Hand-held flares are used to pinpoint the yacht's position, or to raise a distress signal when help is close to hand. They are not as bright as parachute flares, but burn longer. A minimum of four red and four white flares should be carried.

During the day orange smoke signals may be used in lieu of red hand-held flares, being particularly visible to aircraft passing overhead. These may be hand-held or designed to float in the water, the latter type being more powerful; at least two should be carried.

The Radar Reflector

Most ships rely a good deal on radar for collision avoidance, but fibreglass and wood are virtually invisible to radar, and even metal hulls give a poor echo due to their relatively small size. A radar reflector can go a long way to relieve this problem, though, acting as a focused mirror and so reflecting a stronger echo. To be effective it needs to be at least 12 feet above the waterline, and preferably not too close to the mast, which can mask part of the echo.

The most common type of reflector is octahedral, constructed from three squares of metal. Its main advantages are that it is cheap, and it can be folded away into a flat square. To be effective it needs to measure at least 18 inches across the diagonal, and to be hoisted in the 'catch water' position. However, as there are only six 'lenses' available to reflect the signal, it does not give an even response across the horizon, and once heeled it quickly loses its efficiency.

Recently, radar reflectors have appeared consisting of a large number of reflecting surfaces contained inside a plastic casing. These give an almost uniform response right across the horizon, and much better performance when heeled, as well as being easier to hoist and offering less windage.

Emergency Radio Equipment

On many yachts the sole reason for carrying a radio transmitter is to have it for use in an emergency, and so one of the emergency transmitters will generally provide a better, and often cheaper, option compared to a normal transmitter. Even if a radio transmitter is fitted to the yacht, an emergency transmitter is worthwhile as it can alert aircraft, and can also be taken into the liferaft.

Emergency transmitters do not cover VHF channel 16, but do cover one or more of the following distress frequencies:

500 kHz	Marine radiotelegraphy, long range.
2182 kHz	Marine telephony, range about 80 miles.
121.5 MHz	Civilian aircraft, range up to 200 miles.
243 MHz	Military ships and aircraft, range up to 200 miles.

The range of the last two frequencies depends on the height of the aircraft, as the signal is transmitted in an inverted cone with its apex at the aerial. Obviously the ranges quoted will depend upon the power of the transmitter, but are typical for emergency equipment.

The simplest type of transmitter is the EPIRB, or Emergency Position Indicating Radio Beacon. This transmits a Mayday signal as soon as the safety pin is removed, but usually just on the aircraft frequencies. It is powered by batteries which need replacing after about four years, unless non-replaceable batteries are used, sealed into the unit to make it more waterproof, and in this case the whole unit will need replacing.

Slightly more sophisticated units are available that can transmit and receive voice communications on 2182 kHz, as well as transmitting an automatic Mayday signal; they may also be capable of transmitting on the aircraft frequencies. The main advantage of these is that it is possible to transmit one's position, instead of having to rely on the other vessel taking a bearing on your signal. Once again these are battery powered, but usually the batteries are replaceable.

Finally, transceivers are available to full SOLAS (Committee on Safety of Life at Sea) specifications. These are capable of operating in the 8 MHz band, as well as on 500 kHz and 2182 kHz. Although considerably more expensive they

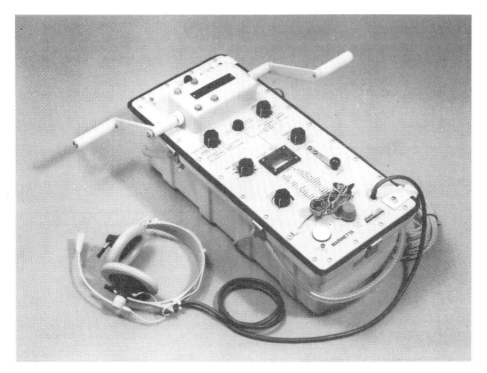

Fig. 10.4. An emergency radio transmitter to full SOLAS requirements. The unit transmits distress signals on 500, 2182 and 8364 kHz, and can also receive on those frequencies and the 8200–8800 kHz band. It is powered by the hand cranked generator, and is fully waterproof. (*Courtesy Skandinavisk Teleindustri Skanti A/S.*)

are much more rugged, and can be powered by a manually driven generator or by batteries, thus freeing them from the limited life of the batteries, which is usually about 200 hours.

The Liferaft

The liferaft must always be regarded as a last resort, only to be boarded if there is no hope whatsoever of saving the yacht. Until this point is reached, staying on board the yacht is always a safer option, no matter how badly damaged. Having said this, a liferaft should be carried on all offshore yachts; the Department of Trade requires sufficient liferafts to carry all crew members, to full SOLAS standards, to be carried on all yachts over 45 feet.

Liferafts are produced to a variety of standards. The highest of these are to specifications laid down by SOLAS, (monitored by the Department of Trade in Britain). These are intended for survival at sea, in any weather, for at least 30 days. They have a self erecting canopy, at least two buoyancy compartments, each of which is capable of supporting the raft, an inflatable double floor to protect the crew from exposure in cold waters, and a very extensive survival pack.

Liferafts built to SOLAS requirements are expensive, and for most yachtsmen a liferaft built to ORC specifications is perfectly adequate. The essential differences are that these are not inspected during manufacture, do not need to have a double bottom (though it may be available as an option), and carry a less extensive survival pack.

Manufacturers are not required to conform to SOLAS or ORC regulations, and many produce liferafts to their own specifications. Some of these are perfectly suitable for offshore use, but others are intended for coastal yachstmen.

As was shown in the first chapter, the stability of a vessel is directly dependent upon its weight. In a liferaft, most of the weight comes from its occupants, and so the liferaft size should be suited to the number of crew on board. In this respect it is better for large vessels to carry, say, three 4-man liferafts rather than two 6-man rafts, particularly if the number of crew on board is variable.

Liferafts may be packed into a waterproof fibreglass canister or a valise. Although cheaper and lighter, the valise is not waterproof, and so must not be stowed on deck if the liferaft is to be relied upon. However, if stowed below it may prove difficult to bring on deck in a hurry, or may prove inaccessible due to fire or flooding. Thus a canister is always to be preferred, stowed in such a way that it can easily be released and launched. Whichever type is carried, the liferaft must be serviced annually by a reputable agent to ensure that it will operate satisfactorily.

Navigation Lights

At night or in reduced visibility all vessels must display navigation lights in accordance with the International Regulations for Preventing Collisions at Sea. As far as the yachtsman is concerned, lights for a power driven vessel, a vessel under sail, and a vessel at anchor will be required.

The various lights required, and the regulations regarding their positioning, are shown in Fig. 10.5. Regulations concerning their range are also laid down; these are based on the power of the light, and take no account of the height at which it is mounted. For vessels up to 20 metres long (65 feet 7 inches) all lights must have a minimum range of 2 miles, with two exceptions: vessels under 12 metres (39 feet 4 inches) need have sidelights with a range of only 1 mile, whilst vessels between 12 and 20 metres must have a masthead (steaming) light with a range of 3 miles.

Whilst under sail, vessels under 12 metres may carry a masthead tricolour light instead of separate side and stern lights. Because of its height this has a greater range than the separate lights, and is less likely to be obscured by waves; it also consumes less power as only one bulb is required. Against this, the side and stern lights still need to be carried for when the vessel is under power, and also changing the bulb is a much more difficult task, especially at sea.

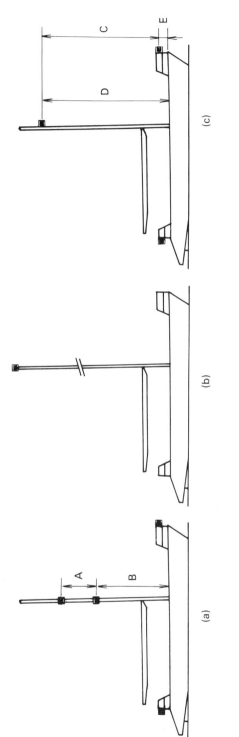

Fig. 10.5. Regulations covering the layout of a yacht's navigation lights.

(a) Vessel under sail with bicolour light, stern light, and optional sailing lights. Dimensions: A minimum 1 metre. B minimum 2 metres.

(b) Vessel under sail with masthead tricolour light. No sailing lights may be carried.

(c) Vessel under power, with bicolour light, stern light and steaming light. A masthead tricolour light is not permitted. Dimensions: C minimum 1 metre on vessels under 12 metres in length. D minimum 2.5 metres on vessels 12–20 metres in length. E maximum three quarters of D, on vessels of any size.

243

Whether under sail or power, the sidelights can be combined into a single bicolour light on vessels up to 20 metres; once again, this offers reduced power consumption compared to two separate lights.

Sailing yachts not using a tricolour light may identify themselves with red over green all round sailing lights up the mast. Although this would make sailing yachts more visible to shipping, it has not caught on due to the extra expense and battery drain involved.

With the exception of the anchor light, nothing is permitted to obscure more than 6° of the arc of navigation lights. This is a thickness of ⅝ inch at a distance of 6 inches from the bulb (not the lens) of the light.

Navigation lights used on yachts need as large a vertical sector as possible; even if not heeled, the boat will be rolling and pitching in the waves. Low power consumption is another requirement, and Fresnel lenses have been universally adopted for this reason; glass lenses tend to absorb slightly less light than plastic ones.

In addition to navigation lights, shapes are required for use during the day, and foghorns for use in poor visibility. When motor sailing, a cone hoisted apex down should be hoisted in the foretriangle; when at anchor a ball should be hoisted.

All yachts must carry some means of making an effective fog signal. A variety of small foghorns powered by lungs or gas cartridges is available, but the chances of their being heard on a board a ship are remote. The electrically powered horns so beloved by motor yachtsmen are considerably more powerful.

The collision regulations require yachts over 12 metres to carry both a whistle and a bell. The whistle, or foghorn, must emit a note between 250 and 700 Hz, and have a range of at least 0.5 miles (a power of 120 dB at 1 metre). The bell must have a diameter of at least 200 mm (8 inches) at the mouth.

Ground Tackle

Adequate ground tackle is essential for the safety of any vessel at anchor; the anchor sizes shown in Fig. 10.6 should prove satisfactory under most circum-stances. At least one kedge anchor, weighing about three quarters the weight of the bower anchor, should also be carried, and this will prove satisfactory for use in good weather.

A variety of different designs of anchor are available, each with their own pros and cons. The traditional Fisherman's or Admiralty anchor is seldom used nowadays, due to its greater weight and awkward shape. Also, when bedded in, one fluke is always exposed, and this may foul the anchor chain, or damage the hull if the boat dries out on top of it. However, it remains the best design for rocky ground or thick weed.

Most yachts are now equipped with one or other of the high holding designs available, the most common of which are the CQR, Danforth and Bruce. The

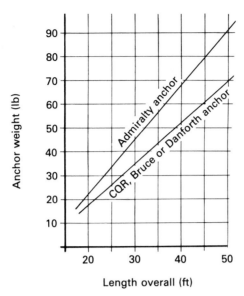

Fig. 10.6. Recommended anchor weights. The upper line is for a Fisherman's or Admiralty pattern anchor, the lower line covers high holding power types such as the Bruce, CQR and Danforth. Kedge anchors should not be less than half the weight of the main anchor.

Bruce is probably the best of the three on rock, and is specifically designed for use with a short scope. However, its awkward shape makes it difficult to stow. The Danforth is probably the best choice for a kedge, as it is very easy to stow and can be used without chain, but its weak point is on a weedy seabed. This leaves the CQR, which is an excellent all-rounder and slightly easier to stow than the Bruce.

The choice between rope and chain must also be made, each having advantages. Chain will not be chafed through by rock or coral, and its weight also means that the boat will swing about less. With a hawsepipe it is also self stowing, and takes up very little space. However, in severe weather its lack of stretch means that the boat's motion may be severely snubbed when the chain becomes taut; this can be prevented by sliding an angel down the chain. It is also undoubtedly heavy, and so is best stowed close to the mast, and not right in the bows as is often the case.

Nylon rope has the advantage of being light, but is also bulky and awkward to stow. It is prone to chafe on the bottom and at the stem fitting; to combat this, and to help the anchor lie properly, there must be at least 3 fathoms, and preferably 4½, of chain between the anchor and the rope. Also, rope less than 12 mm diameter should not be used, to ensure adequate chafe resistance. The larger scope required when rope is used can also present a problem in crowded moorings, as boats' anchor warps may become entwined and the boats will swing round in wider arcs.

Chapter 11

Handicapping Systems

For well over one hundred years handicap rules have been employed, with varying degrees of success, to enable yachts of differing designs to race against each other on an equal footing.

In most cases the boat is given a rating in accordance with some measurement rule, and the handicap is found by applying a time allowance formula, incorporating the boat's rating, to either the time taken to complete the course, or to the assumed distance sailed. This approach lies at the heart of the IOR, the newly introduced American MHS system, and for multihulls, the IOMR. A similar approach is used by the Portsmouth Yardstick and PHRF schemes, though in these cases the rating is found by analysing previous race results instead of by measuring the boat.

Another approach is to have the fleet sailing on a boat-for-boat basis, with no handicap being applied. The classic example of this is the 12-metre rule used for the America's Cup, and the related 6-metre and 5.5-metre classes. Here some latitude is allowed in design, within the framework of a fairly tight measurement rule.

The IOR also has its level rating classes, though their popularity has declined in the smaller classes due to the growth in one design classes. Another example of boat-for-boat racing is found in many of the long distance short-handed races, where boats are divided into classes purely on the basis of overall length.

Inevitably designers try to take advantage of the rating rule under which the boat will race, and so the handicap rule has a marked effect on racing yacht design. This becomes obvious when a 12-metre is compared with a yacht designed under the IOR. It is almost equally inevitable that cruising designs will be influenced by the racing boats of the day, in an attempt to give them a sporty image.

An important facet of designing to a handicap rule is that maximum performance *per se* is no longer important. Instead, the aim must be to obtain the maximum performance for a given rating, which may be completely different. The only exceptions to this are the Portsmouth Yardstick and the PHRF schemes, as these do not use any measurements taken off the boat.

The Portsmouth Yardstick Scheme

The Portsmouth Yardstick scheme assesses a boat's performance from her race results, and not from any measurements of the hull and rig. The corrected time is calculated from the simple formula:

$$C = \frac{E \times 100}{PN}$$

where E is the elapsed time, and PN the Portsmouth Number.

This means that if, say, a boat with a Portsmouth Number of 99 is sailing against one with a number of 107, the latter should take 107 minutes to cover the distance that the former sailed in 99 minutes if they are to have the same corrected time.

Clearly this system is best suited to established mass produced designs, as they will be able to return a greater number of race results, and so obtain a more accurate handicap. Thus the scheme embodies several grades of Portsmouth Numbers, reflecting different levels of accuracy.

Those designs that have had a constant Portsmouth Number over several years and a plentiful return of race results are awarded a Primary Yardstick by the RYA, whilst those showing some variation in performance, or relatively new designs, receive a Secondary Yardstick. New designs or one-offs are awarded a Trial Number by their local club for the first four races, based upon an assessment of their expected performance. After these preliminary results a more accurate Club Number is issued, and once sufficient results have been amassed a Primary or Secondary Number will be issued by the RYA.

The Portsmouth Number is based upon an assumed standard trim: a fixed keel, 150% overlapping genoa, spinnaker close to IOR size, and no engine. Variations from this standard are allowed for by adding or subtracting the appropriate correction factors, for example −1 for a lifting keel, or +4 for a boat with an engine and a fixed three-bladed propeller.

An interesting aspect of the scheme is that the handicap of a class inevitably allows for the average standard of racing within the class. People sailing a high performance racing design will be more likely to get the best out of their boat than those sailing a cruising design, and so the cruising classes will have a higher Portsmouth Number because of the less competitive nature of the people that sail them.

Handicapping by Length

Most short-handed ocean races divide the entrants up into classes according to their overall length, the winner in each class being simply the first to finish.

The most obvious outcome of this is the total domination of multihulls in this type of event, due to the consistently higher speed:length ratios they are able to achieve. It also leads to plumb ended boats, with very short overhangs and a smooth, powerful run to maximise the effective waterline length.

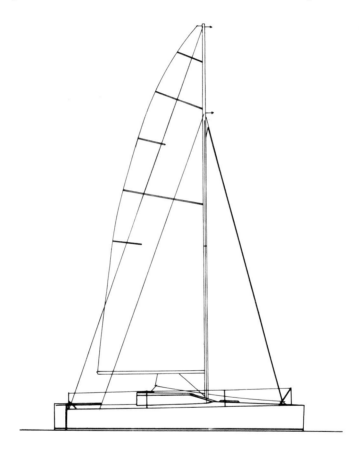

Fig. 11.1 A design for the Mini-Transat Race. Designed to a length limit of 6.5m (21ft 4in), this results in a plumb ended boat with a deep, bulbed lifting keel, and a powerful, high aspect ratio rig. In light airs a spinnaker may be hoisted from the masthead.

As neither sail area nor stability are measured, very large rigs are carried for good light airs performance. However, the sails must be easy to reef in stronger winds, and so roller reefing is the norm. To help support this sail area the boat will have a wide beam to give good stability unless she is a monohull designed primarily for windward work, when most of her stability will come from plenty of ballast carried deep in her keel, or from water ballast which can be dumped when off the wind.

The 6- and 12-metre Classes

These two classes both use the same measurement formula, differing only in the final figure, and so the boats are very similar in concept. The 6-metre class is currently undergoing a revival in popularity, but 12-metres are only built for the America's Cup, the world's most esoteric and exclusive sailing event.

The rule is refreshingly simple. The rating is given by:

$$R = \frac{L + 2d + \sqrt{S} - F}{2.37}$$

and R must not exceed 6 or 12 metres.

The measured length, L, is measured at a height of 1.5% of the rating above the waterline, plus any penalties incurred due to the bow or stern being too full. Artificially distorted ends are avoided by banning any hollows in the hull above the waterline. The girth difference, d, is the difference between the chain girth (which bridges any hollows) and the girth measured along the hull; it is measured at station 5½, from the sheer to a point 12.5% of the rating below the waterline. As this point is relatively deep, it effectively prevents the separate fin keel seen on IOR boats, and forces the designer to draw a deep hull with a bustled stern.

F is the freeboard, averaged between the stem, stern and midships sections; the maximum value is 8% of the rating plus 250 mm.

S is the rated sail area, which is simply the triangulated area of the mainsail plus 85% of the foretriangle area. The boat must have a true three-quarters rig, and there are strict limits on the mast height and size, genoa overlap, spinnaker dimensions and so on.

Both the minimum displacement and the maximum draught increase with the waterline length, and not the measurement length. This means that designers try to minimise the boat's displacement by having long overhangs fore and aft, relying on the boat's full ends to immerse when heeled, and so increase her sailing length.

The hull scantlings are closely controlled by Lloyd's. Originally these were drawn up for timber hulls, but now aluminium is permitted for 12-metres, and fibreglass for 6-metres. As the scantlings were calculated on the basis of equivalent stiffness and strength, wooden metre boats are no longer built as they come out considerably heavier, and so must carry less ballast.

Most designers agree that it does not pay to incur a penalty through d, and so the main trade off is between L (and thereby displacement) and S. Until recently, designs became longer and heavier, with less sail area, the aim being to improve the boat's maximum speed potential. This came about as a result of excessive dependence on tank test results – tank tests are very useful for measuring a yacht's performance in a straight line, but cannot assess properties such as acceleration

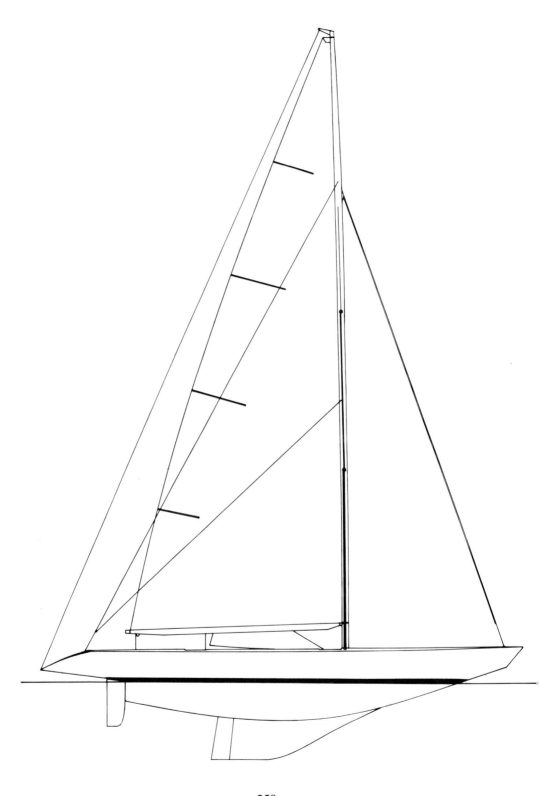

250

and manoeuvrability. However, there is now a trend towards shorter, lighter boats which may have a slightly lower maximum speed in a straight line under steady conditions, but also have greater acceleration and manoeuvrability, and so can realise more of their potential in race conditions. *Australia II's* winged, inverted keel shows how these smaller boats can still maintain sufficient stability.

The 5.5-metre Class

The 5.5-metre rule was formulated in 1949 to provide a three man keelboat that was cheaper to build and more exciting than the 6-metres. Rather than use the same form of rule, a new formula was developed:

$$R = 0.9\left[\frac{L\sqrt{S}}{12\sqrt[3]{D}} + \frac{L + \sqrt{S}}{4}\right]$$

L is measured in the same way as on the other metre boats, but a fuller stern is permitted without penalty, and a lower penalty is placed on full bows.

S is the triangulated area of the mainsail, plus the area of the largest genoa. Limitations are placed on the height of the mast, the size of the foretriangle (again, ensuring a fractional rig), and the minimum genoa size. Once again, the spinnaker dimensions are related to the foretriangle.

D is the displacement, measured in cubic metres and derived by weighing the boat.

Draught, freeboard and beam are all controlled by fixed limits. Note that there is no girth difference measurement, and so 5.5-metres owe more to IOR yachts in their keel and rudder configurations than to the other metre classes. Hull construction is once again governed by Lloyd's, either timber or fibreglass being permitted. However, the fibreglass scantlings have been worked out to give the same hull weight as a timber boat, and so there is relatively little to choose between them.

Most boats are designed to lie close to the maximum limits of *L* and *D*, and so have the minimum sail area. However, an alternative approach that could be at least as competitive would be to go for minimum *L* and *D*, and maximum *S*. The waterline length could be increased by having a straight stem instead of the 12-metre type still prevalent in the class, and a relatively wide and full stern. The reduced stability, due chiefly to the reduced amount of ballast, could be offset by a slight increase in beam, or by using a bulb keel. However, the increase in heeling moment would not be that great, as the height of the rig would not change. This approach would have excellent performance in light airs, and off the wind in a

---

Fig. 11.2. Six-metre design by Ed Dubois. Dimensions: LOA 10.425 m; LWL 7.162 m; Beam 2.857 m; Draft 1.646 m; Sail area 59.7 m^2 (main + No. 1 genoa); Displacement 3.963 m^3. Rule dimensions: *L* 8.377 m; *S* 42.6 m^2; *F* 0.684 m; *d* 0 m. In this drawing the top of the boot top represents the height at which *L* is measured.

Fig. 11.3. '*Victory 82*' 12-metre designed by Ed Dubois. Dimensions: LOA 20.04 m; LWL 13.715 m; Beam 3.784 m; Draft 2.35 m; Sail area 200.5 m^2; Displacement 24.213 m^3.

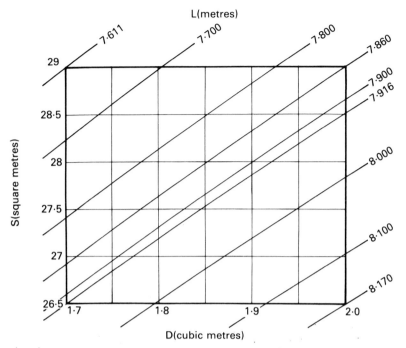

Fig. 11.4. A plot of the combinations of *L*, *S* and *D* permitted under the 5.5-metre rule.

blow; its only possible weakness would be upwind in a blow, but any slight losses here would easily be compensated for on other legs of the course.

The Measurement Handicap System

This rating rule has been developed in the USA as a result of dissatisfaction with the IOR in some quarters. It is based upon the results of tank testing a systematic series of hulls, which have been incorporated into what is perhaps one of the most accurate performance prediction programs currently available. However it does have its weak points, generally overestimating the performance of boats, particularly those with narrow, deep hulls; underestimating tacking angles; and not assessing the effect of the keel particularly well. Also, it is not able to be used for very light displacement designs. These shortcomings are being worked upon, though.

One aspect in which it differs notably from the IOR is that the complete lines of the yacht are lifted off by means of an electronic measuring wand, and the computer uses the entire lines plan, instead of discrete measurement points, to assess the yacht's performance. This inevitably results in fairer hulls than most IOR designs, but does not mean that the rule will not develop a particular style of yacht in time, just as the metre rules and the IOR have done.

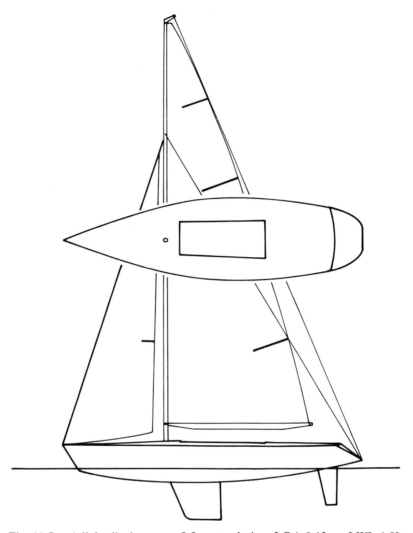

Fig. 11.5. A light displacement 5.5-metre design. LOA 8.12 m; LWL 6.52 m; Beam 2.19 m; Draft 1.35 m; Displacement 1.74 tonnes; Sail area 29 m².

Another good feature of the MHS rule is that it has much more extensive interior accommodation requirements than the IOR, to prevent even the most serious of racing boats from being totally stripped out inside. In fact the whole underlying concept of the rule is biased towards cruiser racers, as is borne out by a ban on bloopers, and limitations on mast bend and the use of hydraulics. However, not all of these regulations are being enforced until the rule is firmly established.

The chief weakness of the rule is that instead of producing just one handicap figure, a table of speed predictions is produced for different true wind strengths and directions, covering between 8 and 20 knots of wind. The race committee

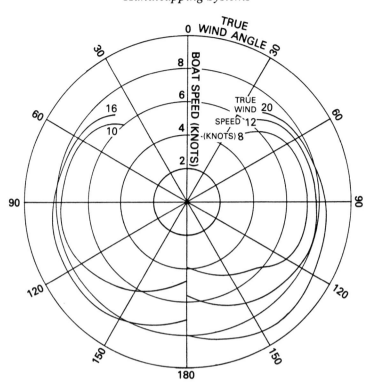

Fig. 11.6. The performance of a 43-foot yacht, as calculated by the Velocity Prediction Program used by the MHS rule. Even allowing for the fact that the program assumes flat water conditions, most designers agree that the predicted speeds are too high. Also note the poor coverage at low and high wind speeds.

assesses the conditions under which the race was sailed, and calculates a mean velocity from the boat's handicap table. Although this may seem ideal at first sight, in practice it is far from ideal. No two boats in a given race are likely to have the same wind conditions, due to different sizes of boat, tidal gates, and other similar factors. Thus some boats will fare better than they deserve and others will be worse off, depending upon the conditions assumed by the race committee. And the above argument assumes that the committee assess the conditions fairly in the first place. However, an average handicap figure is also given on the certificate, which is approximately the same as the figure given for a 10 knot wind.

The International Offshore Rule

The IOR can rate almost any monohull design within the rating band of 16 to 70 feet (about 22 feet to 80 feet LOA). As it is used for almost all top level racing, it is analysed in depth in the next two chapters. Over the years it has been realised that one rule is incapable of rating all designs equitably; thus the Offshore Racing Council, who manage the rule, have redefined its aims, which are now to protect the existing IOR fleet from rapid design changes and premature obsolescence.

This is stated in the rule management policy, placed right at the beginning of the rulebook. It states its policy to be

'...to permit the development of seaworthy offshore racing yachts....The Council will endeavour to protect the majority of the existing IOR fleet from rapid obsolescence caused by...developments which produce increased performance without corresponding changes in ratings...'

This means that the Rule is not interested in developing faster boats, nor is it concerned with developing to a point where all designs will be handicapped fairly. Instead, it is aimed at maintaining the status quo within the existing fleet.

The original rule was perfectly adequate for rating boats in existence at that time. However, designers naturally studied the Rule to seize upon any advantages they could find, the most noticeable of which have been a reduction in displacement and a return to fractional rigs. This has resulted in annual alterations, and we are now on the Mk III version of the Rule, which appears to have achieved some level of stability over the last couple of years.

One of the major weaknesses of the Rule, is the actual measuring system, based on plumb bobs and measuring tapes. Measurement errors of up to about 3% have occurred, particularly where the measurer is assisted by a member of the boat's crew or some other interested party, and so complete remeasurement of boats is avoided wherever possible, unless changes have been made to the boat.

In addition to the full measurement procedure for one-off boats, production boats may be rated upon standardised hull measurements. This offers much more consistent measurements, and the majority of all new boats are measured by this system. Most of the measurements are standardised for the class, with only the freeboards and key rig measurements being taken on each boat.

The competitive life of racing yachts is extended by the Mk IIIA rule, which lowers the boat's rating according to its age and the proportions of its hull and rig. The rule is formulated so that boats with proportions close to the current fleet norm are given a negligible rating reduction in comparison with more old fashioned and less favourably rated designs. Even though new boats can benefit under Mk IIIA, the rule has been formulated in such a way that flat out racing boats cannot benefit.

The IOR only produces a rating, always expressed in feet; it is left to each racing body to develop a handicapping formula. This may be based upon the distance sailed (time on distance), or the time taken (time on time).

Time on time handicapping

The time on time system is chiefly used in Britain, Australia, New Zealand, and Japan. In Britain the RORC formula is used: the time multiplication factor, TMF,

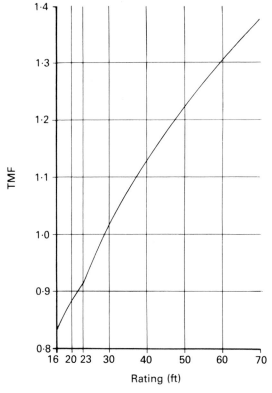

Fig. 11.7. A graph of TMF against rating.

is multiplied by the elapsed time to give the corrected time. The formulae used are:

$$TMF = \frac{0.2424\sqrt{R}}{1 + 0.0567\sqrt{R}} \quad \text{for boats rating 23 feet and over,}$$

$$TMF = \frac{0.4039\sqrt{R}}{1 + 0.2337\sqrt{R}} \quad \text{for boats rating up to 23 feet.}$$

Two formulae are used to allow for the higher speed:length ratios attainable by smaller boats when sailing off the wind. A graph of the *TMF* against rating is plotted in Fig. 11.7.

If we take a three-quarter tonner as scratch boat, with a rating of 24.5 feet, it will give or take the following amounts of time per hour:

Mini tonner	gives	6 min 6 sec
Quarter tonner	gives	4 min 31 sec
Half tonner	gives	1 min 59 sec
One tonner	takes	4 min 57 sec
Maxi rater	takes	28 min 6 sec

257

It is interesting to look at the effect that small changes in rating have on a boat's race results. If we take a half tonner, rating 22.0 feet, it will have a *TMF* of 0.9038. If the rating is reduced by 0.45% to 21.9 feet, the *TMF* drops to 0.9028. This is a change of only 0.111%, or 16 seconds in a 4-hour race. Thus most yachtsmen would benefit more by practising on the water than by spending time and money making small changes to the rating.

The RORC has its own age allowance scheme, in addition to the Mk IIIA rule. It is based upon the launch date of the boat, and not the age date used by the IOR. For every year that the launch date precedes 1978, the *TMF* is reduced by 0.15%, up to a maximum of 4.35% for a boat launched in 1955. In conjunction with the Mk IIIA rule this can make some old boats very competitive indeed.

In races where the wind strength is constant and sufficiently strong for yachts to reach hull speed, time on time handicapping is very fair. However, if the wind drops, or if it is light for the duration of the race, the smaller boats are favoured. On the other hand, in strong winds the bigger boats are favoured, especially when there is a large amount of windward work.

Time on distance

Time on distance is used in the Americas, the Mediterranean countries, Germany and Scandinavia. The USYRU formula is generally used, which assumes that the time taken to sail one nautical mile is:

$$0.6 \left(\frac{3600}{\sqrt{R}} + 306.07 \right) \text{ seconds.}$$

Thus the difference in elapsed time between two boats, sailed equally well, is given by:

$$0.6\left(\frac{3600}{\sqrt{R_1}} - \frac{3600}{\sqrt{R_2}} \right) \text{ seconds per mile.}$$

Figure 11.8 shows the assumed average speed against the rating.

Once again, taking a three-quarter tonner as scratch boat, the following time allowances apply, in seconds per mile:

Mini tonner	gives 1 min 35 sec
Quarter tonner	gives 1 min 6 sec
Half tonner	gives 24 sec
One tonner	takes 45 sec
Maxi rater	takes 2 min 58 sec

An obvious problem with this system lies in deciding upon the distance to be used. For Olympic and short offshore races it is simply the straight line course. However, on long offshore races consideration of the prevailing winds and

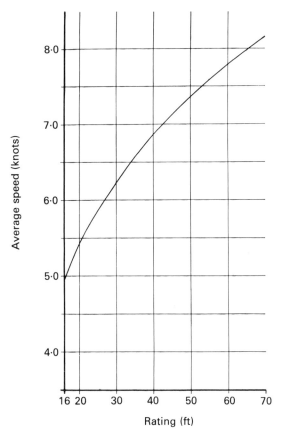

Fig. 11.8. A graph of the average speed assumed by the time-on-distance handicap system.

currents may take the boat well away from the rhumb line; in this case the race committee has to decide upon a distance that represents the course likely to be taken by the bulk of the competitors.

The time on distance system is unaffected by changes in the wind strength, but is affected by the course sailed. The factor of 0.6 is perfectly satisfactory when there is an equal amount of beating, reaching and running, but favours larger boats in windward races, and smaller boats in races off the wind. However, this can be compensated for by increasing the factor for windward races, and reducing it for courses off the wind. It also assumes that the tidal streams cancel out, but if the stream goes with the boats the smaller classes will be favoured, and vice versa.

Level rating classes

The Offshore Racing Council offers boat-for-boat racing in the level rating classes, and both world and national championships are organised.

259

Five classes exist, with the following rating levels (under IOR Mk III or, if eligible, Mk IIIA).

Mini ton	16.5 feet
Quarter ton	18.5 feet
Half ton	22.0 feet
Three-quarter ton	24.5 feet
One ton	30.5 feet

In addition to having a valid IOR certificate, the boats must comply with minimum headroom and accommodation standards, and restrictions on instrumentation, the size of the sail wardrobe, and the number of crew. These are all laid down in the ORC's 'green book'. The ORC safety regulations must also be complied with; generally, category 2 is required for all classes except mini tonners, which usually sail under category 4. Mini tonners also have a maximum beam restriction of 2.5 metres (8 feet 2⅜ inches), which permits them to be towed behind a car.

Chapter 12

The International Offshore Rule (IOR)

Because of the complexities of the IOR, and the annual changes to which it is subjected, an up-to-date copy of the Rule should always be consulted before making any alterations to the boat. The formulae quoted here have in some cases been rearranged from the forms given in the rule book to clarify their meaning, but their content has not been altered.

There are two stages in the measurement procedure. First of all the boat is measured out of the water, where the bulk of the measurements are taken; then the boat is put into the water for the inclining test to be carried out, and for the freeboards to be measured. The immersed depths are then found by subtracting the freeboards from the hull depths. This means that if the ballast is altered, or the interior changed, only the measurement afloat needs to be repeated, and complete remeasurement is reserved for changes to the hull shape. This avoids variations in rating due to the limitations of accuracy inherent in the measuring system.

The IOR Examined

The rating equation

Although the IOR contains a lot of complex detail, only four major and a number of minor parameters are used to calculate the rating.

This is calculated in two stages. Firstly, the measured rating (MR) is given by:

$$MR = \left[\frac{0.13 \times L \times SC}{\sqrt{B \times D}} + \frac{L}{4} + \frac{SC}{5} + DC + FC \right] \times DLF$$

Here the main parameters are:

L Rated length – a measure of the effective waterline length.

B Rated beam – the most fundamental measurement under the rule.

D   Rated depth – measures the mean depth of the canoe body.

SC   Sail value – the square root of the rated sail area.

The product $B \times D$ measures the bulk of the yacht below the waterline, and so is related to the displacement.

The secondary parameters in this equation are:

DC   Draft correction – takes into account the maximum draft of the vessel.

FC   Freeboard correction – encourages high freeboard.

DLF   Displacement length factor – penalises light displacement.

An analysis of the equation shows that an increase of 1% in any parameter produces the following approximate change in *MR*:

L	0.835% increase
B or D	0.229% decrease
SC	0.624% increase
DC or FC	0.500% increase
DLF	1.000% increase

Although the effect of changes in *DC* and *FC* appears large, their magnitude is small, and so their effect on the rating is minimal.

The measured rating is multiplied by several corrective factors to produce the yacht's rating:

$$R = MR \times EPF \times CGF \times MAF \times SMF \times LRP \times CBF \times TPF$$

EPF   Engine and propeller factor – compensates for the extra resistance due to the engine and propeller.

CGF   Centre of gravity factor – taxes an excessively high or low centre of gravity.

MAF   Movable appendage factor – taxes trim tabs etc.

SMF   Spar material factor – taxes exotic spar materials.

LRP   Low rigging penalty – taxes spars with four or more sets of spreaders.

CBF   Centreboard factor – taxes dinghy-type daggerboards.

TPF   Trim penalty factor – penalises boats trying to benefit by a large difference between trim levels ashore and afloat.

In most cases all of these factors, except *EPF* and *CGF*, can be ignored, as the penalties are so high as to make them not worthwhile.

Rated beam, B

The rated beam is in many ways the most important measurement, as it figures in almost every other calculation. It is measured by first of all finding the position of the maximum beam station (*BMAX*), and then measuring *B* at a distance of *BMAX*/6 below the sheer line. If the sheer line is convex, a rated sheer line is used, which is basically a straight line between the stem and stern; however, there

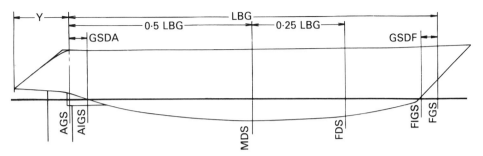

Fig. 12.1. The positions of the girth and depth stations. As is now usual, *AGS* is positioned at the forward end of the transom and a girth difference, *GD*, is measured. Even the large forward overhang on this yacht is only half of the maximum permitted under the rule. The overhang aft, *Y*, has been drawn to the maximum permitted by the rule without incurring a penalty.

is no correction for a concave sheer line. Thus most yachts have a virtually straight sheer to maximise the *B* measurement.

Because of the large benefits for a high value of *B*, the hull is flared out above the waterline to the *B* measurement point, and then the flare is reduced towards the sheer to minimise *BMAX*, thereby increasing *B* by bringing it higher up the topsides. The same result can be achieved by increasing the freeboard.

Rated length, L

Almost all of the complexities of the IOR are to be found in the measurement of *L*, especially at the stern. This is because the original formulae were not sufficiently comprehensive, and as soon as a loophole was discovered the Rule was patched up to prevent the fleet from becoming outdated too quickly.

The length measurement is based upon four girth stations, two at each end of the yacht. The girths (measured from sheer to sheer) are proportional to *B*, and so a large *B* measurement increases the girth lengths. This means that the girth positions are effectively moved in from the ends of the hull, and so the rated length is reduced.

At the bows, the forward girth station (*FGS*) has a girth of 0.5*B*, and the forward inner girth station (*FIGS*) has a girth of 0.75*B*. At the stern, the after girth station (*AGS*) is usually sited at the forward end of the transom, and the amount by which it exceeds 0.75*B* is recorded as the girth difference, *GD*. If the boat has a fine stern giving a negative girth difference, the girth station is brought forwards to a point where *GD* is zero.

The after inner girth station (*AIGS*) is then positioned at the point where the girth is 0.125*B* greater than at *AGS*. However, the distance between the girth stations (*GSDA*) may not be less than 0.1(*B* + *GD*). If *AIGS* would otherwise lie aft of this position, its girth is recorded as *GLAI*; however, *GLAI* is normally zero.

263

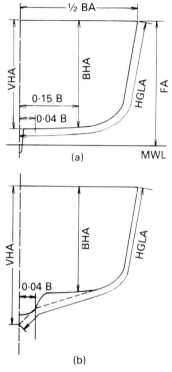

Fig. 12.2. Measurements taken at the aft girth stations. Although only the aft girth station is shown here, measurements at the aft inner girth station are exactly the same, except that *VHAI* is calculated by:

$$VHAI = VHA + (BHAI - BHA).$$

(a) Where there is no skeg, *HGLA* and *VHA* are simply measured to the centreline. Similarly, if there is a skeg narrower than 0.04*B* the skeg is ignored and the hull is projected through it at a tangent to the hull at the 0.04*B* buttock.

(b) By using a fat skeg the girth can be artificially increased. This is often used at the *AIGS* to bring the girth stations closer together. A chain girth is taken to the 0.04*B* buttock, and the girth then follows a line tangential to the hull at the 0.04*B* buttock, though the angle made with the waterline may not be taken as greater than 45°. If used at the *AGS*, *VHA* will be increased, to the detriment of *AOCP*.

If there is a skeg at either girth station, the position is complicated still further. The girth measurement is made up of two parts. First of all a chain girth is measured from the sheer to a buttock line 0.04*B* off the centreline; then the girth measurement to the centreline is calculated by assuming the hull to follow a straight line, tangential to the section at the 0.04*B* buttock. However, the assumed hull shape may not make an angle greater than 45° to the waterline. A skeg is often incorporated into *AIGS* to help bring the two girth stations closer together, as it can create an artificially high girth measurement.

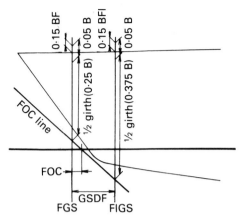

Fig. 12.3. *FOC* measurements. Note that the *FOC* line is almost parallel to a line drawn through the low points of *FGS* and *FIGS*. As is usual, the *FOC* line crosses the waterline aft of *FGS* (ie *FOC* is positive), but forward of the stem.

Now that the girth stations have been set up, the length between girths (*LBG*) is found, measured from *FGS* to *AGS*. Then the forward overhang component (*FOC*) and aft overhang component corrected (*AOCC*) are calculated to find the positions of the ends of the rated length with respect to the girth stations, and subtracted from *LBG* to find *L*. Thus:

$$L = LBG - FOC - AOCC$$

FOC

At the forward girth stations the rule finds the positions of two points, measured below the sheer line at a distance of half the girth, minus 15% of the beam, plus 5% of *B*. It then draws a straight line through these points that cuts the waterline, and *FOC* is the amount by which the point of the intersection of this line with the waterline lies aft of *FGS*. This is all combined into the one formula:

$$FOC = \frac{GSDF(FF - 0.3B + 0.15BF)}{0.125B + (FF + 0.15BF) - (FFI + 0.15BFI) + 0.5GDFI}$$

with the proviso that *FOC* may not exceed 1.5*GSDF*.

In this equation, 0.3*B* is 0.05*B* plus half the girth at the *FGS*, and 0.125*B* is the difference between the half girths at *FGS* and *FIGS*. *GDFI* is zero, except for yachts with a bulbous bow or a hollow at the *FGS*, and so may be ignored. The upper limit of *FOC* may also be ignored, it being there to prevent extremely long overhands being used to gain unmeasured waterline length.

The formula takes no account of the profile of the bow, and so V-sections are employed to give as deep a profile as possible for a given girth measurement, thereby maximising the waterline length. Reducing the freeboard moves the girth stations aft, thus reducing *LBG*; whilst *FOC* is reduced, there is some rating benefit as *FIGS* moves further aft than *FGS*. Fine waterlines with little flare are also encouraged, as the increase in waterline length due to the deeper profile is greater than the rating penalty.

AOCC

At the stern, two lines are constructed to find *AOCP* and *AOCG*, and these are then combined to give *AOCC*. *AOCP* is the profile component of *AOC*, and measures the effective waterline length; *AOCG* measures the rate at which the girth tapers, and thereby assesses the fullness of the stern. In both cases imaginary points are set up at the *AGS* and *AIGS*, and the inverse gradient of the straight line joining them is calculated (*AGSL* and *APSLC*). The height of the line above the water at the *AGS* is then measured, and from this the distance from the *AGS* to the point where the line crosses the waterline is found, giving *AOCP* and *AOCG*.

AOCP   *AOCP* is meant to find the point at which a line drawn $0.018LBGC$ below the hull profile cuts the waterline. *LBGC* is the length between girths that would be found if the *AGS* were moved aft to a point where *GD* would be zero; it is given by:

$$LBGC = LBG + \frac{0.5GD \times GSDA}{HGLI - HGLA}$$

where *HGLA* and *HGLI* are the half girths at *AGS* and *AIGS*.

The inverse gradient of the *AOCP* line is given by:

$$APSL = \frac{GSDA}{(FA - VHA) - (FAI - VHAI)}$$

Although *VHA* and *VHAI* are meant to be the vertical heights on the centreline, it became common practice to increase *VHAI* artificially, and thereby decrease *APSL*, by having a fat skeg or V-ed section at the *AIGS*. Thus *VHAI* is now found by using the slope of the $0.15B$ buttocks and *VHA*, thus:

$$VHAI = VHA + (BHAI - BHA)$$

After this loophole was blocked, designers found it paid to draw normal flat sections, but to bring the girth stations close together with a sharp rise in the buttocks, often with a crease at the *AGS* where the profile reverts to its normal shallow run. To counteract this, a base profile slope (*BAPSL*) is also calculated and *APSLC* is taken as the greater (i.e. least steep) of *APSL* and *BAPSL*, with the proviso that it shall not be taken as greater than 7.0.

BAPSL is given by:

$$BAPSL = \frac{0.4(0.9LBG + GD + Y)}{CMDI + MDI + 2(FA + VHA - 2BHA)}$$

The bracketed term on the top line is double the distance from amidships to the

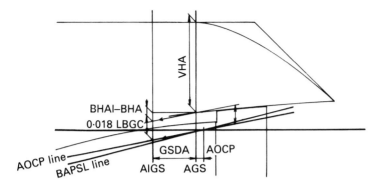

Fig. 12.4(a). *AOCP* measurements. A line is drawn between the low point of *VHA* at the *AGS*, and the low point of the calculated value of *VHAI* at the *AIGS*. The *AOCP* is then drawn parallel to this line, but at a distance of 0.018*LBGC* below it. The *BAPSL* line has also been drawn in for comparison, though in this instance it would be ignored as the *AOCP* line has a shallower slope.

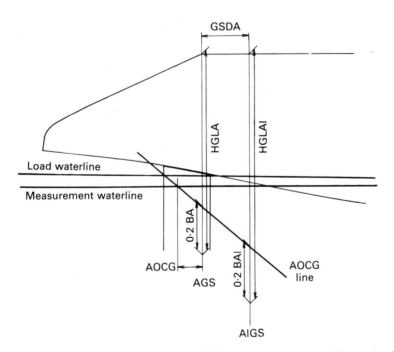

Fig. 12.4(b). *AOCG* measurements. With the present trend for powerful sterns, resulting in high girth lengths at the *AGS* and *AIGS*, *AOCG* is usually negative. Thus by bringing the girth stations close together the *AOCG* line is steepened, and the rating reduced. The same effect can be achieved by a high *BA* and *BAI*, particularly when *BA* is almost as large as *BAI*. The load waterline of this mini tonner has also been drawn in, and the importance of bow-down trim for measurement can clearly be seen.

stern, including the aft overhang Y, and GD is a measure of the fullness of the stern. The first two terms on the bottom line are depths taken at the mid depth station, midway between FGS and AGS. The bracketed term is the height of the $0.15B$ buttock above the waterline, plus the difference between VHA and BHA. Thus the bottom line is effectively double the rise in the hull profile from the mid depth station to the AGS. Combining all these terms gives the inverse gradient of the hull profile if it were a straight line, and multiplying by 0.4 increases the gradient by a factor of 2.5 to allow for curvature in the profile. On new boats the only case where $BAPSL$ is ignored is when GD is zero, the assumption being that a boat with such a fine stern has little to gain from a distortion in the run, as the hull sections are tapering too rapidly.

After the complications of determining $APSLC$, $AOCP$ is refreshingly straightforward:

$$AOCP = APSLC\,(FA - VHA - CCAI - 0.018LBGC)$$

The bracketed term gives the height of the $AOCP$ line above the waterline at the AGS, and multiplying this by $APSLC$ gives the point at which the line meets the water. $CCAI$ is a curvature penalty and is usually zero. If the bracketed term is less than zero, as is often the case, $AOCP$ will be negative and $APSLC$ may not be taken as greater than 6.0; if it is greater than zero $AOCP$ will be positive (i.e. help reduce L), and $APSLC$ may not be taken as greater than 4.0.

There are two approaches to obtaining a good value for $AOCP$. Firstly, the profile can be given a severe inflection between the girth stations to reduce $APSL$ (within the limitations of $BAPSL$). With this approach the girth stations are usually brought well forward so that there is a long, effective overhang aft.

Alternatively, so long as the $AOCP$ line is above the waterline at the AGS, the gradient of the hull profile may be minimised so that the $AOCP$ line cuts the waterline well forward of the AGS. Here the girth stations are normally sited fairly well aft, both to ensure that the $AOCP$ line is clear of the water at the AGS, and to help give a shallow profile slope. Boats designed along these lines are often highly dependent upon bow-down trim, and so a fat skeg may be fitted to increase the buoyancy in the stern.

$AOCG$ $AOCG$ measures the distance from the AGS at which a line, drawn at a distance below the sheer of the half girth of the section minus 20% of the section beam, cuts the waterline.

Once again, the inverse gradient is calculated:

$$AGSL = \frac{GSDA}{(FA - (HGLA - 0.2BA)) - (FAI - (HGLI - 0.2BAI))}$$

This is then multiplied by the height of the line at the AGS to give the girth component:

$$ACG1 = AGSL(FA - (HGLA - 0.2BA))$$

Designers soon found that it paid to offset a shallow hull profile with a steep girth slope, brought about by keeping the girth stations close together and having BA, the beam at the AGS, as large as possible. To block this, the rulemakers decided that if $AGSL$ was found to be less than $0.8APSLC$, a second formula would be applied, giving $ACG2$, and $AOCG$ would be the lesser of $ACG1$ and $ACG2$. $ACG2$ is given by:

$$ACG2 = 0.8APSLC[0.5((FA + 0.2BA - HGLA) \\ + (FAI + 0.2BAI - HGLAI))] + 0.5GSDA$$

The term in square brackets simply finds the height of the $AOCG$ line at a point midway between the girth stations. This is then multiplied by $0.8APSLC$ to find the distance from this point at which a line with a slope of $0.8APSLC$ would cut the waterline, and finally $0.5GSDA$ is added on to find the distance of the intersection from the AGS.

As $ACG2$ must always be numerically greater than $ACG1$, it is only used when the $AOCG$ line lies below the waterline at the AGS, that is when $ACG1$ and $ACG2$ are negative. If the stern is sufficiently fine for the $AOCG$ line to lie above the waterline it is assumed that steepening the girth slope will give such a fine, V-ed stern that no performance benefit can be gained, and so $ACG1$ is always used.

Unless the yacht is intended solely for light airs, it is generally agreed that a relatively high GD is required to give a powerful run for speed off the wind. This means that the $AOCG$ line is usually below the waterline at the AGS, and so the only way of obtaining a good $AOCG$ is to aim for a low $AGSL$.

To some extent the penalty incurred by a high GD can be minimised by having large values for BA and BAI. This, together with the benefits of a small VHA, results in the typical IOR stern: very flat close to the waterline to reduce VHA, and then quickly turning into an almost straight flare to the sheer, so that as much as possible of the section contributes to the effective sailing length.

YCOR   Before we can calculate $AOCC$, an allowance must be made for the overhang aft of the AGS, namely Y. This is done by calculating $YCOR$, and adding it directly onto AOC.

If GD is zero it is assumed that the stern is too fine to benefit from a long overhang, and so $YCOR$ is also taken as zero. Otherwise $YCOR$ is the greater of:

$$0.15LBG - Y \quad \text{or} \quad 1.7VHA - 0.5GD - Y$$

but it shall never be taken as greater than zero.

The first term is the one that usually applies, and it says that when Y exceeds 15% of LBG any excess shall be added to the rated length. The second term permits boats with a large VHA or small GD to have a slightly longer overhang.

269

As the end of a long overhang is seldom that beneficial, hulls are usually designed to make $YCOR$ zero.

Calculating $AOCC$ The first step in calculating $AOCC$ is to find AOC, the aft overhang component. This is the least of:

$$0.5(AOCP + AOCG) + YCOR$$
$$\text{or } 0.05LBG + 0.95AOCP + YCOR$$
$$\text{or } 0.05LBG + 0.95AOCG + YCOR$$

Originally only the first expression was used, simply averaging $AOCP$ and $AOCG$. However, as we have seen, some designers traded off a very large $AOCP$ against a moderate $AOCG$; this resulted in the introduction of the other two terms.

We are now in a position to calculate $AOCC$. If, as is usually the case, $AOC + Y$ is positive, $AOCC$ is set equal to AOC, except that it may not be greater than $1.25GSDA$. However, if $AOC + Y$ is negative, that is, the aft end of the rated length appears to lie beyond the stern, $AOCC$ is negative and the greater of the absolute values of $0.6AOC$ or Y. This brings the aft end of L to the tip of the transom, unless the overhang is very short, in which case the aft end of L will lie abaft of the stern. As a reminder, L is now found by subtracting FOC and $AOCC$ from L.

Rated depth, D

The rated depth is found by setting up two depth stations and taking a series of depth measurements at various distances off the centreline. Amidships the mid depth station, MDS, is sited midway between the AGS and FGS, as has already been mentioned in connection with $BAPSL$. At this station CMD, MD and OMD are measured from the sheer to the $0.125B$, $0.25B$ and $0.375B$ buttocks respectively. The immersed depths $CMDI$, MDI and $OMDI$ are then found by subtracting the freeboard at this point, FMD.

The forward depth station (FDS) is set up midway between the MDS and the FGS, and the immersed depth (FDI) is found by subtracting the freeboard (FFD) from the hull depth measured at the $0.1B$ buttock (FD).

The sectional area at the mid depth station, divided by B, is given by:

$$MDIA = 0.125(3CMDI + 2MDI - 2OMDI) + 0.5OMDI \times \frac{BWL}{B}$$

For a given cross-sectional area no benefit is to be had from varying the proportions of CMD and MD, and OMD is close to zero, so its effect is small.

As we shall soon see, a high value of FDI is rated very beneficially, and this

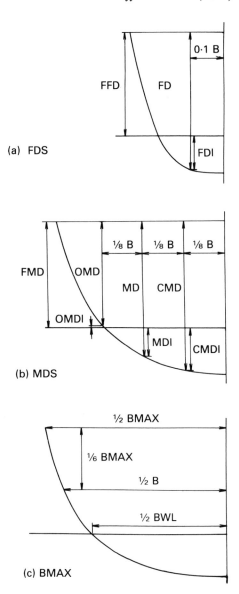

(a) FDS

(b) MDS

(c) BMAX

Fig. 12.5. Measurements at the *FDS*, *MDS* and *BMAX* stations. Note how all depth measurements are taken from the sheerline, and not the waterline. This means that the boat can be remeasured simply by measuring the freeboards at the forward and after girth stations. As the waterline beam *BWL* has a very marked effect on the *CGF* calculations, it is now found by taking the *BWL* at a series of points above and below the estimated waterline, and interpolating a value from the freeboard measurements.

The flat forefoot of IOR designs is due to the distance off centre at which *FD* is measured. Here *FDI* is at its maximum value of 0.475 (*MDI* + *CMDI*).

It can be seen how a flared section at the *BMAX* station reduces *B*, by causing it to be measured lower down where the flare reduces its value.

means that once again a maximum value has had to be imposed. Thus *FDIC* is taken as the smallest of:

$$FDI \quad \text{or} \quad 0.5FDI + 0.2175(MDI + CMDI) \quad \text{or} \quad 0.475(MDI + CMDI)$$

The first expression is used when the Rule deems *FDI* to be moderate, and the last term is the maximum value that may be taken for *FDIC*. The middle term imposes a gradual penalty, and is applicable when *FDI* exceeds $0.435(MDI + CMDI)$.

Now the rated depth is given by:

$$D = 1.3MDIA + 0.9FDIC + 0.055(3FOC - AOCC) + \left(\frac{L + 10}{30}\right)$$

The first two terms are related to the bulk of the hull, but note that *FDIC* is generously rated at almost 70% of *MDIA*. As a result most designs have *FDI* close to the penalty value. The third term is an allowance for the ends of the yacht, and can be ignored as it is only about 3% of the total. Finally, there is a scaling factor, which is notable as one of the few instances in which a high *L* is beneficial.

To obtain the maximum depth measurements for a given cross-sectional area, soft chines often appear at the measurement points, with straight lines in between. This is why IOR boats have a flat section across the centreline for most of their length. However, the extent to which this may be carried out is restricted, as will be seen in the next chapter.

No depth measurement is required at the stern, as for a boat to float in a given trim the centres of buoyancy and gravity must lie in the same vertical line, and so the buoyancy forward must be balanced by the buoyancy aft.

Displacement length factor, DLF

The displacement length factor was introduced after designers discovered that they could produce ultra-light downwind flyers which were still competitive upwind. It penalises the yacht if its displacement falls below a certain level; unfortunately this means a particularly high displacement:length ratio at the smaller end of the fleet, whilst large yachts can have a much lower ratio.

First of all the base displacement ratio is calculated:

$$BDR = \left[\frac{(2.165L^{0.525} - 5.85)^3}{(L \times B \times MDIA)}\right]^{0.125} \quad \text{but may not be less than 1.0}$$

The bottom line, if multiplied by 32, gives the yacht's displacement in pounds, assuming a prismatic coefficient of 0.5 (i.e. $DSPL = 32 \times L \times B \times MDIA$). The upper line gives the minimum penalty-free displacement, once again in pounds if multiplied by 32; this function is plotted in Fig. 12.6.

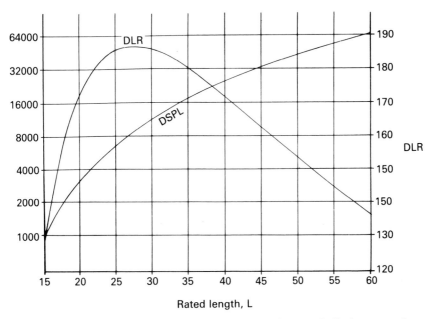

Fig. 12.6. Base displacement curves. *DSPL* is the rated displacement in pounds, calculated as $32 \times L \times B \times MDIA$. *DLR* is the minimum penalty-free displacement:length ratio calculated from *L* and *DSPL*. The *DLR* curve clearly shows the comparatively heavy displacement required by boats with a rated length of 25–35 feet.

Thus *BDR* is simply the ratio of the rule base displacement to the yacht's displacement, raised to the power of ⅛. It has a value of 1.0 whenever the yacht's displacement exceeds the base displacement.

The penalty is then calculated by:

$$DLF = 1 + 5.7(BDR - 1)^{1.75} \qquad \text{but may not be greater than 1.1.}$$

DLF is equal to one, i.e. no penalty is incurred, whenever *BDR* is one. As the boat gets lighter, though, an increasingly heavy penalty is applied, reaching a maximum of 10% of the rating when the displacement is about 47% of the base value. When first introduced some designs incurred penalties of as much as 6%, but nowadays very few designs have a *DLF* exceeding 1.0175, and even this value is restricted chiefly to the smaller classes.

One approach that a designer can use to avoid a *DLF* penalty is to reduce the prismatic coefficient, thereby increasing the value of *MDIA* without an overall increase in displacement.

Freeboard correction, FC

A mean value for the measured freeboard is given by:

273

$$FM = \frac{1.2FF + 0.8FA}{2}$$

and this is compared with the base freeboard:

$$FB = 0.057L + 1.2$$

If, as is usually the case, *FM* is greater than *FB*, then the freeboard correction is given by:

$$FC = 0.15(FB - FM)$$

but if *FM* is less than *FB* a penalty is imposed:

$$FC = 0.25(FB - FM)$$

The effect of *FC* on the rating is small, but in most cases it is beneficial (i.e. negative), as a high freeboard helps to increase the *B* measurement, as well as improving the hull's stiffness against rig loads. However, excessively high freeboard results in unnecessary windage and a poor weight distribution.

Although *FF* is given a more favourable weighting than *FA*, most boats have an almost horizontal sheer line when in measurement trim, due to the beneficial effect that this has on the rated length.

Draft correction, DC

The calculations for the draft correction are basically the same as those for the freeboard correction, though the possibility of a centreboard complicates the issue slightly.

First of all the measured draft, *DM*, is determined. In a fixed keel boat it is simply the maximum draft; in a drop keel boat *DM* measures the maximum hull depth, at a distance off centreline that is the greater of 0.04*B*, or 1.5 times the board thickness. *CD*, the maximum board depth below *DM*, is also measured.

The base draft is related to *L* by:

$$DB = 0.146L + 2.0$$

The rated draft is then given by:

$$RD = (CD^{1.6} + (DM - 0.3DB)^{1.6})^{1/1.6} + 0.3DB$$

where 0.3*DB* shall not be taken as greater than *DM*.

In the case of a fixed keel boat, all that this says is that the rated draft is equal to the measured draft. This also holds for most modern boats with a drop keel, as 0.3*DB* is greater than *DM*; in this case the formula becomes:

$$RD = DM + CD$$

On more traditional designs with a deep profile or a stub keel, though, the actual draft with the board lowered is greater than the rated draft, and the difference increases as *DM* gets larger.

Now the draft correction can be determined by the following formula:

$$DC = 0.07L\left(\frac{RD}{DB} - 1.0\right)$$

As the penalty for a deep keel is not very great, many designers accept one to increase the keel's aspect ratio, thereby increasing the boat's efficiency upwind. This is particularly beneficial when racing in close quarters, where good pointing ability and speed to windward are at a premium. However *Australia II* type winged keels are effectively banned.

Centreboard factor, CBF

The centreboard factor was introduced to eliminate the trend towards ultra lightweight, dinghy-type daggerboard boats that was being pursued around 1975.

Its value is determined by:

$$CBF = 0.95 + \frac{L}{150(DM + CMDI)} \quad \text{but may not be taken as less than 1.0}$$

For any fixed keel yacht, or a centreboarder where the average value of *DM* and *CMDI* is greater than 6⅔% of *L*, *CBF* is 1.0. However, current designs with a *BDR* close to 1.0 and a wide, shallow midships section have values ranging from 4% for a light mini-tonner up to 6¼% for a fairly heavy Admiral's cupper. This would result in *CBF* penalties ranging from 3⅓ to ⅓%. Clearly this penalty is prohibitive for a mini-tonner, and in the larger classes the sail area:wetted surface area is sufficiently high for the performance benefit of a centreboard to be considered negligible.

Movable appendage factor, MAF

The movable appendage factor penalises any attempt at introducing lateral asymmetry into the keel or rudder, and is primarily aimed at trim tabs.

In almost all boats the *MAF* is 1.0, and this covers the rudder and keel or centreboard. A factor of 0.0075 is added to this for every movable appendage on the centreline, and 0.0125 for every movable appendage off the centreline.

For fixed keel boats a movable appendage would be a trim tab, or a keel that could be pivoted in its entirety. For drop keels, any means of gybing the board is included, and this applies to any board that can pivot by more than 2° in its case. In addition, a heavy penalty will also be incurred if bilge boards are fitted.

As far as the rudder is concerned, twin rudders, or a rudder incorporating one or more flaps, will be penalised. This does not include skeg rudders, though, as the skeg is fixed.

Although trim tabs were once popular, the uncertainty of their effect on performance means that they are seldom fitted nowadays. Once again, the Rule imposes penalties not to give fair racing for all yachts, but to push yacht designers along a particular direction towards a hypothetical ideal yacht.

Centre of gravity factor, CGF

The centre of gravity factor is the most contentious part of the IOR. It attempts to measure the height of the centre of gravity, and its initial intention was to favour cruiser/racers, by giving a reduction in rating to a boat with a high centre of gravity. Here the rulemakers assumed that a racing yacht would have a higher ballast ratio due to its stripped out interior and lighter construction, and also that all the ballast would be put into the keel to improve stability. The first assumption is perfectly valid, but the second is not. This is because designers found that they had adequate stability from the high beam encouraged by the Rule; thus by putting a proportion of the ballast inside the hull they improved the weight distribution and lowered the rating.

The first stage in the procedure is to carry out an inclining test to measure the righting moment at one degree of heel. The spinnaker pole is rigged against the hull at the *BMAX* station, horizontal and at right angles to the centreline, with the distance from the centreline to the end of the pole being recorded as *WD*. Weights are then hung on the end of the pole, heavy enough to produce between 1° and 3° of heel; the weight is recorded as *W*.

The angle of heel is measured by a manometer rigged across the boat, graduated in millimetres. The distance from the water container to the scale is designated *PL*, and the difference between upright and heeled water levels at the scale is recorded as *PD*.

This process is repeated four times, once on each side with light weights, and once again with heavy weights. The heavy weights should give about twice the heel angle of the light weights. *W*, *WD* and *PD* are differentiated by the prefix *A*, *B*, *C* and *D* for each measurement.

The righting moment for each inclination is given by:

$$ARM = \frac{AW \times AWD \times PL \times 0.0175}{APD}$$

and similarly for *BRM*, *CRM* and *DRM*. Then the righting moment is obtained by averaging out these values:

$$RM = 0.25(ARM + BRM + CRM + DRM)$$

276

As board boats are measured with their boards raised, their righting moment must be added to obtain *RMC*:

$$RMC = RM + 0.0175((WCBA \times CBDA) + (WCBB + CBDB))$$

where *WCBA*, *WCBB* are the weights of the boards, and *CBDA*, *CBDB* are the vertical drop of their centres of gravity between the fully raised and the fully lowered positions. Obviously for a fixed keel boat *RMC* is equal to *RM*.

A moment's thought will show that these measurements are incapable of being made with a high degree of precision, especially on smaller boats. To begin with, *PL* is usually the minimum permitted length of 1500 mm, and *PD* is read to the nearest millimetre. This gives an error band of about 1.3% with the large weights, and 4% with the light weights. In addition, unless measured in a flat calm in a marina, the wind and waves will swing the boat about and make it more difficult for the measurer to take what will probably be an unsteady reading. All this is borne out in a survey of a number of rating certificates, which show ranges of up to 22% in the inclining tests carried out on a boat, which can affect the rating by 2½%.

Now the tenderness ratio is calculated:

$$TR = \frac{0.97 \times L \times BWL^3}{RMC}$$

The upper line is an approximation to the transverse moment of inertia of the measurement waterline plane, which is proportional to the form stability at small angles of heel. Dividing this by *RMC* gives an indication as to how much of the stability is due to a low centre of gravity. Note how sensitive *TR* is to small changes in *BWL*, a 1% change resulting in a 3% change in the *TR* and *CGF*.

The *TR* formula presents another shortcoming in the *CGF* calculations. One waterline beam is not sufficient to estimate the moment of inertia accurately, particularly as today's full sterns can contribute a sizeable amount to the form stability. This is often particularly apparent when a boat is re-trimmed for measurement, as an increase in bow down trim will reduce *RMC* considerably, yet have only a slight effect on *BWL*, and so *TR* will increase. It also prevents large angles of heel being used in the inclination test, as this would result in *BWL* being even less representative of the hull shape when inclined.

The *CGF* is found from one of two formulae, depending upon the value of *TR*. In either case, it may not be less than 0.968.

$$\text{If } TR \text{ is 35.0 or less: } CGF = \frac{2.2}{TR - 5.1} + 0.8877$$

$$\text{If } TR \text{ is greater than 35.0: } CGF = 0.0064TR + 0.744$$

The first formula results in a minimum value of *CGF* if *TR* lies between 32.5 and 35.0, and it then applies a steadily increasing penalty as *TR* drops and the

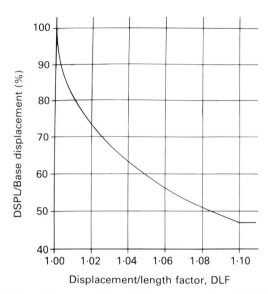

Fig. 12.7. *DLF* penalty curve. The displacement ratio, *DSPL*:base displacement (expressed as a percentage), is plotted against the displacement:length factor, *DLF*. As the displacement is decreased, the rating penalty becomes increasingly severe.

centre of gravity is lowered. The second formula was introduced after doubts were raised regarding the large angle stability of some designs, which is largely dependent upon the position of the centre of gravity. It dishes out a harsh penalty to any boat with a *TR* greater than 35.0, especially as the boat could increase her performance as well as reduce her rating by lowering her centre of gravity. Most boats are designed with a *CGF* close to the minimum permitted, though on boats designed primarily for windward work the *CGF* may rise above 0.98.

Engine and propeller factor, EPF

If a yacht carries an engine that is capable of propelling her at at least $\sqrt{L}$ knots in calm water, she is awarded an *EPF* allowance to offset the extra drag incurred.

This is divided into two parts. Firstly, there is the engine moment factor, *EMF*, allowing for the increased pitching that can be expected from the engine's weight and position. Secondly, there is the drag factor, *DF*, which allows for the extra drag due to the propeller and drive assembly. Obviously an outboard motor is ineligible for a drag factor, though it does receive some slight benefit through the *EMF*. The *EPF* is given by:

$$EPF = 1 - (EMF + DF)$$

This has a maximum value of 1.0 for boats with an inboard or no engine at all, and 0.998 for boats carrying an outboard motor.

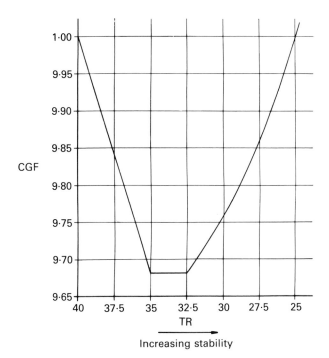

CGF

Increasing stability

Fig. 12.8. *CGF* curve. *TR* is plotted against *CGF*. If *TR* is greater than 35.0, a penalty is incurred as the boat is deemed to have insufficient stability. Boats biased towards beating and strong winds may have a *CGF* in excess of 0.968, but almost always below 1.0.

Engine moment factor, EMF

The two factors determining the effect that an engine has on the pitching of a yacht are its weight and the distance from the pitching centre.

As far as the rule is concerned, the engine weight (*EW*) is the dry weight of the engine, including gearbox, alternator and starter motor, and in the case of sail drives, the drive unit.

The engine weight distance (*EWD*) is the distance from the mid depth station to the centre of the cylinder block, or in the case of an outboard motor, its centre of gravity.

These two factors are then multiplied together to give the engine moment:

$$EM = EW \times EWD$$

This is then related to the size of the yacht to give the engine moment factor:

$$EMF = \frac{0.1EM}{L^2 \times B \times D}$$

This favours large engines fitted towards the ends of the boat. However, the rating benefits are very small, *EMF* usually being 0.01 or less.

279

A large engine can be used to make up the internal ballast that may be carried, thus achieving a slight reduction in rating. It is best sited fairly close to the yacht's actual pitching centre, which usually lies 10 to 15% of the *LWL* aft of station 5. As this is some way aft of the *MDS*, siting the engine close to the pitching centre improves performance and lowers the rating. At one time the engine was placed in the bows to help induce bow down trim, but this is no longer considered worthwhile due to the marked effect it has on the pitching behaviour of the yacht, and in any case outboard motors are no longer allowed to be stowed forward of the mast.

Drag factor, DF
The drag factor is determined from the type of installation, the size and type of the propeller, and its depth below the waterline.

First of all the propeller size (*PS*) is taken to be the lesser of the propeller diameter (*PD*) or four times the maximum blade width (*PBW*). The installation type is then classified into one of three categories (leaving aside propellers sited in an aperture). The first two, exposed shaft and strut drive, cater for a normal shaft and P-bracket and a sail drive installation respectively, but in both cases the installation must comply with a number of measurement restrictions based on *PD*; these are shown in Fig. 12.9. The third category, 'other', covers drive installations that fail to comply with the measurement restrictions. The most popular installation in this category is a short, unsupported shaft emerging from the root of the keel.

Of the dimensions shown, only the strut size and *EDC* or *ESC* may exceed the limits by incurring a penalty; in all other cases the installation will be classified as 'other'. If the strut is too small, whether a P-bracket or sail drive strut, *PRD* may be replaced by *PRDC*, the largest propeller diameter that would make the strut measurements conform. This is often a heavy penalty, but may be avoided by building up the strut with microballoons.

If *EDC* or *ESC* exceed the limits, *PDC*, the propeller depth, is reduced by one of the following formulae:

$$\text{For a sail drive: } EDC - 0.75PRDC$$

$$\text{For an exposed shaft: } \frac{(ESC - 0.75PRDC) \times ESL}{1.5PRDC}$$

For the sail drive this just means that any excess is subtracted from the propeller depth. For an exposed shaft installation, though, the excess is multiplied by the ratio of the shaft length to the minimum shaft length, producing a larger penalty as the shaft length increases.

Now that the installation has been classified, the propeller factor, *PF*, can be read off from Fig. 12.9. If the installation falls into the exposed shaft category,

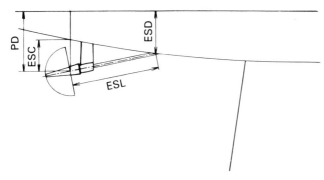

Fig. 12.9(a). Exposed shaft requirements. *ESL*: minimum value 1.5*PRD*. *ESC*: maximum value 0.75*PRD* before penalty incurred. *ESD*: maximum value *CMDI* + 0.3*PRD* before penalty incurred. *ST1*: minimum value 0.05*PRD*. *ST2*: minimum value 0.2*PRD*. *ST3*: maximum value 0.5*PRD*.

Strut measurements

ST1 is the minimum thickness of the strut. *ST2* is the minimum force and aft dimension. *ST3* is the maximum fore and aft dimension, measured above a line 0.3*PRD* above the shaft line. Both *ST2* and *ST3* are measured parallel to the shaft line.

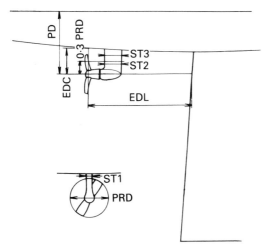

Fig. 12.9(b). Strut drive requirements.
EDL minimum 1.5*PRD*. *EDC* maximum 0.75*PRD* without penalty. *ST1* minimum 0.08*PRD*. *ST2* minimum 0.2*PRD*. *ST3* maximum 0.75*PRD*.

Propeller factors.

Installation type	Propeller type.		
	Folding	Feathering	Solid
Exposed shaft	0.85	0.95	2.05
Strut drive	0.60	0.675	1.33
Other	0.35	0.45	1.05

and the depth of the forward end of the shaft (*ESD*) is greater than *CMDI* + 0.3*PRD*, the following factor must be subtracted from *PF*:

$$K \times \left[\frac{ESD - (CMDI + 0.3PRD)}{0.3PRD} \right]$$

where *K* is 1.0 for a fixed, and 0.5 for a folding or feathering propeller, and the term in square brackets may not be taken as greater than 1.0. This provides an increasing penalty as *ESD* increases, reaching a maximum when *ESD* equals *CMDI* + 0.6*PRD*. It is intended to prevent exposed shaft installations from emerging through the trailing edge of the keel, reducing drag due to the shaft being more nearly parallel to the water flow.

The last measurement to be found is the depth of the propeller below the waterline, *PD*. As the rule favours a deep propeller installation, though, it has been necessary to introduce an upper limit of 0.6*PRD* + *CMDI*, and *PDC* is taken as the lesser of the two.

We are now in a position to calculate the drag factor, *DF*. One of two formulae is applied, depending upon the ratio of *PS:L*:

For *PS:L* greater than 0.03 and up to 0.05: $DF = PF \left(\dfrac{PDC}{DB} \right)^{1/2} \times \dfrac{PS}{L}$

For *PS:L* greater than 0.02 and up to 0.03: $DF = PF \left(\dfrac{PDC}{DB} \right)^{1/2}$

$$\times \left(\frac{PS^2 \times 60}{L^2} - 0.024 \right)$$

If *PS:L* is greater than 0.05, it is taken to be 0.05, to prevent excessively large propellers. If, on the other hand, *PS:L* is less than 0.02, it is taken as 0.02, and so the drag factor is zero.

The middle term in the *DF* equations clearly favours a deep installation, and yet there is no solid evidence to prove that the drag of a propeller increases with its depth. As this term usually has a value of about 0.6 to 0.66 it has a marked effect on the *DF*, and this is the reason for the penalties imposed on an excessively long strut.

As far as propeller size is concerned, it obviously pays to have a value of *PS:L* between 0.03 and 0.05. No rating benefit is to be had from a propeller larger than this, and the benefit for a smaller propeller quickly diminishes. A solid propeller seldom pays unless *PS:L* equals 0.03; it is at its best on an 'other' type of installation. A maximum size folding propeller on an exposed shaft is the usual installation; one of the slim feathering propellers, such as the Max Prop, is probably just as efficient, though considerably more expensive. A strut drive is seldom seen on racing craft, as the increase in performance due to its lower drag is not sufficient to offset the tax in rating it incurs.

Trim Penalty Factor, TPF

Although the Rule has always stated that the shore measurement trim should approximate her trim afloat, this has been difficult to enforce as the Rule specified no tolerances.

The advantages of bow-up measurement ashore are quite high, as it gives an increased *FD*, and reduced *GD*, *BHA*, *BHAI* and *UHA*. This increases D, and also reduces L through both *AOCP* and *AOCG*. To limit this benefit, a penalty is imposed whenever the trim difference exceeds 1°. This is detected by first calculating *TRIM*: *TRIM* = (*FFS* − *FFM*) − (*FAS* − *FAM*), and is taken as positive.

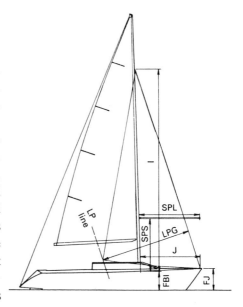

Fig. 12.10. Foretriangle measurements.

If *TRIM/LBG* is less than 0.0175 the trim difference is less than 1°, and *TPF* is set to 1.0. However, if *TRIM* exceeds 0.0175, *TPF* is calculated by: *TPF* = 1 + 1.146 *TRIM/LBG*.

Therefore *TRIM* can be 0.525 ft without penalty on a boat with an *LBG* of 30 ft. If *TRIM* is 0.6 ft, *TPF* is 1.023, whilst at 0.8 ft it rises to 1.031, and at 1.0 ft it is 1.038.

Sail area measurements

The IOR provides a means of measuring almost any one- or two-masted bermudan rig. However, the sloop rig is a must for a competitive boat, whatever her size, and so this is the only rig that will be discussed here.

Although the plan form of the rig is unrestricted, much of this chapter will be devoted to the many restrictions to which the rig is subjected. Unless stated to the contrary, it is not worth incurring any of the penalties inflicted upon a rig deviating from the norm.

First of all, the foretriangle area, *RSAF*, and the mainsail area, *RSAM*, are found. These are combined to give the square root of the rated sail area, *S*, which is converted to *SC* after penalising boats with an excessively large rig in relation to their hull size.

Foresail area, RSAF

The three measurements required for *RSAF* are the foretriangle base, *J*, the foretriangle height, *I*, and the genoa overlap, *LP*.

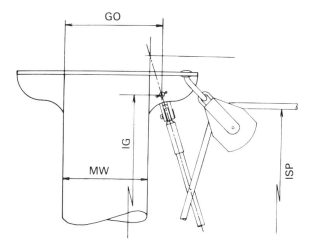

Fig. 12.11 Measurements at the high point of I. The high point of the forestay is calculated by: $(IG + IG(GO - MW)/J - GO + MW)$ which simply projects the forestay to the forward face of the mast. For T terminals and internal shrouds GO equals MW, and so the high point of the forestay is simply IG.

J is simply the horizontal distance from the centre of the forestay to the forward face of the mast. JC is then taken as the greater of J, or the spinnaker pole length SPL, or the maximum spinnaker girth (SMW) divided by 1.8.

The I measurement is more complex. First of all the greater of the height of the spinnaker halyard (ISP) or the forestay height (IG), projected if necessary to where it meets the mast, is taken. Both of these are measured from the sheerline at the base of the mast. Then a factor of $0.04B$ is subtracted from this, to allow for an assumed difference in freeboards between the forestay (FJ) and the base of the mast (FBI). Finally a trim correction factor, TCI, is added on. This is simply any amount by which $FBI + 0.04B$ exceeds FJ, and compensates for bow down trim. This gives the value of I, which is converted to IC by the application of any penalties incurred, shown in Fig. 12.12.

LP is found by adding together two components, LPG and FSP. FSP is double the depth of the luff groove, measured perpendicular to the forestay; if hanks are used it is taken as zero. LPG is the genoa overlap, measured at right angles to the forestay. It may not be taken as less than $1.5JC$, in other words the Rule assumes that all boats carry a genoa with an LP of at least $1.5JC$. The Rule effectively says that the clew of any staysail must also lie forward of the LPG line, as when the clew of a staysail lies aft of this line LPG is replaced by $LPIS$, the distance from the forestay to the clew of the staysail, once again measured perpendicular to the forestay. The rated foresail area is then given by:

$$RSAF = 0.5IC \times JC\left[1 + 1.1\left(\frac{LP - JC}{LP}\right)\right] + 0.125JC(IC - 2JC)$$

ITEM		LIMIT	PENALTY
Jib			
TCI,	correction for bow down trim, $FBI + 0.04B$	Maximum value *FJ*	Excess added to *I*
Spinnaker			
SL,	luff and leach lengths	Max $0.95\sqrt{I^2 + J^2}$	Twice the excess added to *I*
HBS,	headboard width	Max $0.05JC$	Excess multiplied by $1.8SL/SMW$ and added to *I*
SPS,	height of spinnaker pole on mast	Max $0.27ISP$	Excess added to *I*
Mainsail			
BAL,	outer limit of sheeting headsails on main boom	Max 0.5 ft	Excess added to *I*
BD,	maximum depth of main boom	Max $0.05E$	Excess added to *P*
HB,	max width of mainsail in way of headboard	Max greater of 0.5 ft or $0.04E$	Excess multiplied by P/E and added to *P*
MGU,	girth at ¾ height	Max $0.28E + 0.016P + 0.85$ ft	Excess multiplied by P/E and added to *P*
MGM,	girth at ½ height	Max $0.5E + 0.22 P + 1.2$ ft	Excess multiplied by P/E and added to *P*
BLP,	distance along leach from headboard to top batten	Min $0.2P$	Deficit added to upper batten length, *BL1*
BL1,	upper batten length	Max greater of $0.16E$ or $0.1E + 1$ ft	Excess multiplied by P/E and added to *P*
BL2,	lower batten length	As per *BL1*	One sixth of excess multiplied by P/E and added to *P*
BL3,	*BL4*, lengths of two intermediate battens	Max greater of $0.18E$ or $0.12E + 1$ ft	One sixth of excess multiplied by P/E and added to *P*
BL5,	length of additional intermediate battens	0	Multiplied by P/E and added to *P*
BAS,	height of low point of *P* above sheer	Max $0.05P + 0.04B + 4$ ft	Excess added to *P*
RLM,	width of Kevlar reinforcing in leach	Max $E/3$	Ten times excess multiplied by P/E and added to *P*
Mainsail head penalty, $P + BAD - 0.04B + TCI$		Min $0.96I$	Difference added to *P*

Fig. 12.12. IOR rig penalties

The terms before the square brackets simply give the foretriangle area. Then the terms inside the brackets make an allowance for the genoa overlap, and finally a term penalising high aspect ratio is added on. Figure 12.13 shows the effect that

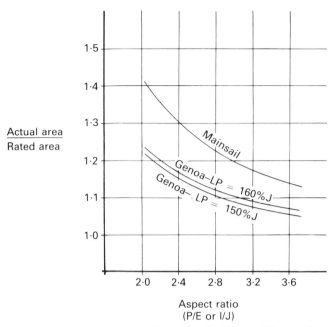

Fig. 12.13. The effect of aspect ratio on rated sail area. The rated area is taken as *RSAF* or *RSAM* (assuming *RGF* is 1.0). The actual area of the genoa is ½luff × *LP*, and for the mainsail it is taken as ½P × E – in other words the genoa area includes the overlap, but the mainsail roach has not been taken into account in either case.

aspect ratio and overlap have on the ratio of rated sail area to actual sail area.

The other factor derived from the foretriangle measurements is *SPIN*, given by:

$$SPIN = 1.01JC \times SL$$

where *SL* is the luff length of the spinnaker.

One of the commonest ways of trimming a boat's rating is to adjust *LP* and *JC*. Clearly there is no benefit to be had from an *LP* less than 1.5*JC*, but increasing it will improve the yacht's windward performance in light airs, particularly if she is short of sail area. Because an increase in *LP* only affects the genoa, and not the spinnaker, the sail area is rated at a lower rate than a sail with a minimum *LP*.

A more drastic move is to increase *JC*, thereby increasing *LP*, *SPL*, *SL*, and *SMW*. Thus not only is the genoa overlap increased, but a larger spinnaker and longer spinnaker pole are also permitted, increasing performance on all points of sail. Obviously the rating increases at a higher rate than if only *LP* is increased, but the penalty is not particularly harsh, especially as the larger spinnaker is likely to be useful over a wider wind range than the larger genoa.

Many yachts find that they are awarded a *TCI* factor due to bow down trim at measurement. The rule assumes that the freeboard at the forestay is 4% of *B* higher than that abreast the mast, and *TCI* corrects for a lower bow by adding the difference to *I*, thus preventing a slight increase in sail area escaping without being rated. To prevent the sheer from being swept up at the forestay in an effort to make *TCI* zero, the rule says that the freeboard at the forestay, *FJ*, shall not be taken as greater than the freeboard that would be obtained by extending a straight line drawn through the sheer at the two forward girth stations.

Mainsail area, RSAM

The mainsail area is calculated from two principal dimensions: *E*, the foot length measured along the boom; and *P*, the luff length measured along the mast. Measurement bands must be painted on to the spars to mark the limits of *P* and *E*, and also the gooseneck position if adjustable, as otherwise the maximum possible dimensions are taken.

Any penalties, listed in Fig. 12.12, are added on to *P* and *E* to give *PC* and *EC*; the rated mainsail area is then given by:

$$RSAM = [0.35(EC \times PC) + 0.2EC(PC - 2E)] \times RGF$$

Once again the second term inside the square brackets penalises high aspect ratios, and its effect is shown in Fig. 12.12.

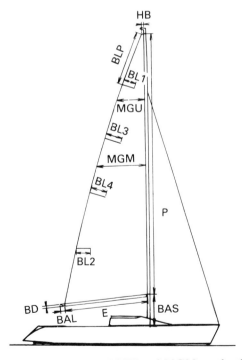

Fig. 12.14 Mainsail measurements. *MGU* and *MGM* are the three-quarter and half height girth measurements, measured from the appropriate point on the leach to the nearest point on the luff. *BAL* is the outermost point on the boom to which headsails may be sheeted, and its position is denoted by a black band.

287

RGF is the ratio of the actual mainsail area to one with the maximum penalty free girths, and is given as:

$$RGF = \frac{(HB + 2MGU + 3MGM + 2E)}{(HB + 2MGUL + 3MGML + 2E)}$$

with a maximum value of 1.0, and a minimum of 0.83. *MGM* and *MGU* are the measured half and three-quarter height girths respectively, whilst *MGML* and *MGUL* are the maximum penalty-free girths. As *RGF* is a simple ratio, there is absolutely no rating benefit to be had from mainsails with a large roach, or for that matter a small one.

Looking at the mainsail penalties, *HB*, *BLP*, and the batten and roach restrictions serve to limit the amount of roach in the sail. Similarly, the boom depth penalty is to prevent booms being used to increase the sail area; a deep boom is advantageous as it can be made lighter and stiffer, and it also acts as an end plate to increase the sail's efficiency. The RLM penalty was introduced to try to keep costs down, by limiting the use of Kevlar.

The other penalties were introduced to combat the trend for mainsails of masthead rigged boats to keep on getting smaller. The *BAS* penalty does this simply by setting a maximum value for the boom height. At the masthead the mainsail head penalty acts in a similar fashion, by saying that the head of the mainsail may not be more than 4% of *I* below the forestay attachment point without penalty.

The final measure taken to preserve mainsails says that all yachts must be rated with a mainsail, and the value of *RSAM* may not be taken as less than $0.094IC^2$. Obviously no benefit is to be had by having a mainsail giving a value below this, but many masthead rigged boats have a mainsail close to the minimum level.

Rated sail area, RSAT
The values of *RSAF* and *RSAM* are weighted in the calculation of *SATC*, and then these three factors are added together to give *RSAT*:

$$SATC = 0.1(RSAF - 1.43RSAM)$$
$$RSAT = RSAF + RSAM + SATC$$

These two formulae can be combined to give:

$$RSAT = 1.1RSAF + 0.857RSAM$$

and so *RSAF* is given a weighting 28% greater than *RSAM*. This means that whilst the large mainsail and small headsails of a fractional rig give a larger upwind sail area for a given *RSAT*, off the wind the large spinnaker of a masthead rig will give it more sail area for a given *RSAT*.

Originally fractional rigs were reintroduced on light, dinghy inspired designs to improve their sail area:wetted surface area, so that they would be able to keep up with the heavier masthead rigged boats when sailing upwind. Over the past few years, though, the fractional rig has become the norm on almost all designs up to about 40 feet, partly because of the trend towards lighter designs, and partly because of its much greater versatility.

Square root of sail area, S
S is taken as the square root of the greater of *RSAT*, *SPIN* and *RSAL*. *RSAT* is usually the greatest of these three, but on some masthead rigged boats *SPIN*, defined in the section on *RSAF*, may be slightly greater. If this is the case, *RSAT* can be increased without penalty until it is equal to *SPIN*, by increasing *LP* or *RSAM*.

RSAL was introduced to prevent people taking advantage of the cheapness of mainsail area in the *RSAT* equation by having a cat-rigged boat. It is defined by:

$$RSAL = 1.3RSAM$$

which effectively means that *RSAF* must have a value of at least 40% of *RSAM*, after the effect of *SATC* has been taken into account.

Sail value, SC
S is multiplied by *SCF*, the sail correction factor, to give *SC*. *SCF* is intended to penalise the large rigs sported by many boats in the Mediterranean and other areas with predominantly light winds.

First of all the sail:hull ratio, *SHR*, is calculated:

$$SHR = \frac{8.66S}{L} + \frac{S}{\sqrt{(B \times MDIA)}} - \frac{L}{100}$$

The first term is the ratio of sail area to length, and the second the ratio of sail area to midship area, which is related to the (sail area:displacement$^{2/3}$) ratio. Finally, there is a scaling factor, giving a lower *SHR* to larger boats due to their greater stability. Using two terms to estimate the relative size of the rig permits heavier boats to have a higher sail area:length ratio than lighter boats of the same size.

If *SHR* is 16.1 or less, *SCF* is taken to be 1.0, and so *SC* is the same as S. However, if *SHR* exceeds this value, *SCF* is given by:

$$SCF = 1 + 0.04(SHR - 16.1)$$

Ignoring the small effect of the final term in the *SHR* equation, this imposes a tax of about 8% onto any sail area in excess of that giving an *SHR* of 16.1.

Ultimate Stability Requirements

Although we have now examined all the factors that make up a boat's rating, before the certificate can be issued a check must be made on the vessel's stability at 90° of heel.

First of all the yacht undergoes a screening test, using data taken off the measurement certificate. If she fails this, though, she must be hauled over to 90° to prove her stability, though on larger boats hydrostatic calculations may be used instead.

Screening value, SV

The screening value checks the yacht's stability at 90° by applying basic principles of naval architecture.

First of all *BCOR* is found, which is intended to be the greater of the waterline beams taken at the *BMAX* and *MDS* stations. The first of these is simply *BWL*, as used in the *CGF* calculations. The second is given by:

$$BWL1 = \frac{3B}{4} + \frac{B \times OMDI}{4 \times (MD - OMD)} \text{ but may not be greater than } 0.8B.$$

The screening value is now given by:

$$SV = \left[\frac{(0.03L \times BCOR^3 \times 64)}{DSPL} + 0.6CMDI - \frac{54RM}{DSPL} - 0.54CMD \right] + 0.25$$

The first term inside square brackets is an approximation of the distance from the centre of buoyancy of the yacht when upright to the transverse metacentre, *BM*.

Then the height of the centre of buoyancy above the low point of the canoe body, *KB*, is estimated to be 0.6*CMDI*. Adding this to *BM* gives *KM*, the height of the metacentre above the canoe body.

The distance from the centre of gravity to the metacentre, *GM*, is estimated by the third term in the *SV* formula, and this is subtracted from *KM* to give *KG*, the height of the centre of gravity.

Now the distance from *K* to the centre of buoyancy at 90° heel, KB_{90}, is estimated to be 0.54*CMD*. Subtracting this from *KG*, we obtain GB_{90}, the righting lever at 90° of heel. A safety factor of 0.25 is then added on to ensure that the righting lever is sufficiently large. If *SV* is zero or negative, the righting lever is at least 0.25 feet, and the boat is assumed to have sufficient reserves of stability.

Within the restrictions imposed by the limited amount of data that can be extracted from the IOR measurements, this calculation is very fair apart from one point. As the safety factor of 0.25 is not related to the boat's size, it represents a much greater reserve of stability for small boats than for large ones, and so it is mostly the smaller boats that have to undergo a stability test.

Stability test

If the screening value is greater than zero the yacht must either undergo a stability test or, if her rated displacement is greater than 17 500 lb, prove that there is

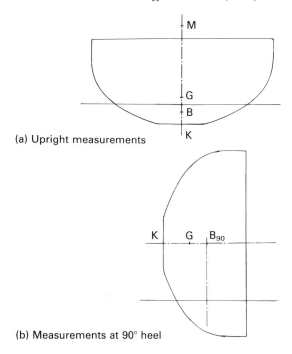

(a) Upright measurements

(b) Measurements at 90° heel

Fig. 12.15. The ultimate stability test. K – base of canoe body. G – position of centre of gravity. M — position of transverse metacentre. B – position of centre of buoyancy (upright). B_{90} – height of centre of buoyancy (90° heel). To pass the test, B_{90} must be at least 0.25 feet above G.

adequate stability by calculations. However, only one boat of each design needs to undergo a stability test.

The yacht is heeled over to 90°, and a weight suspended from the high point of I. The yacht is then released, and to pass the test she must not heel beyond 90°. The weight, in pounds, is given by:

$$W = \frac{1.6(L \times B^2 + (P - 0.5D) \times (5P - 110) + 35R)}{I + 0.67D}$$

The bottom line is representative of the leverage of the weight, and the upper line is meant to relate to the heeling force of the sails. However, any theoretical basis for this formula is very tenuous indeed.

In the top line, the largest factor is the set of terms involving P. Presumably this is meant to represent the heeling moment of the rig. However, if a fractional rig and a masthead rig with the same heeling moment are compared, the value of P for the fractional rig will be considerably higher than for the masthead rig, and so the formula has a strong bias against fractional rigs. Even if P could be used to determine the position of the centre of effort, and the sail area, it would scale as a function of P^3, and not the P^2 used here.

291

The two other terms are different ways of estimating the size of the boat, and require larger yachts to have greater reserves of stability. This is correct in theory, but once again the expressions used seem somewhat arbitrary.

Luckily it is only the smaller boats that have to undergo a stability test, and these can usually get through if put in the right trim.

Rating Older Designs

Over the years designers have gradually discovered the proportions that produce a fast boat for a given rating, and so older boats have become outdated. The Mk IIIA Rule was introduced to reduce the rating of boats whose proportions make them uncompetitive due to being designed to more traditional lines, and thereby to extend their competitiveness.

Another factor concerning older boats is that expensive alterations would be required to avoid some of the penalties imposed by alterations to the Rule. Thus in some cases the Rule changes have incorporated grandfather clauses that either exempt existing boats from compliance, or reduce any rating penalty incurred.

Defining age

Before we can decide upon what age allowances a boat is entitled to, its age must first be defined. Two dates are used, the hull date for the hull, and the rig date for the rig. To determine the hull date, several dates have to be compared.

Age date

The age date is simply the date when the boat was first measured afloat for the IOR, unless it can be proved that the boat was launched before this date.

Series date

A production boat may be given a series date by the national rating authority, so long as all the hulls produced have almost identical measurements. If a series date is awarded, it is simply the age date of the first boat of the class.

This is very useful to the builders of production racing yachts, as it helps to ensure a good competitive life for the series, by giving every boat the same hull date as the first boat built.

Modified hull date

A boat is only given a modified hull date if the hull shape is altered. The only exceptions to this are the restoration of the boat to her original shape by removing bumps at measurement points, and alterations to the keel, skeg or rudder.

If it is intended to alter the hull in such a way that a modified hull date will not be incurred, the measuring authority will inspect the boat before and after the modifications to check that the regulations have been complied with.

Note that the regulations do permit alterations to the ballast without altering the hull date, and so the boat may be retrimmed, or her displacement may be altered, as desired.

Hull date

The hull date determines the boat's eligibility for grandfather clauses in the Mk III rule, and also affects most of the Mk IIIA rule. If the hull has not been modified it is taken as the earlier of the age date and the series date. If the boat has been given a modified hull date, though, this is used instead of the hull date.

Rig date

The rig date is usually the same as the hull date. If this is the case, no restrictions are placed on alterations to the rig. Thus the boat can be given a lighter, multi panel mast, and have her sailplan altered, without affecting the rig date.

If the age date is earlier than 10/1975, and the hull date is 12/1972 or earlier, the rig date is given as 10/1975 so long as certain restrictions on rig alterations have been complied with. These are that since 1 November 1975 the I and J measurements must not have been decreased, and the P and E measurements not increased, by more than 0.1 foot. In other words, that there has been no move towards a fractional rig.

If the rig date is set at 10/1975 by this clause, the value of $RSAT$ is reduced in the Mk IIIA rule for boats with large mainsails; this explains the regulations concerning alterations to the sail plan.

Grandfather clauses in the Mk III rule

Eligibility for the grandfather clauses in the Mk III rule is determined by the yacht's hull date. In chronological order, these are:

Hull date prior to	Grandfather clauses for which eligible
1/75	No upper limit on the propeller depth, *PDC*.
1/79	No penalty on an excessive exposed shaft depth for exposed shaft installations.
1/81	If no skeg is present, and there is no hollow in the hull profile aft of the *AIGS*, *VHAI* is measured directly, and not by the buttock heights. *BAPSL* is taken as zero, so long as *VHAI* is measured directly. *Y*, the after overhang, may be one third longer than the present limit without penalty, and any penalty incurred is halved.
1/83	The outboard motor may be stowed forwards of the mast until the boat is remeasured afloat.
1/84	No radius of curvature penalty is imposed at AIGS. If the hull was first measured before 19 November, 1983, TPF is assumed to be 1.0.

The Mk IIIA rule

Most of the factors used in the Mk III rule remain unchanged in Mk IIIA, but where new values are found they are denoted by the suffix A. All yachts are now eligible for a Mk IIIA rating, being placed into one of three divisions, in accordance with the boat's hull date.

$$\text{Hull date} \begin{cases} \text{prior to 1973} & \text{Division 1} \\ \text{1973 to 1975} & \text{Division 2} \\ \text{1976 onwards} & \text{Division 3} \end{cases}$$

The rule determines new values for DLF, CGF, CBF and SC. It then calculates the measured rating by a new formula, and this is finally converted into the Mk IIIA rating.

DLFA

Yachts in division 1 were all of very heavy displacement compared to current designs. To offset this, $DLFA$ is set at 0.98, giving a 2% rating benefit.

In divisions 2 and 3 a slightly more sophisticated approach is used. The minimum value of BDR is lowered to 0.94, and then $DLFA$ is found by a similar type of formula to that used in the Mk III rule:

$$DLFA = 0.98 + 5.54(BDR - 0.94)^{1.92}$$

This works in exactly the same way as the formula for DLF, but the minimum value for $DLFA$ is 0.98, awarded when BDR is 0.94. The maximum value of $DLFA$ is $0.5(1 + DLF)$ for boats in division 2, and 1.1 for boats in division 3. The reason for this increased penalty on light displacement is that the rulemakers associate it with modern design, and so it is penalised here to offset rating benefits obtained elsewhere in the rule.

If a boat incurs a $DLFA$ penalty it may prove worthwhile to increase her displacement by adding internal ballast.

CGFA

For boats in division 1, the value of $CGFA$ is given by:

$$CGFA = 0.5(CGF + 0.963)$$

As the minimum value of CGF is 0.968, this gives a rating reduction. It compensates for the very high CGF of these boats, especially when compared with the size of their rigs. The rating benefit is 0.25% for a boat with a minimum CGF, rising to 2% for a design with a CGF of 1.002.

A more complex approach is used for boats in divisions 2 and 3. First of all, a factor is introduced to determine whether the midship section is broad and shallow, or narrow and deep:

294

$$CGFC = \frac{0.375B}{OMDI + MDI + CMDI} - 0.5$$

This term may not be less than 0.5, nor greater than 1.0. The narrower and deeper the section, the lower the value of *CGFC*.

Now the value of *CGFA* is found:

$$CGFA = CGFC(CGF - 0.968) + 0.968$$

If *CGFC* has a value of 1.0, *CGFA* will have the same value as *CGF*. For older designs, with a lower *CGFC*, *CGFA* will be progressively reduced, until at the minimum value of *CGFC* the value of *CGFA* will lie midway between the boat's *CGF* and 0.968.

CBFA

Boats in division 3 were designed after the introduction of the *CBF* factor, and so *CBFA* always taken on the value as *CBF*.

For those boats in divisions 1 or 2 with a *CBF* greater than or equal to 1.0, *CBFA* is set at 1, and so no penalty is imposed. If *CBF* is calculated to be less than 1.0 the boat is assumed to be a traditional deep hulled centreboarder, and a 1% rating benefit is given by making *CBFA* 0.99.

SA

In most cases no value for *SA* is calculated, and *S* is used. The exception is those boats in division 1 that have been awarded a rig date of 10/75, as these frequently had a masthead rig with a large mainsail, which does not give a very beneficial rating.

The values for *RSAF* and *RSAM* are maintained, but a new formula is used for *SATCA*:

$$SATCA = 0.3(RSAF - 2.2RSAM), \text{ with a minimum value of } -0.25RSAF$$

RSATA is then found by adding up *RSAF*, *RSAM* and *SATCA*. Combining these, we obtain:

$$RSATA = 1.1RSAF + 0.34RSAM,$$

$$\text{with a minimum value of } 0.75RSAF + RSAM$$

Comparing this with the formula used in Mk III, *RSAF* is given the same multiplier, but *RSAM* is about 40% cheaper. The minimum value effectively prevents fractional rigs from benefitting from this formula, as it applies whenever *RSAM* exceeds 83% of *RSAF*. *SA* is, of course, the square root of the greater of *RSATA*, *SPIN* or *RSAL*.

SCFA

SCFA is intended to operate in a similar way to *DLFA*, favouring older designs with small rigs and penalising modern designs with generous sailplans. The cut-off point between a small and a large rig is when *SHR* equals 15.5.

In division 1, those boats with an *SHR* greater than 15.5 have *SCFA* set at the same value as *SCF*, this being almost always 1.0. Where the boat has an *SHR* below 15.5, a rating benefit is given by:

$$SCFA = 1.0 + 0.24(SHR - 15.5)$$

Thus the smaller the *SHR*, the greater the rating benefit. For example, a boat with an *SHR* of 14.0, which is low but still relatively common on boats of this vintage, would be given an *SCFA* of 0.64, a very considerable rating reduction.

Boats in division 2 were given larger sailplans, and so *SCFA* is simply the same as *SCF*, with no benefit being given for boats with small rigs.

In division 3, the rig size has carried on rising, and fractional rigs are firmly established. To differentiate between masthead and fractional rigs, a new term is introduced to replace *RSAT*:

$$MSAR = 0.5(PC \times EC + IC \times LP)$$

This is intended to measure the actual area of the mainsail and genoa; it is 3.25% greater than *RSAT* on a minimum main masthead boat, and about 15% greater on a fractional rig. The sail:hull ratio is then found by using the square root of *MSAR* in place of *S*:

$$SHRA = \sqrt{MSAR} \left(\frac{8.66}{L} + \frac{1.0}{\sqrt{B \times MDIA}} \right) - \frac{L}{100}$$

and the sail correction factor is given by:

$SCFA = 1.0 + 0.04(SHRA - 15.5)$, but it shall not be taken as less than 1.0.

The combined effects of setting the penalty level of *SHRA* at 15.5, and of using *MSAR* in place of *RSATA*, mean that masthead rigs begin to be penalised when their sail area is about 93% of the maximum penalty free area under the Mk III rule, but for fractional rigs a penalty is incurred at only 80% of the value used in Mk III.

For boats in division 1 sailing in areas with a reasonably high average wind strength, it may well pay to reduce the sail area to reduce the rating. The only point to watch is that this may make the boat ineligible for *SA* calculated on the basis of *RSATA*, due to the rig date changing.

Boats in division 2 are in some ways in the best position. Although there are no rating formulae to take advantage of, neither are there any restrictions on the rig. There is nothing to stop the boat from being updated with a large fractional rig if so desired.

In division 3, on the other hand, the heavy penalty imposed on fractional rigs makes it worthwhile to revert back to a masthead rig. This would allow a considerably greater sail area before a penalty is imposed. In addition, if *SHRA* exceeds 15.5 it will almost undoubtedly pay to avoid the *SCFA* penalty by reducing the rig size.

SCA
If the boat has had its sail area calculated by *SA*, *SCA* is given by:

$$SCA = SA \times SCFA$$

Otherwise, it is given by:

$$SCA = S \times SCFA$$

MRA
MRA is determined by one of two formulae, the lowest value being used. First there is a formula based on the one used in the Mk III rule:

$$M1 = \frac{0.13L \times SCA}{\sqrt{B \times D}} + \frac{L}{4} + \frac{SCA}{5}$$

Secondly, we have:

$$M2 = SCA\left(\frac{0.077SCA}{\sqrt{B \times D}} + 0.2216\right) + L\left(\frac{0.0659L}{\sqrt[3]{L \times B \times MDIA}} + 0.1738\right)$$

From these, $MRA = ((M1 \text{ or } M2) + DC + FC) \times DLFA$. This replaces the terms relating *L*, *B*, *D* and *SCA* with two new terms. The first multiplies *SCA* by the sail area:midship area ratio; this term is low for boats with a low sail area:displacement ratio. The second term multiplies the length by the inverse of the displacement:length ratio, and so is low for boats with a high displacement for their length.

Thus the older designs, with their heavier hulls and smaller rigs, will have *MRA* determined by *M2*, whilst more modern designs will use *M1*.

RA
The Mk IIIA rating is determined by the same formula as used by the Mk III rule:

$$RA = MRA \times EPF \times MAF \times SMF \times LRP \times CGFA \times CBFA \times TPF$$

but it may not be taken as greater than the Mk III rating, nor less than 85% of Mk III, except for boats with a hull date of 1/1982 or later, for which the minimum value is 96.8% of the Mk III rating.

Chapter 13

The IOR and the Owner

Thankfully yachtsmen do not need to be aware of all of the intricacies of the IOR dealt with in the last chapter. But they do need to know how to prepare the boat for measurement, how the rule restricts the sail plan, and perhaps also how to adjust the rating. In addition, the ORC's Special Regulations need to be complied with, governing minimum standards for safety equipment and internal accommodation.

Owner's Requirements

It is solely the owner's responsibility to ensure that the yacht has a valid rating certificate, and that the yacht's measurements conform to those given on her certificate. Once the certificate has been issued, a copy must always be carried on board when racing. The certificate needs to be revalidated annually, or when the yacht changes hands.

Once the yacht has been measured, the owner is required to inform the national rating authority (the RORC in Britain) of any changes that may affect her rating. Clearly this includes any changes to the shape of the hull, and any changes in the amount or position of ballast. However, alterations to the interior joinery or to the yacht's tanks will affect her trim and stability, and therefore require some remeasurement. Also, any changes to the propeller or engine will affect the EPF.

As far as the rig is concerned, any repositioning of the measurement bands, or changes in the position of the mast or forestay, will affect the rating. If the spars are changed this may well affect the results of the CGF inclination test, even if no alterations are made to the rig measurements. All mainsails, spinnakers, and jibs with an LP greater than $1.3J$ need to be measured, and it is the owner's responsibility to ensure that all sails comply with the rule and the measurement certificate.

Provision is also made for limiting the number of crew that may be carried on board during the race, in order to stop racing yachts gaining unmeasured stability by carrying large numbers of crew sitting out on the weather rail. For example, before the Rule change, a one tonner may have carried a crew of fourteen, but the maximum now permitted is ten.

The maximum number of crew is given by: $INT(0.4R + 0.02) - 2$, where INT signifies that the term within the brackets is rounded down to the nearest whole number. The Rule states that the race committee may waive this rule, and hopefully this will be done for all normal club races.

Sail Limitations

To help to moderate the cost of racing, the IOR incorporates restrictions on the size of sail wardrobe carried on boats rating under 45 feet, and the sail-cloth on boats rating less than 60 ft, using the Mk III rating.

One mainsail and one spare may be carried, a storm trysail, a storm jib and a heavy weather jib. The second mainsail must be a genuine spare; thus a light and a heavy weather mainsail would not be permitted. The storm trysail must be smaller than the mainsail when close reefed. The storm jib is limited to a maximum area of $0.05IG^2$ square feet, and a maximum luff length of $0.65IG$. The heavy weather jib also has its area restricted, to a maximum of $0.135IG^2$; in addition, it may not be fitted with reef points. On boats rating less than 60.0 ft, the use of Kevlar in jibs is banned unless LPG is less than $1.1J$, and the sail is not the storm jib; as discussed in the previous chapter, the use of Kevlar in the mainsail is also severely restricted. The limitations imposed on sails in addition to those mentioned above are given in Fig. 13.1.

Fig. 13.1 IOR sail limitations on jibs and spinnakers. In addition to the sails listed above, the boat may carry one mainsail, together with a spare, a storm trysail, a storm jib and a heavy weather jib. Two-masted vessels are also permitted a number of between mast sails in addition to a mizzen or foresail. No sail restrictions are placed on yachts rating 45.0 feet or more.

Rating (feet)	Jibs	Spinnakers
Up to 16.5	4	2
16.6–22.9	5	3
23.0–28.9	6	4
29.0–32.9	7	4
33.0–39.9	8	5
40.0–44.9	9	6

Jibs are defined as headsails with a girth, measured between the midpoints of luff and leach, not greater than half the foot length; spinnakers must have a mid girth of at least three-quarters the foot length, and also be symmetrical about the centreline. Note that no headsails are permitted that lie between the jib and the spinnaker measurements. Bloopers, or big boys, comply with the jib measurements, but cruising chutes are not permitted.

There are a number of additional restrictions imposed on jibs and spinnakers. Firstly, when trimmed along the centreline no jib may be set so that its clew falls

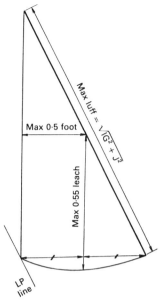

Fig. 13.2 Restrictions on jib dimensions. The cross girths are usually also checked at the quarter and three-quarter heights.

aft of the *LP* line, or so that more than half of its area lies aft of the mast. These limit how far aft spinnaker staysails may be tacked down, and incidentally limit the *LP* of jibs to a pretty hefty 1.9*J*.

The size of big boys is limited by imposing a maximum luff length of $\sqrt{(IG^2 + J^2)}$ on jibs, in other words the length of the forestay. The maximum tack pennant length is also restricted to 2.5 feet.

The amount of roach in the foot of the jib is limited to 5% of the leach length, and no headboard is permitted. Also, only one sheeting point is permitted, thus outlawing quadrilateral jibs, and clewboards are only allowed on self tacking jibs. Up to four equally spaced battens are permitted in the leach, so long as their forward end lies forward of the mast, and their length does not exceed 0.08*J*. Finally, under the IYRU rules all jibs and staysails set on the wind must be tacked down close to the centreline.

The spinnaker and its gear are much freer of restrictions. Basically the pole must be set to windward, with one end on the mast and the other close to the tack of the sail. The IOR says that a jib may only be set as a spinnaker if there is no undamaged spinnaker on board, or if it is the only sail in the foretriangle and the wind is abaft the beam.

It is permitted to set twin boomed-out jibs when running in heavy weather, though, so long as neither the spinnaker nor the mainsail are set. The jibs may be sheeted to twin spinnaker poles, or to the main boom and one spinnaker pole.

Sail numbers are required on the mainsail, all spinnakers, and jibs with an *LP* greater than 1.3*J*. The numbers must be on both sides of the sail, with the starboard numbers uppermost on the mainsail. On spinnakers and jibs they must be sited at approximately half height, whilst on the mainsail the numbers must lie in the upper third of the sail.

A few restrictions are placed on the spars and standing rigging. A forestay must be fitted, and it may not be adjusted whilst racing unless the shrouds are swept aft, in which case they may not be adjusted. This is to prevent hydraulics being used to alter the rake of the mast. Under no circumstances may the shrouds be adjusted or disconnected whilst racing.

No method of adjusting the mast at the heel or at deck level is permitted, though free movement at deck level of up to 10% of the maximum fore and aft or athwartships mast dimension is allowed. Rotating or permanently bent masts are banned, but this does not prohibit pre-bending the mast by tensioning the rigging.

ORC Special Regulations

Although responsibility for the safety of the yacht and her crew must always lie with the owner, the ORC do lay down minimum standards for safety equipment to try to ensure that all yachts are adequately equipped. There are also some extremely basic requirements for internal accommodation, which just manage to prevent IOR yachts from becoming completely bare inside.

Obviously, an ocean race demands a greater amount of safety equipment to be carried than an afternoon's racing round the cans, and so races are classed into one of five categories. Category 0 is for ocean races, which last for a considerable period, during which the boats must be totally self-reliant no matter what happens. Category 1 is for races well offshore, where the boats cannot count on any rescue facilities. Most offshore races fall into category 2, and differ from category 1 in having sheltered waters fairly close to hand, and some rescue facilities are probably available in emergencies. With the exception of mini tonners, level rating events are generally held under this category. Category 3 races are short offshore events, held in fairly protected waters close to the shore. Finally, category 4 races are short inshore races, held in sheltered or warm waters. This category covers races round the buoys, and is also the one used by mini tonners.

There is no point in listing the equipment requirements here, but they do provide a useful guide to the safety equipment required for cruising as well as racing yachts. A similar set of regulations, though not quite as comprehensive, is published by MOCRA for use by multihulls. All these regulations are to be regarded as the minimum amount of equipment required, and may need to be supplemented to meet the needs of particular events or craft.

Preparing for Measurement Ashore

As no variables such as freeboard or stability are measured ashore, but just the fixed hull and rig measurements, comparatively little preparation is required.

301

Fig. 13.3. The waterline beam is measured at five trial waterlines, and then calculated from the freeboards measured afloat.

The boat needs to be in an accessible place, properly supported, with the weight of the keel taken by a support. The boat must be level both longitudinally and athwartships, and the standing rigging must be slack. Level longitudinal trim means having the boat set up close to the anticipated measurement trim when afloat. Although it is advantageous to have bow-up trim, it is very important to avoid incurring a *TPF* penalty.

The mast and sails are also measured ashore. All sails that are to be used must be declared, as well as where they are to be set; this is primarily to determine the position of the *LP* line. Spar measurement bands must be painted on; coloured adhesive tape is not allowed, as its position can be changed too easily.

Preparing for Measurement Afloat

As the yacht's rating is highly dependent upon her trim, the requirements for measurement afloat are laid down in some detail to try to ensure a standard trim condition. The boat needs to be in measurement trim for the freeboard measurements, the inclining test used to determine the *CGF*, and if necessary the stability test.

To be measured the boat must be fully completed, rigged and ready to sail, with the standing rigging and fittings in their normal position; the yacht's head may not be depressed by lying to a mooring. Any centreboard or drop keel must be in the fully raised position. The bilges, heads, bilge and waste pipes must be dry, but any hydraulic systems are required to be full. If the boat is measured with an outboard motor it must be stowed in its special locker or stowage bracket, which must be abaft the mast.

Fig. 13.4. The freeboards FF and FA are measured at the forward and after girth stations, with all the other freeboards being calculated from these values and the datum waterline used ashore.

To prevent retrimming of the boat after measurement, the weights and positions of all heavy items are recorded on the measurement inventory, which now forms part of the yacht's rating certificate, and a sticker marks their position inside the boat. This covers internal ballast, the batteries, toolbox, anchors and chain, and any other heavy equipment found on board. All of these items must have secure stowage positions. At least one anchor must be on board when the boat is measured, and the anchor rope may not be stowed forward of the mast; if any extra anchors have to be carried to comply with the sailing instructions these must be stowed forward of the mast.

The condition of the yacht's water, fuel and sump tanks will clearly affect her trim. To avoid having one set of tanks for measurement and another for racing, the rule states that the tanks (including any voids in the keel, which may not be free-floating) shall be in the condition that will maximise the rating. This usually means empty tanks forward and full ones aft, thus minimising the bow down trim. If there is any doubt in the measurer's mind about the conditions required, or if any tanks lie between 0.65 and $0.75LBG$ aft of the *FGS*, the owner or designer is required to supply a signed statement giving his opinion as to the correct tank conditions. For measurement purposes tanks shall be either completely full or completely empty.

Fig. 13.5. To determine the boat's stability for the CGF, weights are hung from the end of the spinnaker pole, and the angle of heel is measured by a manometer laid across the stern.

The mast is to be set up with the maximum possible amount of rake; the boom must be at the low point of P, and the spinnaker poles in their normal stowages. All halyards and any running rigging forward of the mast shall be taken to the base of the mast; those lying aft of the mast must be taken to their aftermost position, except that the main halyard may be used to support the boom. All halyards and running rigging shall be hauled tight, with the halyard tails taken to their normal working positions.

Any sheets, guys or running rigging not permanently carried on the spars, together with any portable deck equipment such as winch handles and snatch blocks, are to be laid on the cabin sole aft of the mast.

The mainsail must be furled on the boom, and the other sails placed on the cabin sole between the mast and a line $0.65LBG$ aft of FGS; if it is necessary to pile the sails up, the lighter ones shall be placed on top. The number of sails that may be on board at the time of measurement is limited to one mainsail, one storm trysail, two spinnakers, and four jibs, including the smallest and the largest.

The amount of stores and equipment that may be on board is also limited. No bedding, clothing, food or stores are allowed on board, nor are the yacht's dinghy, danbuoy and liferaft. On the other hand the navigation and cooking equipment shall be on board, with any portable gear normally stowed forward of the mast laid on the cabin sole aft of the mast. Mattresses, cushions and pillows must all be on board, stowed in their normal bunks.

As the rating is reduced by giving the boat bow down trim, the aim should be to increase the bow down trim for measurement purposes, and then restore the boat to normal trim for racing. Thus no equipment should be stowed forward of the mast, as it has to be brought aft of the mast for measurement purposes. Also any equipment not required to be on board during measurement should be stowed well aft, though also bearing in mind that this will have a detrimental effect on the weight distribution.

Optimising the Rating

On receipt of the boat's certificate it is well worth checking it over to ensure that no measurement errors have occurred, and also that no unwanted penalties have been imposed, particularly regarding the rig. Many owners want to go further than this and adjust the rating slightly to enter a certain level rating band, or to improve some aspect of the boat's performance. This generally requires the assistance of a yacht designer, who will be able to call upon previous experience to advise on the best ways of achieving the desired results, and will probably have a computer to enable him to study many possibilities in a comparatively short time.

Checking the certificate

Although the use of computers has made arithmetical errors extremely unlikely, errors may have occurred when the boat was measured. Thus it is always worth comparing the measurements taken with those predicted by the designer or, in the case of production boats, with those on the certificate of another boat in the class. If the yacht is in a class that uses standardised measurements, then only the freeboards and rig measurements will require checking.

The next stage is to ensure that no unwanted penalties are being incurred. Any alterations made will, of course, have to be reported to the rating authorities, and will usually require partial remeasurement.

The areas that deserve most attention are the rig and the propeller installation. Taking the latter first, there is no point in having a propeller large enough to make $PS:L$ greater than 0.05, but it generally pays to go right up to this limit. Nor is it worth having the rated propeller size reduced by an undersized P-bracket; this can easily be remedied by some filler.

There are a considerable number of rig measurements that may attract penalties, and these have been listed in Fig. 12.13. None of these should be incurred, unless it has been decided to accept a penalty in LP or JC. An important point to note, though, is that the rule uses the largest, or where appropriate the

305

smallest, measurement found on any of the sails. Thus if one spinnaker luff is overlength, the rule will assume that all spinnaker luffs are overlength. Similarly, with *JC* and *LP*, if a penalty is incurred in one measurement it is assumed to have been accepted in all related measurements. However, some tolerance is allowed in sail measurements, as they are measured to the nearest 0.1 of a foot, as opposed to the nearest 0.01 of a foot used for the hull measurements, headboard, and batten lengths.

On a masthead rig the values of *RSAT*, *SPIN* and *RSAM* should also be inspected. Often, *RSAM* is below the stipulated minimum value, and so the mainsail measurements can be increased slightly without penalty. Similarly, *SPIN* may be greater than *RSAT*, in which case *RSAT* may be made to equal *SPIN* by increasing *LP* or the mainsail size.

Adjusting the rating

Before making any major alterations to a yacht, her performance should be assessed. Once this has been done any changes can be aimed at improving weak points in her performance, or accepting a slight reduction in areas where her performance is above par. Without assessing her performance, any changes made are as likely to worsen as to improve her results.

Bumping the hull

As far as the hull is concerned, apart from major reshaping operations all that can be done is to bump out the measurement points with blisters of foam or filler. This fools the rule into thinking that the hull is wider or deeper than it actually is. Not surprisingly, the rulemakers have clamped down on the amount of bumping permitted, as it can lower the rating with only a negligible effect on performance. They achieve this by placing limits on the local curvature at the measurement stations, as shown in Fig. 13.6. There are severe penalties or alternative measurement procedures for boats on which the curvature limits have been exceeded, and as these negate any gain to be had from the increased hull measurements they will not be described here.

Bumping at the *B* measurement point lowers the rating in two ways. Firstly, the value of *B* is increased; secondly, the girth lengths are increased, which reduces *LBG* and *GD*, thereby reducing *L*.

If the hull is bumped at *BWL* the tenderness ratio *TR* will be increased, and so the *CGF* will be reduced. The exception to this is when the yacht previously had a *CGF* of 0.968, in which case the *CGF* will remain unchanged. It may even be increased if the new *TR* lies above 35.0, as this will bring the boat into the penalty area.

Bumping the depth stations can be very profitable. The most obvious effect is an increase in *D* due to the increases in *FDI* and *MDIA*. However, the increase in *MDIA* will also reduce any *DLF* or *SCF* penalty incurred, whilst the increases in *CMDI* and *MDI* may also reduce the rated length through an increase in *BAPSL*. The only drawback is that *BCOR* will be increased, and so the boat will not find it quite so easy to pass the screening test. Clearly there is nothing to be gained in bumping *FDI* if it already lies on the limit of *FDIC*. Finally, the stern may be bumped at BHA1. This has the twofold effect of reducing GSDA and, more

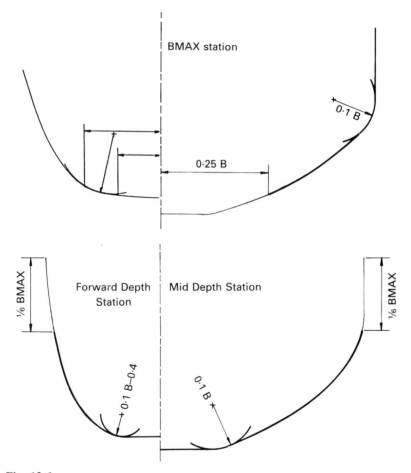

Fig. 13.6.
(a) Curvature limits in the sections. The extent of the restrictions is shown by the heavy line. If the curvature is greater than shown, a penalty is applied to the depth measurements, and an alternative measurement system is used to determine *B* and *BWL*, giving lower values in each case. At the forward depth station a fair line is drawn through any hollows. No hollows are permitted within 0.25*LBG* of the mid depth station (within the area governed by curvature limits).

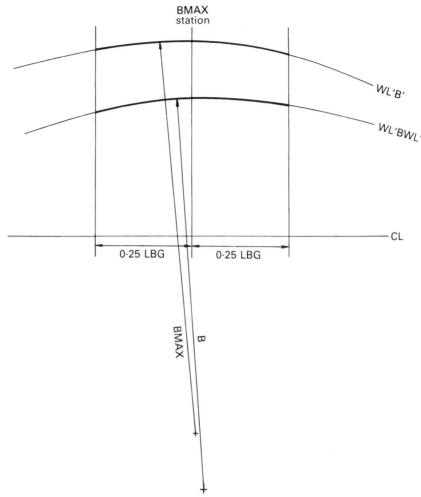

(b) Curvature limits in the waterlines. If the maximum curvature is exceeded, an alternative measurement system is applied, once again resulting in lower values for *B* and *BWL*.

importantly, increasing BHAI, and thereby the computed value of VHAI. Thus both the profile line and, to a lesser extent, the girth line are steepened, reducing L. However, this must be carried out with care if the increase in drag is to be minimised.

Altering the ballast

Another way of altering the hull's rating is to change the amount of bow down trim or the displacement of the boat. In addition to adding or moving any internal ballast, the anchors, batteries or outboard motor may have their locations altered.

Increasing the bow down trim can have a dramatic effect on the rating, but performance will also suffer due to the shorter waterline length, fuller bow, and having the run raised higher out of the water. Naturally these effects make themselves felt most once the boat attains hull speed.

As can be seen in Fig. 13.7, the shallower slope of the *AOCP* and *AOCG* lines compared to the *FOC* line means that, although *FOC* is reduced, the net effect is a reduction in rated length. This will cause any *DLF* penalty to be reduced, but there will also be a very slight reduction in *D*. Even though the boat becomes more tender with increased bow down trim, *TR* is still usually reduced. Thus some increase in *CGF* can be expected, though the exact amount is dependent upon the vagaries of the inclining test. The reduction in *RMC* and the increase in *MDIA* will make it easier for boats to get through the stability screening test, though.

As far as the rig is concerned, the reduction in *FJ* may result in a *TCI* penalty being incurred, resulting in an increase in *RSAF* and *SPIN*, and therefore in *RSAT*. The reduction in *L* will also cause an increase in *SCF*, and so if the boat has a big rig an *SCF* penalty might be incurred.

Another possible approach is to increase the yacht's displacement. This route is not very profitable in terms of rating, though, as the sinkage results in an increased rated length. However, a slight reduction in rating is normally obtained through an increase in *D* and, more importantly, a reduction in any *DLF* or *SHR* penalty present. As the extra displacement will also reduce the yacht's speed, this route is only likely to pay in the case of light, overcanvassed boats as a means of increasing the sail carrying power. If the yacht's *TR* is close to 35.0 it may be possible to add the weight in the form of a lead shoe to the keel, and increase the stability with no increase in the *CGF*.

The propeller installation

One of the easiest ways of adjusting the rating is to fit a different propeller. Generally, it has been found most beneficial to have a maximum sized folding or feathering propeller, with the folding propeller proving most popular due to its low cost. However, a minimum sized solid propeller will give an increase in *DF* of up to 45% for an exposed shaft installation, 33% for a strut drive, and a massive 80% for an 'other' installation. Although this change will reduce performance it may prove worthwhile, especially in 'other' installations, so long as the boat has plenty of sail for her size to offset the extra drag.

Before carrying out any changes, the installation dimensions should be checked to ensure that an exposed shaft or strut drive installation will not be reclassified as 'other' due to the new propeller, as this will cause the rating to increase. The *P* bracket or strut drive width and thickness can easily be altered with filler, but any other alterations will prove expensive.

It is worth noting that no account is taken of the size of prop shaft fitted. Thus some reduction in drag can be had by fitting a minimum diameter shaft of a high strength alloy such as Monel K500, flared out to fit the bearings and propeller if necessary.

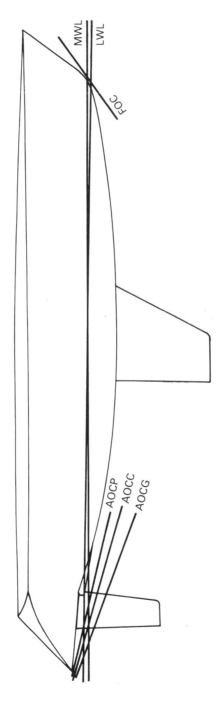

Fig. 13.7. This half tonner is shown trimmed to her measurement and load waterlines. In measurement trim her rated length is 25.275 ft, but when trimmed down by the stern in her load condition *L* increases to 25.9 ft.

Rig alterations

Another fairly simple way of altering the rating is to modify the sail plan. Obviously there is no point in using this approach to reduce the rating of a boat that is already short of sail area, or to increase the rating of a boat that is well endowed in this respect.

Clearly any changes to the rig measurements will require the sails to be altered or replaced, except for small changes to *P* and *E*. However, it is not always necessary to have the spars modified: *E* can be changed, and *P* reduced, by moving the measurement bands, whilst *J* can be changed by moving the mast at deck level. Similarly, an *LP* penalty requires no change to the spars, and a *JC* penalty only requires a longer spinnaker pole.

If the rating is being optimised for one of the level rating classes, changes to the rig are particularly useful. This is because most hull alterations, including reballasting but excluding fitting a new propeller, require remeasurement of the boat afloat, complete with the difficulties of predicting the outcome accurately. However, once a satisfactory rating has been obtained for the hull, small changes can be made to the rig, knowing exactly what effect they will have on the rating.

The simplest modification is to accept an *LP* penalty. A considerable increase in genoa area can be had for only a small increase in rating; however, only the largest genoa benefits, and so performance will only be improved when beating or fetching in light airs. For this reason this avenue is seldom followed nowadays.

A penalty on *JC*, on the other hand, gives improved performance all round. It allows a larger *LP*, a longer spinnaker pole, and a larger spinnaker with increased luff and girth measurements. However, once again the rating can only be increased, and not reduced.

Perhaps the most radical change that can be made to the rig is to cut something off the heel of the mast, thus reducing the size of the foretriangle. This will have little effect on reaching performance, but will reduce performance on and off the wind until reefing is required.

311

Appendix A

List of symbols and abbreviations

ABS	American Bureau of Shipping
a.c.	Alternating current
AM	Amplitude modulation
A_S	Sail area (mainsail and No. 1 genoa unless stated otherwise)
b	Breadth of a beam or girder
B	Centre of buoyancy (upright)
B_θ	Centre of buoyancy (heeled to $\theta°$)
B_{90}	Centre of buoyancy (heeled to 90°)
BM	Bending moment
$BMAX$	Maximum beam of a boat
BWL	Waterline beam
CE	Centre of effort of the rig
CLR	Centre of lateral resistance of the hull
C_P	Prismatic coefficient
d	Thickness of a beam
DA	Dellenbaugh angle
d.c.	Direct current
E	Young's modulus
E	Mainsail foot length
F_D	Drag force developed by the rig
F_H	Side force developed by the rig
F_L	Lift force developed by the rig
F_R	Driving force developed by the rig
F_T	Total force developed by the rig
FM	Frequency modulation
G	Centre of gravity position
GRI	Group Repetition Interval
GZ	Righting lever
h	Heeling arm of rig

I	Moment of inertia
I	Height of foretriangle
J	Base of foretriangle
l	Lead between CE and CLR
LOP	Line of position
LWL	Waterline length
M	Metacentre
MF	Medium frequency
MOCRA	Multihull Offshore Cruiser Racer Association
ORC	Offshore Racing Council
P	Mainsail luff
PEP	Peak envelope power
PN	Portsmouth Number
RM_1	Righting moment at 1 degree of heel
SF	Multihull stability factor
SG	Specific gravity
SSB	Single side band
T_c	Depth of canoe body
VDF	Voltage drop factor
VHF	Very high frequency
x	Depth of a girder or beam
y	Distance from the neutral axis of a body to its outermost element
$\triangle$	Displacement, tons
$\triangledown$	Displacement, cubic feet
δ	Angle made between the foot of a headsail and the projection of the sheet lead
λ	Angle of leeway
ρ	Density
θ	Angle of heel
σ_f	Maximum permitted flexural stress

Appendix B

Derivation of the factors used to compare material properties

From simple beam theory: $BM_{max} = \sigma_f \times \dfrac{I}{y}$

where BM_{max} is the maximum permitted bending stress

       σ_f is the maximum permitted stress

       I is the moment of inertia of a section through the beam

       y is the distance from the neutral axis to the furthest element.

For the local strength condition, the situation is taken as that of a rectangular beam of unit width.

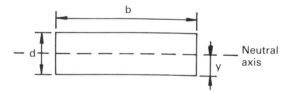

Fig. B.1.   Beam model for local properties.

Thus $I = \dfrac{1}{12} \times b \times d^3$

$y = \dfrac{d}{2}$

Therefore local strength factor $= \sigma_f \times \dfrac{1/12 \times b \times d^3}{d/2}$

$= \dfrac{1}{6} \times \sigma_f \times b \times d^2$

But $b = 1$

Therefore local strength factor $\propto \sigma_f \times d^2$

Appendix B

Local stiffness is taken as the radius of curvature of a simple beam.
Thus local stiffness factor $\propto E \times I$ for unit bending moment

$$\propto E \times \frac{1}{12} \times b \times d^3$$

$$\propto E \times d^3$$

The overall properties are taken as those of two parallel plates in simple bending, connected by a web or core of negligible weight.

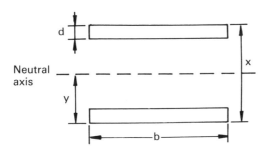

Fig. B.2. Beam model for overall properties. The members are assumed to be joined by a lightweight core or web – the sandwich core when applied to the local properties of sandwich structure, or the hull sides when applied to the hull's overall stiffness.

$$\text{Thus } I = 2 \times \frac{1}{12} \times b \times d^3 + 2 \times b \times d\left(y - \frac{d}{2}\right)^2$$

As the skin thickness is small compared to the hull depth, the first term, giving the moment of inertia of the two individual plates, can be assumed to be small, and $\left(y - \frac{d}{2}\right)^2$ held approximately equal to y.

Therefore $I \approx 2 \times b \times d \times y^2$

Therefore I is approximately proportional to $b \times d$

Now overall strength $= \sigma_f \times \dfrac{I}{y}$

$$\propto \sigma_f \times \frac{b \times d}{y}$$

But b is unitary, and y is independent of the material used.
Therefore overall strength factor $\propto \sigma_f \times d$
Similarly, overall stiffness factor $\propto E \times I$

$$\propto E \times d$$

On the basis of equal weight, material thickness is inversely proportional to the density. Thus we have:

Local stiffness factor $\quad = \dfrac{E}{\rho^3}$

Local strength factor $\quad = \dfrac{\sigma_f}{\rho^2}$

Overall strength factor $= \dfrac{\sigma_f}{\rho}$

Overall stiffness factor $= \dfrac{E}{\rho}$

On the basis of equal local strength, $\sigma_f \times d^2$ is constant.

Therefore $d^2 \qquad \propto \dfrac{1}{\sigma_f}$

Therefore $d \qquad \propto \sqrt{\dfrac{1}{\sigma_f}}$

But weight $\qquad \propto \rho \times d$

Therefore weight $\propto \rho\sqrt{\dfrac{1}{\sigma_f}}$

Similarly substituting $\sqrt{\dfrac{1}{\sigma_f}}$ for d in the other expressions, we find:

Local stiffness factor $\quad = \sqrt{\dfrac{E^2}{\rho^3}}$

Overall strength factor $= \sqrt{\sigma_f}$

Overall stiffness factor $= E\sqrt{\dfrac{1}{\sigma_f}}$

On the basis of equal overall strength, $\sigma_f \times d$ is constant.

Therefore $d \qquad \propto \dfrac{1}{\sigma_f}$

Thus weight $\qquad \propto \dfrac{\rho}{\sigma_f}$

Overall stiffness $\propto \dfrac{E}{\sigma_f}$

Local strength $\quad \propto \dfrac{1}{\sigma_f}$

Local stiffness $\quad \propto \dfrac{E}{\sigma_f^3}$

Bibliography

Adlard Coles Ltd
Aerohydrodynamics of Sailing, Marchaj (1979).
Designed to Win, Roger Marshall (1979).
Electrics and Electronics for Small Craft, French (1981).
From a Fibreglass Hull, Collins (1979).
Further Offshore, 6th ed, Illingworth (1969).
High Speed Sailing: Design Factors, Norwood (1979).
Sail Power, Ross (1975).
Sailing Theory and Practice, 2nd Ed, Marchaj (1982).
Sailing Yacht, The, Baader (1979).
Sailing Yacht Design, Phillips-Birt (1976).
Sails, 5th ed, Howard-Williams (1983).
Technical Yacht Design, (1975) Hammit

Bodley Head
Yacht Joinery and Fitting, Saunders (1981).

David & Charles
Boat Electrics, Watney (1981).
Boat Engines: A Manual for Work and Pleasure Craft, Bowyer (1979).
Sailing and Boating: The Complete Equipment Guide, Jarman (1981).

Hollis & Carter
First Ferro-Boat Book, The, Greenfield (1978).

John Murray
Complete Amateur Boat Building, Verney (1979).

Nautical
Boatbuilding in Aluminium Alloy, Sims (1978)
Self-steering for Yachts, Dijkstra (1979)

Stanford Maritime
Metal Corrosion in Boats, Warren (1980).
Power for Yachts, Cox (1975).

The New York Society of Naval Architects and Marine Engineers (SNAME)
Hydrodynamics in Ship Design, Saunders (1957–65).

Index

Page numbers in bold type indicate an illustration.